ECONOMICS
IN TWO
LESSONS

ECONOMICS IN TWO LESSONS

*Why Markets Work So Well,
and Why They Can Fail So Badly*

JOHN QUIGGIN

PRINCETON UNIVERSITY PRESS

Princeton and Oxford

Published by Princeton University Press
41 William Street, Princeton, New Jersey 08540
6 Oxford Street, Woodstock, Oxfordshire OX20 1TR

press.princeton.edu

Library of Congress Control Number 2018962708
ISBN 978-0-691-15494-7

British Library Cataloging-in-Publication Data is available

Editorial: Sarah Caro, Hannah Paul, and Charlie Allen
Production Editorial: Jill Harris
Text Design: Pam Schnitter
Jacket Design: Faceout Studio, Lindy Martin
Production: Erin Suydam
Publicity: James Schneider and Caroline Priday
Copyeditor: Karen Verde

This book has been composed in Garamond Premier Pro

Printed on acid-free paper. ∞

Printed in the United States of America

1 3 5 7 9 10 8 6 4 2

CONTENTS

∎

ACKNOWLEDGMENTS   xi

Introduction   1
    Outline of the Book   8
    Further Reading   9

LESSON ONE, PART I: THE LESSON   11

Chapter 1. Market Prices and Opportunity Costs   13
    1.1. What Is Opportunity Cost?   14
    1.2. Production Cost and Opportunity Cost   17
    1.3. Households, Prices, and Opportunity Costs   22
    1.4. Lesson One   24
    1.5. The Intellectual History of Opportunity Cost   25
    Further Reading   27

Chapter 2. Markets, Opportunity Cost,
    and Equilibrium   30
    2.1. TISATAAFL (There Is Such A Thing As
    A Free Lunch)   32
    2.2. Gains from Exchange   35
    2.3. Trade and Comparative Advantage   37
    2.4. Competitive Equilibrium   40
    2.5. Free Lunches and Rents   44
    2.6. Adam Smith and the Division of Labor   45
    Further Reading   48

Chapter 3. Time, Information, and Uncertainty   50

3.1. Interest and the Opportunity Cost of (Not) Waiting   51
3.2. Information   59
3.3. Uncertainty   62
Further Reading   64

LESSON ONE, PART II: APPLICATIONS   67

Chapter 4. Lesson One: How Opportunity Cost
Works in Markets   69

4.1. Tricks and Traps   69
4.2. Airfares   71
4.3. The Cost of (Not) Going to College   75
4.4. An Exception That Proves the Rule: The Boom
and Bust in Law Schools   77
4.5. TANSTAAFL: What about "Free" TV, Radio,
and Internet Content?   79
Further Reading   83

Chapter 5. Lesson One and Economic Policy   85

5.1. Why Price Control Doesn't (Usually) Work   85
5.2. To Help Poor People, Give Them Money   89
5.3. Road Pricing   96
5.4. Fish and Tradable Quota   100
5.5. A License to Print Money: Property Rights
and Telecommunications Spectrum   108
5.6. Concluding Comments   111
Further Reading   111

Chapter 6. The Opportunity Cost of Destruction   114

6.1. The Glazier's Fallacy   115
6.2. The Economics of Natural Disasters   118
6.3. The Opportunity Cost of War   119
6.4. Technological Benefits of War?   125
Further Reading   128

LESSON TWO, PART I: SOCIAL OPPORTUNITY COSTS 131

Chapter 7. Property Rights and Income Distribution   134

7.1. What Lesson Two Tells Us about Property Rights
and Income Distribution   135
7.2. Property Rights and Market Equilibrium   136
7.3. The Starting Point   138
7.4. Property Rights and Natural Law   142
7.5. Pareto and Inequality   145
7.6. Conclusion   148
Further Reading   149

Chapter 8. Unemployment   150

8.1. Macroeconomics and Microeconomics   151
8.2. The Business Cycle   153
8.3. The Experience of the Great and Lesser Depressions 155
8.4. Are Recessions Abnormal?   159
8.5. Unemployment and Opportunity Cost   162
8.6. The Macro Foundations of Micro   165
8.7. Hazlitt and the Glazier's Fallacy   167
Further Reading   169

Chapter 9. Monopoly and Market Failure   171

9.1. The Idea of Market Failure   171
9.2. Economies of Size   173
9.3. Monopoly   177
9.4. Oligopoly   184
9.5. Monopsony and Labor Markets   185
9.6. Bargaining   187
9.7. Monopoly and Inequality   191
Further Reading   193

Chapter 10. Market Failure: Externalities and Pollution 196

10.1. Externalities   197
10.2. Pollution   200

10.3. Climate Change 203
10.4. Public Goods 208
10.5. The Origins of Externality 210
Further Reading 212

Chapter 11. Market Failure: Information,
Uncertainty, and Financial Markets 214

11.1. Market Prices, Information, and Public Goods 215
11.2. The Efficient Markets Hypothesis 218
11.3. Financial Markets, Bubbles, and Busts 221
11.4. Financial Markets and Speculation 223
11.5. Risk and Insurance 226
11.6. Bounded Rationality 228
11.7. What Bitcoin Reveals about Financial Markets 232
Further Reading 235

LESSON TWO, PART II: PUBLIC POLICY 237

Chapter 12. Income Distribution: Predistribution 239

12.1. Income Distribution and Opportunity Cost 240
12.2. Predistribution: Unions 242
12.3. Predistribution: Minimum Wages 249
12.4. Predistribution: Intellectual Property 254
12.5. Predistribution: Bankruptcy, Limited Liability,
and Business Risk 262
Further Reading 267

Chapter 13. Income Distribution: Redistribution 270

13.1. The Effective Marginal Tax Rate 272
13.2. Opportunity Cost of Redistribution: Example 275
13.3. Weighing Opportunity Costs and Benefits 278
13.4. How Much Should the Top 1 Percent Be Taxed? 282
13.5. Policies for the Present and the Future 285
13.6. Geometric Mean 286
Further Reading 286

Chapter 14. Policy for Full Employment   288

    14.1. What Can Governments Do about Recessions?   289
    14.2. Fiscal Policy   290
    14.3. Monetary Policy   297
    14.4. Labor Market Programs and the Job Guarantee 299
    14.5. One Lesson Economics and Unemployment   301
    14.6. Summary   306
    Further Reading   306

Chapter 15. Monopoly and the Mixed Economy   308

    15.1. Monopoly and Monopsony   309
    15.2. Antitrust   311
    15.3. Regulation and Its Limits   314
    15.4. Public Enterprise   315
    15.5. The Mixed Economy   319
    15.6. *I, Pencil*   322
    Further Reading   326

Chapter 16. Environmental Policy   328

    16.1. Regulation   330
    16.2. Environmental Taxes   332
    16.3. Tradeable Emissions Permits   334
    16.4. Global Pollution Problems   335
    16.5. Climate Change   336
    16.6. Summary   341
    Further Reading   342

Conclusion   343

BIBLIOGRAPHY   345

INDEX   371

ACKNOWLEDGMENTS

The idea for this book was suggested to me back in 2011 by Seth Ditchik, my publisher at Princeton University Press, encouraged by then PUP director Peter Dougherty. Like many books, this was a long time in the writing, so long that both Seth and Peter had moved on by the time I finally had my ideas straight. Sarah Caro, who picked up the project in 2016, gave me the encouragement and prodding I needed to turn my scrappy draft into a final manuscript. I thank Seth, Peter, and Sarah for making this book happen. I am also grateful to the PUP production and marketing teams, including Bob Bettendorf, Jill Harris, Dimitri Karetnikov, Hannah Paul, Stephanie Rojas, Julie Shawvan, and Karen Verde, for their work in turning my manuscript into a real book.

I thank Roger Backhouse and another anonymous reader for PUP for their enthusiastic reaction to the book and useful suggestions for improvements. I also received valuable comments and positive feedback from academic colleagues, including Max Corden, Simon Grant, Jacob Hacker, Raja Junankar, and Flavio Menezes.

In addition to these traditional sources of feedback, I posted excerpts from the book on my blog, johnquiggin.com, and on the academic group blog, crookedtimber.org. I got so many useful responses in different media, some under pseudonyms, that I am sure to miss some. Undeterred by this, I will thank "Anarcho," "Anarcissie," Rob Banks, Stephen Bartos, Jim Birch, Graeme Bird, Mark Brady, "ccc," "CDT," "Cervantes," Harry

Clarke, Paul Davis, "DCA," Tim Dymond, Kenny Easwaran, Geoff Edwards, "Equalitus," Mike Furlan, Christian Haesemeyer, Mike Haines, Nicholas Haines, Nigel Harden, Sebastian Holsclaw, Hubert Horan, Hugo, "Ikonoclast," "J-D," Valerie Kay, "Keshav," Ian Kirkegaard, "LFC," Peter Ludemann, Greg McKenzie, Robert Merkel, Zoe Mithen, "Nastywoman," Mark Nelson, "Newtownian," Peter T, Philip, Greg Pius, "Plasmaatron," Quentin Reynolds, "Richie Rich," David Richardson, G. Branden Robinson, "Sandwichman," Scott P., Simon, Matthew Smedberg, Smith, "stostosto," "Tabasco," Robert Vienneau, Bruce Wilder, and James Wimberley, with apologies to those I've inevitably left out.

Special thanks go to three readers. My long-standing colleague David Adamson provided comments on all the chapters. Mike Huben read and commented in detail on all the chapters and also pointed me to useful links on his *Critiques of Libertarianism* site, http://critiques.us. Most of all, my beloved wife and colleague, Nancy Wallace, brought both her training as an editor and her skills as a critical reader to bear on the book, catching lots of errors and never letting me get away with a sloppy argument. Without her love and support, I could never have finished this book.

ECONOMICS IN TWO LESSONS

INTRODUCTION

Moral: To understand economics you need to know not only fundamentals but also its *nuances*. Darwin is in the nuances. When someone preaches "Economics in One Lesson," I advise: Go back for the second lesson.

—Paul Samuelson, An Enjoyable Life Puzzling
Over Modern Finance Theory, *Annual Review
of Financial Economics*, Vol. 1, p. 30

As the name implies, this book is, or at least began as, a response to Henry Hazlitt's *Economics in One Lesson*, a defense of free-market economics first published in 1946. But why respond to a seventy-year-old book when new books on economics are published every day? Why two lessons instead of one? And where does opportunity cost fit into all of this?

The first question was one that naturally occurred to me when Seth Ditchik, my publisher at Princeton University Press, suggested this project. It turns out that *Economics in One Lesson* has been in print continuously since its first publication and has now sold more than a million copies. Hazlitt's admirers have embraced the message that all economic problems have a simple answer, and one that matches their own preconceptions. Adapting Hazlitt's title, this simple answer may be described as One Lesson economics.[1]

---

[1] One-lesson economists do not describe themselves in these terms, typically preferring terms like "free market." As I shall show, however, the concept of a "free"

Broadly speaking, Hazlitt's simple answer is "leave markets alone, and all will be well." This may be summed up, in the pithy expression of eighteenth-century French writer and free trade advocate, René de Voyer, Marquis d'Argenson, as *laissez-faire* (let [business] do it).

Hazlitt, as he makes clear, was simply reworking the classic defense of free markets by the French writer Frédéric Bastiat, whose 1850 pamphlets "The Law" and "What Is Seen and What Is Unseen" form the basis of much of *Economics in One Lesson.* However, Hazlitt extends Bastiat by including a critique of the Keynesian economic model, which was developed in response to the Great Depression of the 1930s.

Both where he was right and where he was wrong, Hazlitt's *One Lesson* is relevant today, and has not been improved on by today's advocates of the free market, who may fairly be referred to as One Lesson economists. Indeed, precisely because he was writing at a time when support for One Lesson economics was at a particularly low ebb, Hazlitt gave a simpler and sharper presentation of the case than many of his successors.

Hazlitt presented One Lesson economics in clear and simple terms that have not been sharpened by any subsequent writer. And, despite impressive advances in mathematical sophistication and the advent of powerful computer models, the basic questions in economics have not changed much since Hazlitt wrote, nor have the key debates been resolved. So, he may be read just if he were writing today.

---

market is illusory and misleading. All markets operate within legal systems that enforce certain kinds of property rights and contracts and disregard others. A free market is one in which currently existing private property rights take precedence over all others. There are many other terms used to describe One Lesson economics, mostly used pejoratively. These include "Chicago School economics," "neoliberalism," "Thatcherism," and the "Washington Consensus." In my previous book, *Zombie Economics*, I used the term "market liberalism."

Hazlitt worked in the tradition of "microeconomics," that is, the study of the way prices work in particular markets. The central question, which will be the main focus of this book, is whether the prices of goods and services reflect, and determine, all the costs involved for a society in providing those goods and services, summed up in the concept of "opportunity cost."

The opportunity cost of anything of value is what you must give up so that you can have it.

Opportunity cost is critical both in individual decisions and for society as a whole.

Reading Hazlitt, the centrality of opportunity cost isn't immediately evident. Hazlitt states his One Lesson as:

The art of economics consists in looking not merely at the immediate but at the longer effects of any act or policy; it consists in tracing the consequences of that policy not merely for one group but for all groups.

This isn't particularly helpful: it seems to say only that economists should do a thorough job. But, on reading *Economics in One Lesson* it becomes clear that Hazlitt, as an anti-government activist, wants to make a much stronger claim. When economics is done properly, Hazlitt argues, the answer is always to leave the market alone. So, the One Lesson may be restated as:

Once all the consequences of any act or policy are taken into account, the opportunity costs of government action to change economic outcomes always exceed the benefits.

The simplicity of Hazlitt's argument is his great strength. By tying many complex issues to a single principle, Hazlitt is able to ignore secondary details and go straight to the heart of the case against government action. His answer in every case flows from his "One Lesson."

Hazlitt's claim to teach *Economics in One Lesson* is similar in its appeal to other best sellers like *The Secret* and *The Rules*. He provides a simple answer to problems that have puzzled humanity since the dawn of civilization. As with these other best sellers, Hazlitt is offering a delusion of certainty. His One Lesson contains important truths about the power of markets, but he ignores equally important truths about the limitations of the market.

So, we need *Economics in Two Lessons*.

Two lessons are harder than one. And thinking in terms of two lessons comes at a cost: we can sustain neither the dogmatic certainty of One Lesson economics nor the reflexive assumption that any economic problem can be solved by government action. In many cases, the right answer will remain elusive, involving a complex mixture of market forces and government policy. Nevertheless, the two lessons presented here provide a framework within which almost any problem in economic policy can usefully be considered.

One Lesson economics, of the kind propounded by Bastiat, had come under severe criticism from leading economists by the time Hazlitt rose to its defense. Decades before Hazlitt, economists such as Alfred Marshall and A. C. Pigou had developed the concept of "externalities," that is, situations in which market prices don't fully reflect all the relevant opportunity costs. The classic example is that of air or water pollution generated by a factory. In the absence of specific government policies, the costs of pollution aren't borne by the owner of the factory or reflected in the prices of the goods the factory produces. To understand the problem, we need to go beyond individual opportunity costs and consider costs for society as a whole. We must modify the original definition (changes in capitals):

The SOCIAL opportunity cost of anything of value is what you AND OTHERS must give up so that you can have it.

Externalities are just one example of a large class of problems referred to by economists as "market failures." In all these cases, prices differ from social opportunity costs. In some cases, but not all, the problems may be remedied by appropriately designed government policies. A typical intermediate course on microeconomic policy begins with a catalog of market failures and goes on to examine arguments about the desirability or otherwise of possible policy responses.

When I began writing this book, I envisaged it as a nontechnical guide to microeconomic policy, based on the concepts of opportunity costs and market failure. As I worked on the book, though, I felt dissatisfied.

Externalities and related market failures are big issues; the problem of climate change has been aptly described by Sir Nicholas Stern as "the biggest market failure in history." But at a time of chronic economic recession or depression in much of the developed world, and of rapidly growing economic inequality, a book on market failure alone could scarcely justify the title *Economics in Two Lessons*.

I started to think more about the problem of unemployment and how it is treated in Hazlitt's work. Much of *Economics in One Lesson* can be read as an attack on the work of John Maynard Keynes, the great English economist, whose *General Theory of Employment, Interest and Money* was published in 1936 and gave rise to the entire field of macroeconomics (the study of disturbances affecting aggregate levels of employment, interest rates, and prices).

Experience shows that the economy frequently remains in a depression or recession state for years on end. Keynes was the first economist to present a convincing account of how a market economy could operate for long periods at high levels of unemployment. By contrast, despite the then-recent experience of the Great Depression, Hazlitt implicitly assumed that the economy is always at full employment—or would be if not for government and trade union interference.

As I worked on the problem, I reached the conclusion that the central issue could be stated in terms of opportunity cost. In a recession or depression, markets, and particularly labor markets, don't properly match supply and demand. This means that prices, and particularly wages, do not, in general, reflect or determine opportunity costs.

That insight doesn't tell us what, if anything, governments can do to restore and maintain full employment. But it does lead us to a crucial observation, ignored not only by Hazlitt but by the majority of mainstream economists today. It is normally assumed that, in the absence of obvious market failures in some particular part of the economy, Hazlitt's *One Lesson* is applicable. But a recession or depression affects the economy as a whole. Under conditions of recession, opportunity costs will not, in general, be equal to market prices in any sector of the economy.

The other crucial issue of the day is the distribution of income and wealth, which is becoming steadily more unequal. Although he does not say so explicitly, Hazlitt implies that the existing market distribution of income (or rather, the one that would emerge after the policies he dislikes are scrapped) is the only one that is consistent with his One Lesson.

The market outcome depends on the system of property rights from which it is derived. In fact (as we will see later), when markets work in the way Hazlitt assumes, any distribution of goods and resources where prices equal opportunity costs can be derived from some system of property rights. So, Hazlitt's One Lesson tells us nothing useful about the distribution of income or about government policies that may change that distribution.

While markets are exceptionally powerful social institutions, they cannot work unless governments establish the necessary framework in which they can operate. The core of the economic framework in a market economy, and a central role of government, is the allocation and legal enforcement of property rights. The choices that determine property rights are subject to the logic of opportunity costs just as much as the choices made within a market setting by firms and households.

Between them, microeconomics, macroeconomics, and income distribution cover all the critical issues in economic policy. To master any one of these fields requires years of study. In microeconomics, for example, it is necessary to deal with the theory of supply and demand, first by manipulating the graphical representations given in a typical Economics 101 course, and then with more complex algebraic and numerical techniques.

But this level of analysis is required only for specialists who need, for example, to give quantitative answers to questions like "How much will a change in tariffs on steel imports affect employment in the automobile industry?" For most of us, it's sufficient to understand that protecting the steel industry will have an opportunity cost, and that part of that cost will be the loss of jobs in the automobile industry.

Most of the questions of principle involved in public policy can be illuminated by a careful application of the idea of opportunity cost and its relationship to market prices. For this purpose, as I argued above, we need only two lessons.

Lesson One: Market prices reflect and determine opportunity costs faced by consumers and producers.

Lesson One describes the way markets work and explains why, under certain ideal circumstances, Hazlitt's One Lesson economics provides the right answer. Lesson Two is the product of more than two centuries of study of the way markets work under circumstances that are less than ideal and why they may not deliver the desired results:

> Lesson Two: Market prices don't reflect all the opportunity costs we face as a society.

The problem of how markets work and why they fail is at the core of most of the economic policy issues that drive political and social debate. I hope this book, and the two lessons it contains, will help to clarify these issues.

Outline of the Book

The book is divided into four parts, two for each lesson.

Lesson One, Part I, shows how a market economy functions under conditions that ensure that prices are equal to the opportunity costs faced by producers and consumers.

Lesson One, Part II, is a series of applications of Lesson One. We will consider how policies based on the concepts of prices and opportunity costs can be used to achieve the goals of public policy.

Lesson Two, Part I, shows that market prices may not reflect the opportunity costs faced by society as a whole. In fact, any market equilibrium is the product of social choices about the allocation of property rights. Market prices tell us nothing about the opportunity costs associated with those choices.

Equally important, not all opportunity costs associated with consumer and producer choices are reflected in the opportunity costs they face. There are many different ways in which market prices can fail to reflect opportunity costs. These "market failure" problems include unemployment, monopoly, environmental pollution, and inadequate provision of public goods. Lesson Two will help to show how these disparate problems can all be understood in terms of opportunity costs.

Lesson Two, Part II, contains applications to a wide range of policy problems. First, we will consider the problem of income distribution. We will show that, more often than not, the best way to help poor people, at home and abroad, is to give them money to spend as they see fit, rather than tying assistance to particular goods and services. In other words, it is better to fix the inequitable allocation of property rights in the first place than to fix the resulting market outcome. Next we will consider how macroeconomic problems, the most important of which is mass unemployment, may be addressed using fiscal and monetary policy. Finally, we will examine a range of public policies more conventionally associated with the idea of market failure.

In an effort to make the book more readable, but still adhere to academic standards of referencing, I've dispensed with the standard, but cumbersome, apparatus of endnotes. Instead, I've included a short section at the end of each chapter, giving sources for factual claims and suggestions for further reading, which may be followed up using the bibliography at the end of the book. I've used footnotes sparingly, to cover peripheral issues and for occasional asides.

Further Reading

Hazlitt (1946) is still in print and is also available online at the Mises Institute. Apart from *Economics in One Lesson*, Hazlitt is best known for his (1959) book, *The Failure of the "New Economics,"* a line-by-line response to Keynes's (1936) *General Theory of Employment Interest and Money*. Hazlitt (1993) is a representative collection of his writing, published in the year of his death. Bastiat's writings have been translated into English a number of times (Bastiat 2012a, 2012b, 2013).

Marshall's *Principles of Economics*, first published in 1890, was the classic economic textbook of its day, and remained influential for much of the twentieth century. It went through many editions, culminating in the eighth edition (Marshall 1920), which remains the most-used and most-cited version. Pigou's (1920) analysis of *The Economics of Welfare* introduced the modern concept of "externality," which became one of the archetypal forms of "market failure." One of the first typologies of market failure was that of Bator (1958).

Other works cited in this introduction are Byrne's *The Secret* (2006), and Fein and Schneider's *The Rules* (1996). The quotation at the chapter opening is from Samuelson (2009).

LESSON ONE

■

PART I

The Lesson

> Two roads diverged in a wood, and I—
> I took the one less traveled by,
> And that has made all the difference.
> —Robert Frost, *The Road Not Taken*, 1916

Part I is a discussion of Lesson One, showing how a market economy functions under conditions that ensure that prices are equal to the opportunity costs faced by producers and consumers.

Chapter 1 begins with an exposition of the core idea of this book, opportunity costs. We will then consider the relationship between opportunity cost and more familiar measures of the cost of production. Next, we will examine opportunity cost in relation to the choices we face, as consumers, workers, and households. The last section discusses the intellectual history of the concept of opportunity cost.

Chapter 2 shows how, under ideal conditions, markets reach an equilibrium where prices and opportunity cost are equal and where all opportunities for mutually beneficial trade have been realized. First, we will show that, contrary to many perceptions, economic interactions can provide everyone with a "free lunch." Next, we will discuss voluntary exchanges and show how both parties to such an exchange must benefit, though not always equally. In the special case of international trade, these ideas lead to the crucial concept of comparative advantage. Finally, we show how the competitive equilibrium prices that emerge from exchange are determined and how they reflect opportunity costs.

The standard treatment of market equilibrium found in introductory economics textbooks is static (fixed at a point in time) and deterministic (no uncertainty), largely because the standard treatments of time and uncertainty are difficult and complex. This often leads to the impression that Lesson One only works in a static and deterministic world. In chapter 3, we show that, in principle, Lesson One is applicable to choices that take place over time and under conditions of uncertainty. However, the conditions under which equilibrium prices equal opportunity costs are considerably more stringent than in the static and deterministic case. Chapter 3 begins with a discussion of interest rates, considered as the opportunity cost of time. Next, we consider information and uncertainty. We begin with the role of prices as a social mechanism for aggregating and transmitting information about demand and opportunity cost. We then consider risk and uncertainty. We show how insurance markets information about perceived risks and the opportunity costs associated with the various possible outcomes of risky choices. We will return to these issues later in the book.

CHAPTER 1

▓

Market Prices
and Opportunity Costs

Remember that Time is Money. He that can earn Ten Shillings a Day by his Labour, and goes abroad, or sits idle one half of that Day, tho' he spends but Sixpence during his Diversion or Idleness, ought not to reckon That the only Expence; he has really spent or rather thrown away Five Shillings besides.
    —Benjamin Franklin, *Advice to a Young Tradesman Written an Old One*, 1748

Most introductory economics textbooks start with a discussion of opportunity cost. Once discussed in a couple of pages, however, the concept of opportunity cost typically disappears, to be replaced by a diagrammatic exposition of the way in which prices are determined by supply and demand. This exposition can be further elaborated using the idea of elasticity (a measure of price responsiveness) to show how prices respond to changes in the conditions that determine supply and demand.

All of this is useful and necessary, as the starting point in the training of professional economists, although many of them would benefit from a more thorough grounding in the idea of opportunity cost.[1] However, the technical apparatus of supply and demand analysis is largely unnecessary to understand the economic questions commonly raised in public discussion, and may even get in the way.

So, what is opportunity cost?

1.1. What Is Opportunity Cost?

Economists are famous for disagreeing among themselves. Keynesians argue with monetarists about fiscal policy. Members of the Chicago School, including a string of Nobel Memorial[2] Prize winners, advocate unfettered markets, while the case for government intervention in the economy is championed by economists such as Paul Krugman, Amartya Sen, and Joseph Stiglitz, all of whom have also been awarded the Prize. As George Bernard Shaw is supposed to have observed, "If all the economists in the world were laid end to end, they still wouldn't reach a conclusion."

And yet, there is an economic way of thinking that separates any serious economist, regardless of their views on policy, from just about anyone who has not studied economics. Some people, such as Benjamin Franklin, grasp the concept without any formal training. Franklin's observation, cited above, that "time is money," has become such a truism that it is often taken to be a traditional proverb rather than the acute observation it was when he made it. Franklin's explanation leads toward a broader

---

[1] A well-known, though controversial, study reported that only 22 percent of 200 economists attending the 2005 annual meetings of the American Economic Association gave the correct answer to a simple question on opportunity cost measures.

[2] The Economics Prize is not one of the original Nobel Prizes, and its full name is The Bank of Sweden Prize in Economic Sciences in Memory of Alfred Nobel.

point, which forms the basis of the central idea in economics: opportunity cost.

The idea of opportunity cost is inseparably bound up with choice. When we make a choice between alternatives, choosing one implies forgoing the other. To paraphrase Robert Frost, the opportunity cost of walking down one road is whatever would have been found on the road not taken. It is this road not traveled, and not any monetary measure, that is most properly regarded as the cost of our choice.

To sum up:

> The opportunity cost of anything of value is what you must give up to get it.

This is an idea that seems simple enough when it is first presented but turns out to be unexpectedly subtle. The lesson of opportunity cost is easy to state, but hard to learn. A large part of a good course in introductory economics needs to consist of attempts to lead students to an understanding of the idea.

Let's consider a few examples, starting with some textbook cases. For people who are largely self-sufficient producers, or who trade mainly through barter, opportunity cost can be described in simple terms. This is why introductory economics courses spend so much time worrying about Robinson Crusoe, alone on his island, or engaged in barter transactions with Friday.[3]

If Crusoe spends a day fishing, when the best alternative was to pick coconuts, the opportunity cost of the fish he eats for dinner is the coconut he might have enjoyed if he had spent the day foraging on land instead.

---

[3] In Defoe's novel, Crusoe's relationship with Friday was that of master and servant rather than, as in economic textbooks, trading partner. We will discuss this further in subsequent chapters.

Alternatively, perhaps, Crusoe might have traded his fish to Friday in return for, say, some roast goat. If the trade takes place, then Crusoe's opportunity cost for his goat dinner is the fish he traded. For Friday, the reverse is true. He gets fish for dinner, and the opportunity cost is the goat.

The benefit of the trade to Crusoe is the opportunity cost of obtaining the goat some other way. If this cost is greater than the opportunity cost of fishing, then the trade is a good one from Crusoe's viewpoint. The same is true for Friday and the fish.

These examples are oversimplified and conceal a range of complexities. A couple are worth mentioning straight away. First, Crusoe can't know for sure what will happen if he goes foraging for coconuts instead of fishing. The problem of uncertainty is inescapable and, often, intractable. Second, in discussing barter, we haven't said how Crusoe comes to have the fish, and Friday the goat. We'll look at both of these issues, and the complexities they raise, later on.

Introducing money complicates the problem even more and provides plenty of opportunities for fallacious reasoning. The lesson of opportunity cost is that, contrary to the popular view, economics is not "all about money." In fact, the lesson of opportunity cost is harder to learn, the more accustomed you are to thinking about costs and benefits in monetary terms. The principle of opportunity cost is relevant to decisions of all kinds, whether or not there is any monetary cost associated with those decisions.

Sometimes, as we will see, the money price of a good or service is a good measure of its opportunity cost. But very often, as Franklin points out, it is not. The sixpence spent on idle diversion is only part of the opportunity cost of a day off. And even adding the forgone earnings of five shillings may not capture the entire cost. Perhaps the hardworking tradesman might have built up goodwill, leading to future demand for his services; this is also part of the opportunity cost.

Opportunity cost is equally relevant to public policy. This is obvious in relation to decisions to provide some particular good or service to the public. In making such a decision, governments forgo opportunities, including alternative expenditure items, cuts in taxation, or reductions in public debt (allowing for higher spending in the future). The opportunity cost of a particular item of public expenditure is the value of the best available alternative.

Sometimes, the way in which choices are presented makes it appear that an attractive good can be obtained at no cost. A careful consideration of the alternatives often, though not invariably, shows that there is an opportunity cost involved. As we go on, we will see numerous examples of this.

1.2. Production Cost and Opportunity Cost

How does opportunity cost relate to ideas about costs with which we are more familiar, such as the cost of production? And how does this relate to prices?

The cost of production is the value, at market prices, of the resources the producer uses in producing a good or service, including raw materials, the labor of employees, the capital employed in production, and the time and effort of managers.

Think about a small business, such as a garment maker, specializing in, say, making jackets. For any particular jacket, some of the costs (materials, cutting, sewing, and so on) are specific to that item, while others are "overhead" or fixed costs required to keep the business running however many jackets are produced.

The prices paid for these inputs reflect the opportunity costs their owners face when they supply them. For the landlord, this is the rent they could collect from another tenant. For the suppliers, it is the price they could get from another buyer.

For workers and the owner-manager, it is their best alternative, whether this is another paid job, work at home, or leisure.

It's easy enough to see that, for purchased inputs like cloth and other materials, the opportunity cost facing the buyer and seller is just the market price. The price charged for cloth by a textile manufacturer will be the same for any buyer of medium-sized quantities, whether it is used for jackets, skirts, drapery, or sold in a retail haberdashery store. This price is the amount the manufacturer forgoes by selling to one buyer rather than another and is the same whoever buys the cloth.

The same is true, in most cases, of rent on shop space. Provided the rent is paid, and the building maintained, landlords do not care whether they rent to a garment maker or to another tenant, say, a shoe repair business. Similarly, the garment maker has a choice of comparable locations and will be unwilling to pay a premium price. So, the rent will reflect the opportunity cost of the space.

To sum up:

> When markets are competitive, with many buyers and sellers, the cost of production at market prices reflects the opportunity cost of the inputs used, as perceived by input suppliers.

1.2.1. Fixed Cost, Variable Cost, Marginal Cost, and Sunk Cost

To understand opportunity cost more fully, it's useful to look at the cost of production in more detail. One way of breaking down the cost of production is to classify costs as either "fixed" or "variable."[4] The fixed costs are those that arise from a decision to undertake production in the first place; for example,

---

[4] In business parlance, fixed costs are often called "overheads."

rent on premises, the cost of necessary capital equipment, and so on. Variable costs are those that depend on the amount produced, such as the cost of input materials and the wages of production workers.

This distinction isn't hard and fast, and it depends on the length of time over which choices are made. On any given day, staff who have turned up for work have to be paid, so the only variable costs are those of the raw materials actually used that day. Over a period of years, it's possible to invest (or not) in additional machinery, move to new premises, and so on, so that nearly all costs are variable. Nonetheless, the distinction is a useful one.

Having drawn the distinction between fixed and variable costs, we can deepen our understanding of the opportunity costs of production. First, let's consider the increase (or reduction) in variable cost that arises when more (or less) of some good or service is produced. This is called the "marginal cost of production."

Assuming that the firm is concerned only about profits, it will choose to produce more only if the market price is at least as high as the marginal cost of production for one extra unit. This is an example of Lesson One, with marginal cost as the relevant form of opportunity cost.

While producers must adjust their production up or down in response to market prices on a regular (say, daily) basis, they must also pay attention to their business as a whole and consider whether it is better to continue in business or to close down. A decision to shut down altogether saves all the variable costs of production, and potentially some of the fixed costs, such as the need to pay rent on premises.

The crucial distinction here is between those fixed costs that can be avoided by shutting down and those that cannot. Only avoidable costs represent part of the opportunity cost of continuing production. Costs that cannot be avoided or recouped, whatever choice is made, are called "sunk costs." One of the crucial insights of opportunity cost reasoning (echoed in the folk wisdom "don't throw good money after bad") is that sunk costs should not influence our decisions, since there is nothing we can do to change them.

The relevance of sunk costs goes far beyond business decisions. In all long-term projects, from university studies to personal relationships, we face the decision of whether to persist. The problem of sunk costs arises mostly when, in retrospect, we regret our decision to begin the project. Sunk costs can lead us astray in two different ways.

On the one hand, we may think that, having invested heavily in a project, we should see it through, regardless of future costs and benefits, rather than waste all our effort. On the other hand, we may conclude that, no matter what happens in the future, the project as a whole is bound to have had more costs than benefits and that we should therefore abandon it immediately. Both forms of reasoning are rejected by the logic of opportunity cost. What matters to a choice are the alternatives available now, not the costs that have been incurred in the past.

1.2.2. Labor and Wages

The logic of opportunity cost is clear enough for items such as materials and rent. However, because labor is the most important input to production in any economy, the cost of producing any good or service is determined, to a substantial extent, by the wage cost of the labor time required. Does the analysis of opportunity cost apply to work and wages?

At one level, the answer is "Yes."

The workers who produce a given good or service could have spent their time on another job (assuming other jobs are available), or at home, working around the house or enjoying leisure activities. In the first case, the opportunity cost of labor time is the wage that workers could have received if they took their "outside option," that is, the best available alternative job. The "wage" consists not merely of the hourly rate, but of employer-provided benefits and working conditions, including those that affect the enjoyability, safety, and security of the job.

Under conditions of full employment, it is easy enough for workers with generic skills to move from one job to another. And, in competitive labor markets, wages and working conditions are typically much the same for jobs with similar requirements and responsibilities.

An employer who offers wages below the opportunity cost of workers' time will not lose all their workers immediately. But their most mobile workers (usually including the best ones) will start looking for new jobs and will be hard to replace when they leave.

In the long run, therefore, an employer in a competitive labor market must pay the market wage. Under these circumstances, the market wage is, in general, a good measure of the opportunity cost for buyers and sellers. In a competitive labor market, where jobs are plentiful and workers can choose between employers, wages will therefore tend to reflect the opportunity costs workers face.

In reality, though, labor markets are rarely like this. When unemployment is high, workers are not free to move from one job to another. Even in situations of full employment, workers with specialized skills may have only a limited choice of employers. And, with labor market institutions such as employer-funded health insurance, switching jobs may be costly. To understand employment, unemployment, and wages, we need two lessons, not one. We will look at this in more detail in chapters 8 and 14.

1.3. Households, Prices, and Opportunity Costs

We've just seen how the logic of opportunity cost applies to producers. What about consumers? When we make our own daily decisions about what and how much to buy, market prices usually determine the opportunity costs we face.

Consider the age-old problem of balancing the family budget. Despite the good advice we receive, few of us do this in the systematic manner prescribed by manuals of home economics. Rather, most of us pay the bills that have to be paid, buy what we see as necessities, and then decide how to spend, or save, what is left over.

Sometimes, there's enough spare cash that we can pick and choose among optional expenditures. In this case, the logic of opportunity cost is clear enough. We can afford either a nice new jacket, made by the garment shop mentioned in the previous section, or a pleasant restaurant meal, but not both.

If we choose the jacket, its opportunity cost is the meal we might have enjoyed with the same expenditure. The market price of the jacket tells us how much, in the way of eating out or other optional expenditures, we must give up in order to get it.

At other times, the choices may be more difficult. There may not be enough money to pay for the necessities, let alone the luxuries. In these circumstances, the choices are either to go without (effectively redefining "necessities") or to go into debt, for example by running up the balance on the credit card.

If the decision is to go into debt, the opportunity cost of resolving the immediate problem of paying the bills is the increased difficulty of the choice that will have to be made in a month's time, when the credit card debt, plus interest, will be added to the regular bill. One way or another, the logic of opportunity cost is always relevant.

On the other side of the ledger, we must earn the money to pay our bills. For most households, this money comes primarily from wage employment. Under conditions of full employment, we always have the opportunity to find a job at the market wage. One Lesson economists assume that this is always the case, but in reality, full employment is more the exception than the rule (see section 8.4).

Depending on the nature of the job, we may be able to work more (or fewer) hours, gaining (or giving up) extra income from overtime. In the longer term, a couple's household must choose whether both members will seek full-time work or one will spend more time at home. This dilemma is particularly acute for couples with children, where the opportunity cost of time spent at work is time for childcare.

1.3.1. Household Production

When we talk about "the economy," most of the time we mean the world of paid work and production of goods and services for sale on the market (or, perhaps, provision by government, funded by taxation). However, thinking about opportunity cost brings home the fact that much economic activity takes place outside the market, mostly within the home, or, in the jargon of economics, the household sector. Time at home can be allocated to household work, childcare, or leisure. The wage that could otherwise be earned in the market sector is the opportunity cost of this time.

Household work substitutes more or less directly for market goods and services. A home-cooked meal is an alternative to eating out, a shopping trip is an alternative to home delivery, and so on. In each case, the choice is between using time to produce the good or service directly, or using the time to work to earn money, which can be used to buy goods and services on the market.

In this context, it's worth mentioning the concept of gross domestic product (GDP). GDP is a measure of the total output of the market sector of the economy. The concept was developed to assess whether the market sector was in a boom (in which case, it would attract unemployed workers back into work) or in a slump (in which case those workers would return to the household sector to engage in household work or involuntary idleness).

GDP was not intended as a measure of society's total productive activity or of economic well-being. Unfortunately, it is often (mis)used in this way, particularly by One Lesson economists. Advocates of lower corporate taxes and business-friendly regulation commonly argue that these policies will increase GDP. Even when this is true, it does not mean that society as a whole will be better off.

Although we have seen a lot of change over the past 50 years or so, most household work is still done by women and most market work by men.[5] The misuse of GDP as a measure of economic well-being devalues the work of women and reinforces existing inequalities.

1.4. Lesson One

These everyday choices illustrate Lesson One:

Market prices (including wages) tell us about the opportunity costs we face as consumers and workers.

---

[5] According to the Bureau of Labor Statistics, American men spend an average of 4.3 hours per day on paid work and related activities, and 1.8 hours per day on household activities, including childcare. Women spend 2.9 hours per day on paid work, and 2.7 hours per day on household activities.

But market prices are only one side of the equation that determines our possible choices. On the other side of the equation is income: the more we have, the wider the range of choices open to us. Incomes in turn are determined by the allocation of property rights, including financial wealth, access to education, obligations to pay debts including taxation, and rights to receive income from others, or from government programs like Social Security and Medicare.

Hazlitt, like other One Lesson economists, assumes the allocation of private property rights to be preordained and natural, while treating government programs like Social Security as an arbitrary intervention. In fact, all property rights are constructions of government and law. We will develop this point further in chapter 7.

In some cases, these constructions are obvious and immediately visible: in others they are decades or centuries old. Either way, the set of property rights is logically prior to the determination of property rights.

A huge amount of intellectual effort has gone into determining the prices that will emerge from a given set of property rights, production technologies, and consumer preferences. In the next chapter, we will examine the outcomes of this effort in the light of Lesson One.

1.5. The Intellectual History of Opportunity Cost

The idea of opportunity cost is a natural consequence of modernity. In a traditional society, most economic decisions are made on the basis of custom, or of fixed obligations (what Marx and Engels called "motley feudal ties"). The central idea of tradition is to do whatever has been done before. In a modern society, we are faced with new choices all the time, regarding how to spend our household income, how to manage the business of production, and how to determine public policy.

We have already seen what is, perhaps, the first presentation of the idea of opportunity cost, given by Benjamin Franklin. Franklin presented the idea as a piece of practical wisdom, naturally applicable in a modern commercial society, and particularly for the "tradesman" to whom his advice was addressed.[6] But it is equally applicable to anyone making the complex choices entailed by modern life.

Frédéric Bastiat was the first to deploy the idea of opportunity cost (though not the name) as a polemical weapon. Bastiat demolished spurious arguments for a variety of proposals to assist particular industries by pointing out that the proponents had focused on the benefits of the path they proposed without taking account of the opportunity costs of the (unseen) path not taken.

Bastiat is well known in the history of economic thought. The same cannot be said of Friedrich von Wieser, the Austrian economist who coined the term "opportunity cost" (*Opportunitätskosten* in German) along with the equally notable term "marginal utility."

For von Wieser, the concept of opportunity cost was applicable, not only to decisions made in markets but also to the distribution of wealth and resources for the community as a whole. A highly unequal distribution of wealth means that the luxury consumption of the rich takes precedence over the basic needs of the poor. As von Wieser sharply observes:

> It is therefore the distribution of wealth that decides what will be produced, and leads to a consumer of a more anti-economic variety: a consumer wastes on unnecessary,

---

[6] The term tradesman at the time encompassed shopkeepers as well as self-employed crafts workers.

guilty enjoyment that which could have served to heal the wounds of poverty.

Von Wieser used this idea to justify a progressive income tax.

The idea of opportunity cost was brought into the mainstream of economics by Austrian and Austrian-influenced economists, most notably F. A. Hayek, Ludwig von Mises, and Lionel Robbins. Unfortunately, all three were dogmatic One Lesson economists, who stripped von Wieser's idea of its egalitarian implications.

Mainstream economists largely accepted Robbins's dictum that interpersonal comparisons of well-being should be rejected as "unscientific" and sought to rebuild welfare economics without reference to such concepts as marginal utility. By the 1970s, when theorists such as Peter Diamond and James Mirrlees returned to the problem of optimal tax, the link to von Wieser's work and to the concept of opportunity cost was lost.

Meanwhile, rather than applying the opportunity cost concept to the actual problems of economics, von Wieser's students Hayek and Mises pursued a far less fruitful aspect of his work: the sterile nineteenth-century controversy over the "theory of value." By subordinating economic analysis to dogmatic market fundamentalism, Hayek and Mises drove the Austrian school of economics into a blind alley from which it has never escaped.

Further Reading

Among the vast number of introductory textbooks presenting the mainstream view of microeconomics, McCloskey (1982) is, in my opinion, the most idiosyncratic and enjoyable. Unfortunately, even this classic follows the usual pattern, stressing the importance of opportunity cost in the opening sections, but making little use of the concept in the main body of the work.

It's worth looking at a critical companion to such texts, pointing out the problematic assumptions, especially those that aren't spelled out. Fine's *Microeconomics: A Critical Companion* (2016) is a good choice. The companion volume, Fine and Dimakou, *Macroeconomics: A Critical Companion* (2016), is also worth reading. It stresses the point, developed in section 8.6, that analysis of the macroeconomy cannot be subordinated to One Lesson microeconomic reasoning. Rather, One Lesson reasoning depends on the assumption that the economy is operating under conditions of full employment.

The quotations at the beginning of section 1.1 are from Franklin (1748) and Frost (1921). *Robinson Crusoe* was first published as Defoe (1719). An accessible version is Defoe (2003). The study described in footnote 1 is reported in Ferraro and Taylor (2005). The quotation about economists' disagreement is unsourced, although it is often (incorrectly, as far as can be determined) attributed to George Bernard Shaw.

Philip Mirowski (2011), in a video currently available on YouTube, has some interesting remarks on how the Nobel Memorial Prize in Economics came into existence. A more detailed account, spelling out the relationship between One Lesson economics and the establishment of the Prize, is given in *The Nobel Factor* (Offer and Söderberg 2016).

Marilyn Waring's (1988) *Counting for Nothing* provides a feminist critique of GDP, the elements of which are sketched out in section 1.3.1. Estimates of paid and unpaid work are derived from the American Time Use Survey (Bureau of Labor Statistics 2018). Also of interest is Diane Coyle's (2015) *GDP: A Brief but Affectionate History*, which addresses these issues (notably in the introduction to the paperback edition).

Von Wieser's systematic presentation of the theory of opportunity cost and its relationship to marginal utility was presented in *Natural Value* (von Wieser 1893). Von Wieser's broader views were presented in his *Social Economics* (von Wieser 1927). Both are available in translation in Google Books. Streissler (1990) provides an accessible account of the first generation of the Austrian School. Robbins (1932) is an early and influential example of the fallacious idea that a value-free economics can have anything useful to say.

The Diamond and Mirrlees (1971a, 1971b) presentation of the theory of optimal taxation is highly mathematical, and accessible only to trained economists. We will give a simple presentation of some of the issues in chapter 13.

Other sources cited are Marx and Engels (1848).

CHAPTER 2

∎

Markets, Opportunity Cost, and Equilibrium

An economist is someone who knows the price of everything
and the value of nothing.[1]
—Popular adaptation of Oscar Wilde,
Lady Windermere's Fan

Economists talk a lot about markets and prices. Yet markets
are only one of the ways in which we balance the benefits and
opportunity costs of our choices. We've already looked at how
much economic activity takes place within families, and the opportunity costs of different choices they make. Governments
also make choices on behalf of society as a whole. In a properly
functioning democratic society those choices broadly reflect
the wishes of the voting public. As we will argue in more detail
when we discuss Lesson Two, the logic of opportunity cost is
just as relevant to governments as to firms and households.

Even in the business sector, markets often play only a sub-
ordinate role. Within a large corporation, decisions are made
through a hierarchical system that differs only in details from

---

[1] Wilde referred to "cynics" rather than economists, but the use of his turn of
phrase to describe economists has been widespread.

that of a centrally planned economy.[2] Other decisions involve contractual relationships with suppliers and large customers. It is only in the sale of final goods and services to households that market prices play the kind of role described in introductory textbooks.

What, then, is special about markets? The answer is: prices. When we make a market choice, between one item and another, the opportunity cost of one item is determined by its price relative to that of the alternatives. The same is true for a firm deciding what, and how much, to produce for the market.

These observations raise a number of questions.

- How are prices determined?
- How can the same price reflect opportunity costs for both producers and consumers?
- Do exchanges at market prices benefit everyone, or does one party (say, the seller) always benefit at the expense of the other?

Lesson One provides an answer to these questions, though not a complete answer. Under some stringent conditions, a competitive market equilibrium illustrates a strong form of Lesson One:[3]

In an ideal competitive equilibrium, market prices will equal opportunity costs, leaving no free lunches on the

---

[2] This observation was first made by the great Chicago economist Ronald Coase in the 1930s. At the time, Coase was shifting from his early socialist sympathies to a more market-oriented viewpoint and was able to encompass both positions in his analysis of the firm.

[3] One Lesson economists generally assume that these conditions hold, without bothering to spell them out. In the case of Hazlitt, writing in 1946, this was understandable, since the conditions weren't worked out precisely until the 1950s, with the work of Arrow and Debreu. His successors have no such excuse.

table. For a given distribution of property rights, exchanges at market prices benefit everyone.

2.1. TISATAAFL (There Is Such A Thing As A Free Lunch)

The acronymic adage TANSTAAFL (There Ain't No Such Thing As A Free Lunch, pronounced /tan′-stah-fl/) was popularized, particularly in propertarian circles, by Milton Friedman and, a little earlier, by Robert Heinlein's science fiction classic *The Moon Is a Harsh Mistress*.[4]

The adage is derived from a marketing ploy used by nineteenth-century saloons, which offered a "free" lunch to customers, on the assumption that they would wash it down with beer or other drinks. Naturally, the cost of the lunch was incorporated into the price of the drinks.

The key idea may be restated in terms of the broader point that it is opportunity cost, rather than just monetary cost, that matters when making economic decisions. Although there is no explicit charge for the lunch, patrons can only consume it at the opportunity cost of forgoing cheaper beer to go with the lunch.

Propertarians commonly use the TANSTAAFL adage to point out that services provided "free" by governments will, in general, have an opportunity cost. "Free" provision of some

---

[4] Advocates of this viewpoint normally describe themselves as "libertarian." I'm using the term "propertarian" for two reasons. First, ownership of the term libertarian is strongly contested by left-wing libertarians, who regard the enforcement of property rights by government as an assault on freedom. Second, an emphasis on the desirability of protecting markets and the existing system of property rights from government intervention need not be associated with any concern about liberty in general. This has become increasingly evident under the Trump administration.

service must be funded either by higher taxes or by reductions in other areas of public expenditure. The more general point, that it's necessary to look at the full opportunity cost of any good or service, and not just the immediate price, is yet another version of Lesson One.

But there is a contradiction here. Most economists think that improved economic policy can yield better outcomes for everyone, even though they may disagree about which policies would yield this result. Propertarians, who extol the benefits that might be realized by rolling back state control and giving markets free rein, are no exception to this rule.

A free lunch is "something for nothing," that is, a benefit obtained with no opportunity cost. Conversely, TANSTAAFL holds if and only if there are no free lunches left on the table, which in turn will only happen if the economic system is functioning perfectly. So, if economic outcomes can be improved for everyone, the correct statement is TISATAAFL (There Is Such A Thing As A Free Lunch).

The TANSTAAFL adage embodies an important truth applicable to many apparent "free lunches," in which the true opportunity cost is carefully hidden. However, if TANSTAAFL were literally true, humanity could never have risen above subsistence.

The more important truth, argued by economists beginning with Adam Smith's *The Wealth of Nations*, is TISATAAFL. The poorest person in a modern developed economy enjoys, with less effort and toil, a range of goods and services that were unavailable to our ancestors. The improvements in living standards generated by a modern economy are, for us, a free lunch. In fact, economics tells us about two kinds of free lunch, technological innovations and improved allocation of resources.

Technological innovations are the most obvious kind of free lunch. Technological innovations that allow us to produce a given output with less of every kind of input, including labor, provide us with the classic example of free lunch. Adopting the new technology allows us to increase output without using any additional resources. So, the opportunity cost of the additional output is zero. The only thing required to improve production and consumption possibilities in this way is information.

The second kind of free lunch, the core concern of economics, arises from improved allocation of resources. Lesson One leads us to think about improvements that can be generated by allowing markets to work. In Lesson Two we will see that public policy can yield improved resource allocation when markets fail to match prices and social opportunity costs.

Exchange through trade and markets can generate benefits for everyone, compared to a situation where everyone relies on themselves. When Crusoe trades fish for Friday's goat, each obtains a meal that would have had a higher opportunity cost in the absence of trade. The improvement is a (partly) free lunch, or maybe a free dinner.

By contrast, the saloon story underlying TANSTAAFL, in which an apparent bargain turns out to be nothing of the kind, stands in stark opposition to the economic idea of exchange as a bargain in which both parties benefit. It is in line with the premodern view of trade as a zero-sum game, in which any gain to one part is a loss for the other.

With a correct economic analysis, the saloon story illustrates TISATAAFL. Suppose that the customer would be willing to pay the saloon's price for the beer alone. Then, compared to the situation in the absence of exchange, the lunch really is free. For the lunch not to be free, the price of beer in the saloon must be more than the opportunity cost of obtaining the beer some other way, for example, at another saloon or through home brewing.

However, assuming the saloon is not operating at a loss, its price must cover the saloon's opportunity cost of providing both the beer and the lunch. If this cost is the same as that facing businesses where the beer and the lunch are priced separately, then the price of the lunch is fully included in the price of the beer. There is a net gain from exchange between the saloon and the customer, whether the beer and lunch are priced separately or sold together.

Under ideal conditions, the market outcome will ensure that there are no free lunches left on the table. These are the conditions of perfect competitive equilibrium, which we will consider in section 2.4. But first, we will look in more detail at the idea of gains from exchange.

2.2. Gains from Exchange

Understanding opportunity costs leads us to a central idea of economics. This is the idea of gains from exchange, or, more precisely, the idea that a voluntary exchange of goods and services can, and ordinarily will, leave both parties better off.

At first glance, this idea seems paradoxical, and throughout history, many people have viewed any kind of trade as a zero-sum game. That is, whatever one party gains must be at the expense of the other. The most recent example of such thinking is demonstrated by US president Donald Trump.

The reasoning underlying Trump's apparently plausible view is simple, particularly where goods are traded for money. An item has a "true value" or "just price." If the item is sold for more than its true value, the seller gains at the expense of the buyer, and vice versa.

It is perhaps not surprising that Trump should see trade in this way. Speculative real estate transactions are, in large measure, zero-sum deals in which the seller (or buyer) wins by getting a price that is higher (or lower) than the market value. Trump's book, *The Art of the Deal*, exemplifies this thinking. Indeed, the book itself is a minor instance, since buyers weren't told that they were reading the words of a ghostwriter, rather than those of Trump himself.

Opportunity cost reasoning shows why trade isn't generally zero-sum. Sticking with books as the example, suppose that F. A. von Hayek offers a copy of his classic free-market polemic, *The Road to Serfdom*, to Keynes, in return for a copy of Keynes's *The General Theory of Employment, Interest and Money*. The opportunity cost to Hayek of the copy of Keynes's book is a copy of his own book and vice versa.

Since each of these famous authors has presumably read his own book, and probably has more copies on hand, the opportunity cost associated with giving up one copy of their own book is small. It might perhaps be the opportunity to give the book as a present to a family member.

On the other hand, since it is important to understand one's intellectual adversaries, both Keynes and Hayek would naturally want to read what the other had written.[5] So, the value of the book received in exchange would be greater than the opportunity cost of the book given away, even though both authors presumably would regard their own arguments as more convincing.

Of course, it might be that one or both of the authors doesn't value the opportunity to read the other's work as highly as the opportunity cost of giving up a copy of their own book. In this case, trade would indeed be harmful to at least one party. Under these circumstances, however, the trade won't take place. So, the fact that trade takes place is sufficient to conclude that both parties are better off, relative to the alternative of not trading.

---

[5] In this case, the adversarial nature of the relationship was somewhat one-sided. Hayek rejected Keynes's *General Theory*, but Keynes later wrote to Hayek in quite complimentary terms about *The Road to Serfdom*. Moreover, Hayek was not particularly notable among the critics of the *General Theory*. The supposed Keynes-Hayek contest really reflects Hayek's latter-day reputation as the prophet of market liberalism and the "Austrian school" of economics.

The argument doesn't change at all if, instead of bartering goods, the transaction involves money. For the buyer, the opportunity cost of the purchase price of an item is the goods or services the money could have been used for otherwise, and the purchase will go ahead only if the value of the item exceeds this opportunity cost. For the seller, the value of the sale is the value of the goods that can be bought with the proceeds, while the opportunity cost is the good itself, or the resources required to replace it.

Once again, trade will take place only if the value gained for both parties exceeds the opportunity cost, so that both parties are better off than they would be without the trade. In fact, trade using money allows us to put things more simply. A sale will take place only if the price is less than the value of the item to the buyer and more than the value of the item to the seller.

The fact that both parties gain from voluntary exchange does not mean that the outcome of such exchanges is fair to both. Before exchange can take place, property rights must be defined and enforced. If property rights are unequally and unfairly allocated in the first place, they will remain unequal and unfair after voluntary exchanges have taken place.

Moreover, trading between two people may close off opportunities for others to trade, and thereby make them worse off. When a new supplier offers products at lower prices, its customers are better off, but the firms that formerly supplied those customers are not. So, moving from restricted to unrestricted trade need not make everyone better off.

2.3. Trade and Comparative Advantage

International trade is a special kind of exchange, and one that has always been more complex and controversial than ordinary market purchases and sales between residents of the same country, using the same currency. The language in which international trade is commonly discussed, centered on terms like "competitiveness," "surplus," and "deficit," tends to reinforce the view that exchange, at least between different countries, must be a zero-sum game.

Economists have long rejected this view. Their key arguments are based on the concept of comparative advantage, first developed by the great classical economist David Ricardo. Although the term is used mostly in relation to international trade, it's equally applicable to any kind of trade.

The idea of comparative advantage is subtle, powerful, and surprising. An understanding of comparative advantage, and the resulting theory of gains from trade, is one of the things that separates economists from just about everybody else. Not surprisingly, economists are very fond of the idea; sometimes too fond.

Ricardo used the example of trade between Portugal (then and now a producer and exporter of wine) and England (then, but not now, a producer and exporter of cloth). I'll try to bring things up to date by looking instead at the United States and Australia. In keeping with the general idea of this book, focusing on ideas rather than graphs and calculations, I'll also forgo the presentation of a numerical example.

On a superficial look at the two economies, it might seem that Australian producers can't compete with the United States in any important industry. The United States is more technologically advanced and US farmland is richer and more fertile than Australia's. Australia produces lots of coal and iron ore, but the United States also produces more of these commodities than it needs for domestic use.

Unsurprisingly, the United States exports a lot of manufactured goods, such as boats, to Australia. On the other hand, Australia exports a wide variety of agricultural products to the

United States, notably including beef, and would sell more if not for a variety of restrictions on market access, imposed with the aim of protecting US farmers.

To see why, let's apply Lesson One, and think about the opportunity cost of producing beef in Australia and in the United States. To keep things simple, suppose that the alternative is to produce boats.

Suppose Australia were to produce more boats, to replace boats imported from the United States. That might be done by converting cattle ranches into timber plantations from which to make boats, and re-employing Australian farmworkers as boatbuilders. Unfortunately, the land on which beef cattle is mostly raised in Australia is low in fertility and doesn't get reliable rainfall. That makes it less productive as cattle country, but it's even less well suited for producing timber. The opportunity cost of using land for beef is the value of the timber that might otherwise be grown, and that value is very low.

The same point applies to labor. In our example, the opportunity cost of farmworkers' labor used in beef production is the extra boats the same workers could produce if they were retrained as boatbuilders. For a variety of reasons, output per hour in most Australian manufacturing industries is lower than in the United States, so the number of extra boats produced for each ton of beef forgone would be small, well below the number that could be produced by transferring US workers from agriculture (beef) to manufacturing (boats). That is, in the US case, the opportunity cost of beef is higher, and the opportunity cost of boats is correspondingly lower.

Putting these points together, we can see that to produce more boats, Australia would have to give up a lot of beef production. By contrast, the opportunity cost of boats and other manufactured goods in the United States is much lower. So, in a simple system of barter, it would make sense for Australians to trade their beef for American manufactures, exactly as happens in reality.[6]

2.4. Competitive Equilibrium

Let's restate Lesson One:

> Market prices reflect and determine the opportunity costs faced by consumers and producers.

We've seen how market prices determine the opportunity costs we face in making economic decisions as consumers, workers, and producers of goods and services. We can't, as individuals, change the market prices we face for goods and services in general, so we must take them as given in looking at the opportunity cost of different choices.

But Lesson One says something more, namely that market prices also *reflect* opportunity costs. That is, just as the opportunity costs of our choices are determined by market prices, those market prices are determined by our choices. Under ideal conditions, those choices, aggregated over all the members of a society, will reflect the opportunity costs for that society as a whole.

There is a large branch of economic theory devoted to proving results of this kind using formal mathematics. But the core of the idea may be approached using the idea of "no free

---

[6] It's true that the United States sells more goods and services to Australia than it buys; that is, the United States has a surplus in its bilateral balance of trade with Australia. But this doesn't reflect an absolute US advantage. China runs a surplus in its trade with the United States and a deficit in its trade with Australia. This pattern of "triangular trade" is found quite commonly. It makes sense because trade is determined by comparative advantage, not absolute advantage.

lunches" or, more precisely, "no benefits without *equal* opportunity costs," as discussed in section 2.1.

As we saw then, this condition requires that all production be technologically efficient. If not, there is always a free lunch to be had by making production more efficient, thereby producing more with the same inputs.

The second "no free lunch" requirement is that there should be no gains from mutually beneficial exchange remaining to be realized. It's easy to see that this requirement is closely related to market prices.

Example 1: Suppose that you own a new jacket that you would be willing to trade for tickets to tonight's baseball game, while I have tickets and would be willing to trade them for your jacket.

Now let's look at market prices. If the market price of the jacket is greater than the price of the tickets, there is no need for you to trade with me. You can sell the jacket at the market price, use the proceeds to buy the tickets, and have money left over. Since you make the best possible choices, that's what you will do. If I want to complete the trade, by selling my tickets and buying the jacket, I will have to make up the price difference.

On the other hand, if the market price of the jacket is less than that of the tickets, the fact that this price prevails indicates that there must be someone else willing to sell jackets and buy tickets at those prices. So, I can sell my tickets and use the proceeds to buy a jacket, making an exchange that benefits both me and the other parties involved. You, on the other hand, are out of luck. At the prevailing prices, no one is willing to trade tickets for a jacket, and there are no remaining exchanges to be made.

This simple example gives a flavor of the argument that leads to Lesson One. Intuitively, it suggests the conclusion that trade at market prices will capture all the potential gains from mutually beneficial exchanges, so that no free lunches will be left on the table. In other words, in market equilibrium, TANSTAAFL holds.

This is where casual presentations of Lesson One commonly stop. But the simple story above embodies a lot of assumptions about the way markets work.

The most important are:

(A) Everyone faces the same market-determined prices for all goods and services, including labor of any given quality, and everyone can buy or sell as much as they want to at the prevailing prices.

(B) Everyone is fully aware of the prices they face for all goods and services, including how uncertain events might affect those prices.

(C) No one can influence the prices that they face.

(D) Everyone makes the best possible choices given their preferences and the technology available to them.

(E) Sellers bear the full opportunity cost of producing the good, and buyers receive the full benefit of consuming it, no more and no less. That is, no one can shift costs associated with production or consumption to anyone else without compensation (for example, by dumping waste products into the environment) and no one else receives benefits for which they do not pay.

We can go back to the ticket-for-jacket example above to see where each of these conditions fits in.

If the market price of the jacket is greater than the price of the tickets, there is no need for you to trade with me. You can (assumption A) sell the jacket at the market price (which is unaffected by assumption C), use the proceeds to buy the tickets, and have money left over. Since you make the best possible choices (assumption D), that's what you will do. If I want to complete the trade, by selling my tickets and buying the jacket, I will have to make up the price difference. By assumption (E), no one else is affected.

This more complicated version of the story can be formulated in mathematical terms to show that, under the stated conditions (and some additional technical requirements), a competitive equilibrium will arise in which there are no free lunches; that is, any potential benefit entails an opportunity cost that is at least as great.[7]

In this "perfectly competitive" equilibrium, the price of any particular good is equal, for everyone who consumes that good, to the opportunity cost of a change in consumption, expressed in terms of the best alternative use they could make of the money paid for the good. Similarly, firms can maximize profits only if the prices of the goods they produce are equal to the opportunity cost of the resources that could be saved by producing less of those goods.

This point is the core of Lesson One. In a perfect competitive equilibrium, prices exactly match opportunity cost. There are no "free lunches" left. More precisely, any additional benefit that can be generated for anyone in the economy must be matched by an equal or greater opportunity cost, where opportunity cost is measured by the goods and services forgone, valued at the equilibrium prices. This opportunity cost may be borne by those who benefit from the change or by others.

---

[7] The proof of this result by Kenneth Arrow and Gerard Debreu in the 1950s was arguably the greatest theoretical achievement of mathematical economics. However, as we will see, its implications for economic theory and economic policy are routinely misunderstood. Moreover, the result says nothing about whether, and how fast, the economy will actually reach this equilibrium.

One Lesson economists like Hazlitt implicitly assume something much stronger: that if prices reflect opportunity costs, there is no room for improvement in public policy. In particular, he assumes that any policy that benefits one group at the expense of others is undesirable. To put it more strongly, the distribution of income associated with the competitive market equilibrium we might observe if all government intervention were removed is assumed to be optimal.

This idea is false. As we will see, there are a vast number of possible outcomes in which there are no free lunches, each corresponding to a different allocation of rights and a different market equilibrium.

2.5. Free Lunches and Rents

Whenever there's a free lunch left on the table, there is a gap between prices and opportunity costs.[8] If the price of a good or service is higher than the opportunity costs, some potential producers who would benefit from selling are not doing so. On the other hand, those who do sell are getting a price that exceeds their opportunity cost. The same is true, in reverse, for buyers, in the case where price is less than opportunity cost.

Economists use a variety of names for the difference between the price and the opportunity cost, including "economic profit," "true profit," and, most commonly, "economic rent." A competitive equilibrium is characterized by the absence of economic rent. Moreover, a common way of generating rents is to exclude rivals from a market, either through dubious business practices or by enlisting the aid of governments to restrict market access

---

[8] The idea for this section was suggested by an anonymous reader for Princeton University Press.

to a favored few. For both these reasons, economists tend to view rents with suspicion and the term "rent-seeking" is invariably used pejoratively.

Rents are not always bad, however. The first firm to bring a new and improved product to market earns rents, at least until rivals can copy their innovations. And the wage premium workers receive when they form an effective union is a kind of rent. In situations of high inequality, like those that currently prevail in the United States, an increase in incomes flowing to workers is likely to be socially beneficial, whether or not it is consistent with competitive market equilibrium. These issues are discussed in chapter 12.

2.6. Adam Smith and the Division of Labor

Although there were previous writers on economic topics, and although he thought of himself as a moral philosopher rather than as an economist in the modern sense, Adam Smith's classic *The Wealth of Nations* is rightly regarded as marking the beginning of economics in its present form. Smith was the first economist to give a systematic exposition of the gains from trade. He was equally insightful when it came to technological change.

Smith sought to understand the processes by which living standards could increase over time. His primary focus was on technological progress arising from the division of labor.[9]

His famous example of the pin factory illustrates the point and is worth quoting in full.

---

[9] Smith was by no means the first writer to stress the importance of the division of labor, or even its importance in the manufacture of pins. His great insight was to see the crucial role of the division of labor in technological progress.

To take an example, therefore, from a very trifling manufacture; but one in which the division of labour has been very often taken notice of, the trade of the pin-maker; a workman not educated to this business (which the division of labour has rendered a distinct trade), nor acquainted with the use of the machinery employed in it (to the invention of which the same division of labour has probably given occasion), could scarce, perhaps, with his utmost industry, make one pin in a day, and certainly could not make twenty. But in the way in which this business is now carried on, not only the whole work is a peculiar trade, but it is divided into a number of branches, of which the greater part are likewise peculiar trades. One man draws out the wire, another straights it, a third cuts it, a fourth points it, a fifth grinds it at the top for receiving the head; to make the head requires two or three distinct operations; to put it on, is a peculiar business, to whiten the pins is another; it is even a trade by itself to put them into the paper; and the important business of making a pin is, in this manner, divided into about eighteen distinct operations, which, in some manufactories, are all performed by distinct hands, though in others the same man will sometimes perform two or three of them. I have seen a small manufactory of this kind where ten men only were employed, and where some of them consequently performed two or three distinct operations. But though they were very poor, and therefore but indifferently accommodated with the necessary machinery, they could, when they exerted themselves, make among them about twelve pounds of pins in a day. There are in a pound upwards of four thousand pins of a middling size. Those ten persons, therefore, could make among them upwards of forty-eight thousand pins in a day. Each person, therefore, making a tenth part of forty-eight thousand pins, might be considered as making four thousand eight hundred pins in a day. But if they had all wrought separately and independently, and without any of them having been educated to this peculiar business, they certainly could not each of them have made twenty, perhaps not one pin in a day; that is, certainly, not the two hundred and fortieth, perhaps not the four thousand eight hundredth part of what they are at present capable of performing, in consequence of a proper division and combination of their different operations.

Smith goes on to spell out three sources of technological progress. First, the acquisition through education and experience of specialized skills. Second, the savings in time that are realized by doing a single task repeatedly, rather than switching between a number of tasks, each requiring appropriate equipment. Finally, the benefits of improvements in the design of machinery, some discovered by workers on the job and others by specialist researchers.

In modern economic jargon, these are referred to as "human capital," "economies of scale," and "technological innovation," respectively.

The logic of opportunity cost and specialization explains why people in developed economies spend much of their time producing goods and services for sale, then exchange their earnings for goods and services produced by others.[10]

A skilled worker, with specialized equipment, say a bricklayer, can lay a large number of bricks in the time that it would take him to stop laying bricks and perform some other task, such as repairing his car. The same is true in reverse for a mechanic,

---

[10] Although not all of their time. A large part of economic activity, particularly for women, consists of the production of services, and to a lesser extent goods, for the use of their own household.

who might think about taking time off work to lay a brick wall around her garden. So, the opportunity cost of car maintenance is higher for the bricklayer than for the mechanic and vice versa. This allows for gains from trade that take the form of productivity gains from the division of labor.

Further Reading

Unusually among Nobel Prize–winning economists, Coase wrote comparatively little. His fame rests almost entirely on two articles: "The Nature of the Firm" (Coase 1937) and "The Problem of Social Cost" (Coase 1960), which will be discussed in subsequent chapters.

Wikipedia traces the phrase "There Ain't No Such Thing As A Free Lunch" back to a 1938 article in the *El Paso Herald-Post*, where it is the punchline of a joke. This implies that readers already understood the point of the adage, which had presumably circulated in oral form for some time. Heinlein (1966) put the phrase into wider circulation.

Heinlein began his career as a supporter of the radical writer Upton Sinclair, author of such works as *The Jungle* (Sinclair 1906), which included a critical description of the "free lunch" saloons of the late nineteenth century. Over time, however, Heinlein moved to the political right. Riggenbach (2010) quotes a study by the Society for Individual Liberty, claiming that one propertarian activist in six had been led to propertarianism by reading Heinlein's novels, of which *The Moon Is a Harsh Mistress* (Heinlein 1966) is the most overtly propertarian.

Milton Friedman (1975) used the more conventionally phrased "There's No Such Thing as a Free Lunch" for a collection of essays and columns critical of arguments for government regulation.

Smith's *Wealth of Nations* is one of the few economics "classics" that is still worth reading. It can't be fully understood without also reading his *Theory of Moral Sentiments*. I've listed free online versions of both in the bibliography, but there is no general agreement as to which is the best text.

Keynes (1936) and Hayek (1944) are also important in understanding contemporary debates, although Hayek's book is (in my view) spectacularly wrong (Quiggin 2010). The (mis)understanding of Hayek as Keynes's leading intellectual adversary is evident in videos like https://www.youtube.com /user/EconStories.

Ricardo's theory of comparative advantage was presented in his major work, *The Principles of Political Economy and Taxation* (Ricardo 1817), but in this case, I'd recommend getting the more accessible version presented in an introductory microeconomics text, such as McCloskey (1982), rather than going to the notoriously obscure original.

Debreu's (1959) little book, *Theory of Value*, which gives his mathematical proof of the existence of competitive equilibrium, is a gem, though one that can be appreciated only with the benefit of a mathematical education. Arrow and Debreu (1954) jointly presented the results of their work to prove this result.

CHAPTER 3

∎

Time, Information, and Uncertainty

Again I saw under the sun that—the race is not to the swift,
nor the battle to the strong, nor food to the wise, nor riches to
the intelligent, nor favor to those with knowledge; but time
and chance happen to them all.
    —Ecclesiastes 9:11, Modern English Version (MEV)

The discussion of Lesson One in the previous chapter, like most
introductory discussions of economics, deals with a timeless
world of perfect certainty. Goods are exchanged once and for
all. Everyone knows what they are giving up, what they are getting, and the price at which the exchange can take place.

Is Lesson One still relevant when we think about a more realistic representation of the world, where choices are made over
time, and with limited information about the future? If so,
what are the market prices in question and how much can they
tell us about opportunity costs?

In this chapter, we will show that the answer to the first question is "Yes." Interest rates, insurance premiums, and the market
values of financial assets are all special kinds of prices. When
financial markets function smoothly, they tell us about the opportunity cost of choices between the present and the future
and between different possible future contingencies. Lesson
One is as important as ever.

3.1. Interest and the Opportunity Cost of (Not) Waiting

Interest rates are prices that express the cost of current expenditure, financed by borrowing, in terms of the future repayment that must be made. Interest rates can be expressed in many different ways, but the most common and useful is the annual percentage rate (APR). If the APR is equal to, say, 5 percent, $100 borrowed today converts to a repayment of $105 in a year's time. Longer terms may be calculated using the standard formulas for compound interest.

What does this mean in terms of opportunity cost? A useful device is the "rule of 70," which states that a sum invested with compound interest at a percentage rate of interest r doubles its value in approximately $70/r$ years.[1] For example, a dollar invested now at 2 percent will be worth two dollars in 35 years' time. That is, the opportunity cost of spending a dollar today is the two dollars of spending that would be available 35 years from now.

A rate of 2 percent may seem low, but, in fact, it is the correct starting point for thinking about the opportunity costs involved in choices between the present and the future. Where repayment in full is taken as certain (as was the case until very recently for US government bonds), and where inflation is not a major problem, interest rates are normally around this level. Over the past two centuries, the "risk-free" rate of interest, after adjusting for inflation, has averaged about 2 percent. At the time of writing it is below 1 percent.

---

[1] For the mathematically inclined, the basis for the rule is the fact that the natural log of 2 is approximately 0.7, while the natural log of the return on investment, $1+r$, is approximately equal to r for small values of r.

How are interest rates determined? As with every price, it is necessary to look at the issue from the perspective of both consumers and producers.

3.1.1. The Production Side

On the production side, the nature of technology is such that an investment made now can return its value, and more, in the future. The earliest (and still an important) illustration of this came with the discovery of agriculture in the Neolithic era. Before agriculture, humans gathered goods in much the same way as other animals, though with the use of tools and enhanced cooperation. They collected grains and other plant products to eat and killed wild animals for their meat.

Provided population pressure was low enough, the opportunity cost of hunting and gathering was very low. The animals and plants consumed in one season were replaced by the ordinary processes of reproduction.

If population pressure was too great, animals that were hunted for food could be driven to extinction or reduced in population to a level where the opportunity cost of collecting food one day was to have less available the next. Successful hunter-gatherer societies evolved institutions, such as tribal boundaries and taboos, that took this opportunity cost into account. Such institutions were essentially stationary in nature, maintaining populations at a stable sustainable level.

The key discovery for agriculture was that, by saving some grain and sowing it where the new plants could be protected, the initial seed would be returned manyfold. Similarly, by keeping some animals alive, and under control, each female would bear many young. Against this benefit must be set the added costs of managing crops and livestock. However, as long as there is sufficient land, there is still a net surplus.

Under suitable conditions, such as those prevailing in the Fertile Crescent of Western Asia and in the river valleys of Egypt, India, and China, the discovery of agriculture enabled a massive increase in the amount of food that could be produced in a given area, and therefore in the human population it could support. Expanding agricultural populations, seeking more land, rapidly drove hunter-gatherer societies out of areas suitable for cropping and grazing, and into more marginal hill and forest country.

In an agricultural society, the opportunity cost of consuming an extra meal of grain, say wheat, today is the amount of food that could be produced the following season if the grain was saved for seed. Similarly, a steak dinner today comes at the cost of the amount of meat that could be produced next year if the animal were saved for breeding or fattening.

Under normal conditions, the quantity used as seed is less than the amount harvested in the future. However, this need not be the case. In a year of particular abundance, and in conditions where storage is difficult or impossible, there may be so much grain left over that it makes sense to sow it on marginal ground, where the yield may be less than the original investment of seed.

John Maynard Keynes expressed these ideas in terms of the "wheat rate of interest." If, for example, 100 bushels of wheat used as seed grain today would produce 110 bushels next harvest, the wheat rate of interest is 10 percent. As Keynes observed, while the wheat rate of interest is normally positive, it may, in some circumstances, be negative.[2]

---

[2] In his anti-Keynesian polemic, "The Failure of the 'New Economics': An Analysis of the Keynesian Fallacies," Hazlitt missed the point completely, claiming that "a negative rate of interest is a foolish and self-contradictory conception." In reality, a negative rate of interest will arise naturally in an agricultural society in any

In a society with productive opportunities that yield a positive net return, interest may be seen as the opportunity cost of consuming now, rather than investing and consuming more in the future. More succinctly, interest is the opportunity cost of not waiting.

The abstract economic reality of opportunity cost was soon translated into the concrete social institutions of money and debt. Agricultural societies produced a food surplus, which could be used to sustain specialist trade workers. Rather less usefully, the surplus could be extracted by military rulers in the form of taxes and compulsory gifts.

The obligations of subjects to rulers, and of the poor to the rich, gave rise to the institution of debt. The logic of opportunity cost then ensured that the settlement of debts required the repayment not only of the amount originally owed (the principal) but also of the additional opportunity cost (interest). Resentment over this exaction, and the power imbalance with which it has typically been associated, has been a constant theme in political, social, and religious conflict between creditors and debtors ever since.

While the conceptual idea of an "own-rate of interest" for commodities such as wheat is useful, debts and interest are most naturally expressed in terms of money. For kings and specialist lenders alike, money provides a common unit of account and store of value. That is, money arose from debt, and only later came into use as a medium of exchange.[3] This idea overturns

---

period where food is unusually abundant but not storable. Hazlitt was presumably led astray by thinking about money, which can be stored at little or no cost.

[3] In his recent book, *Debt: The First 5000 Years*, David Graeber made this point, and derived a range of interesting and controversial conclusions. In the course of my research, I discovered that the same observation had been made, much earlier, by my namesake, Alison Hingston Quiggin, in her classic work, *A Survey of Primitive Money*.

the standard (but entirely ahistorical) economists' story in which money arose as a way of overcoming the inconveniences of barter, and more complex financial instruments such as debts were derived from it.

Money has many advantages, but it can also obscure and mystify. Modern economic life involves numerous financial transactions: depositing into and withdrawing money from bank accounts, borrowing to finance a house purchase or business investment, and so on. Interest rates are clearly a kind of price, but it's not immediately obvious how this price is, or should be, determined. That's why it is useful to consider how the own-rate of interest idea applies to the opportunity costs of borrowing and lending in a modern economy.

Modern manufacturing technology faces the same logic of opportunity cost as agriculture. An investment of resources not consumed today can produce a larger amount in the future. In addition, the rapid technological progress that characterizes modern society has generated a new source of opportunity cost. The resources required to produce a given quantity and quality of final output are declining steadily. This process may be slow and gradual, as in the case of improvements in agricultural productivity. Alternatively, the process may be rapid, as in the case of information and communications technology, where Moore's Law predicts that the number of transistors in a dense integrated circuit will double approximately every two years. In some cases, the rate of technological progress may be essentially zero, as in the case of services such as haircuts, where there is hardly any change in productivity.[4]

----

[4] One implication is that the own-rate of interest will be higher for goods subject to rapid technological change, such as computers, than to manufactured goods in general, and lower in the case of services. This might seem to create a problem, given that the producers and consumers of all these goods and services face the same rate of interest on money. The problem is resolved by changes in prices over time. The price

Overall, the annual rate of growth in productivity is around 2 percent, which is approximately equal to the risk-free interest rate. As will be discussed in the following subsection, this equality is about what would be expected on the basis of sensible judgments about the opportunity cost trade-off between present and future consumption.

3.1.2. The Consumer Side

Every market transaction involves a buyer and seller, and market equilibrium involves opportunity costs for both producers and consumers. It is necessary to consider how interest rates affect the opportunity costs facing consumers and, conversely, how choices between present and future consumption help to determine market interest rates.

The existence of a positive interest rate implies that the opportunity cost of a given amount of consumption expenditure now is a larger amount in the future. Conversely, the opportunity cost of a given amount of consumption expenditure in the future is a smaller amount in the present.

The crucial factor is that in a growing economy, most people expect to consume more in the future than at present. Conversely, we expect our unmet needs and desires for consumption expenditure to be more pressing now than in the future. For the opportunity cost trade-off to be balanced, consumption forgone in the present must be matched by a larger increase in the future.[5]

---

of services like haircuts has risen by more than the rate of inflation, while the price of computers has fallen, even as their computing capacity has risen dramatically.

[5] An alternative, or sometimes complementary, explanation is that people are inherently impatient, and will always prefer present to future consumption. In particular, it is often suggested that members of the current generation (or at least, those in a position to make economic decisions) place more value on their own well-being than on that of later-born generations. There is not much evidence to support this

How big must the increase in future consumption be to outweigh the opportunity cost, namely the forgone opportunity to increase current consumption? One answer, which seems close to the views typically elicited when people are asked questions of this kind, is to treat equal proportional increases in consumption as being equally desirable. That is, an increase from $10,000 to $11,000 is just as desirable as an increase from $20,000 to $22,000. Conversely, if the opportunity cost of the $10,000 benefit to the high-income earner is a loss to the low-income earner of more than $1,000, the cost exceeds the benefit.

As this example shows, when total future consumption doubles, so does the additional future consumption required to justify the opportunity cost of a given amount of consumption forgone today. As we can see from the rule of 70, this balance will arise if the rate of interest is equal to the rate of growth of consumption. For example, if consumption is growing at 2 percent per year, it will double in 35 years. And, if the rate of interest is 2 percent, any given amount saved and invested today will double, with compound interest, over the same period of 35 years. More generally, the interest rate is the same as the rate of growth of consumption.

3.1.3. Which Rate of Interest?

In the discussion above, we looked at an idealized concept of the rate of interest, which is the same for all borrowers and lenders. This idealized concept corresponds to the risk-free interest rate, typically about 2 percent.

---

view. On the contrary, the more prevalent pattern is one of parents sacrificing their own welfare to improve the lives of their children. At least in well-functioning political systems, the same pattern can be observed in our collective decisions: governments routinely make long-term investments, both in physical infrastructure and in education, that will mostly benefit future voters rather than current ones.

In actual market settings, a wide variety of interest rates may be observed, from very low to very high. Standard "investment-grade" corporate bonds offer a higher interest rate than US Treasury bonds. The rate of interest on lower-grade "junk" bonds is substantially higher, and the rate on most kinds of consumer debt, higher again.

Explaining the differences between low and high interest rates is a complex exercise, beyond the scope of this book. But the crucial factor is risk; more precisely the "default risk" that a debt will not be repaid. Debt subject to default risk is subject to rates of interest (or expected rates of return) substantially higher than the risk-free rate, even after making an allowance for the average loss associated with default.

Equity (investment in the stock market or in private companies) is riskier again. The average rate of real return on equity, after allowing for the risk of corporate failure, has historically been around 8 percent. The difference between the rate of return on equity and the rate of interest on bonds is referred to as the "equity premium" and is substantially larger than can be explained by economic models based on Lesson One. We will look more closely at the "equity premium puzzle" in chapter 11 and show that its existence undermines many of the assumptions implicit in One Lesson economics.

There are much larger differences in the interest rates faced by individual borrowers. The rates charged by "payday lenders" to borrowers with poor credit history and little collateral can be as high as 400 percent.

This difference could not exist if it were not for default risk, which makes lenders like banks unwilling to make loans to borrowers with bad credit. However, the difference is much more than can be accounted for by default risk alone, or even by a premium for risk bearing. Once excluded from the regular credit market, borrowers are vulnerable to all kinds of predatory practices that force them to pay far more than is justified by default risk.

3.2. Information

It is cliché to say that we are living in an "information economy." The ubiquity of computers, mobile phones, and other digital devices makes it obvious that the great majority of us are engaged, to a greater or lesser extent, in dealing with information. In reality, though, information has always been central to economic activity.

Human beings differ from other animals in two crucial respects: our capacity to make and use tools, and our ability to communicate with each other. Both are crucially connected with information and with our ability to reason.

The information embodied in technology and our capacity to communicate it have enabled humans to develop large and complex societies. This development solves many problems but creates new ones: the information needed for a complex human society to operate is far more than any one person can acquire or process.

These problems are particularly severe in relation to economic activity. In any modern society, we depend on others for the great majority of our needs and wants, while our own labor is part of a complex production process no single person can fully understand. How do disparate parts of this system fit together to produce and distribute the goods and services we consume?

As Hayek and others have pointed out, markets provide one solution to this problem. It is worth quoting Hayek's classic article, "The Use of Knowledge in Society," at length on this point.

> Fundamentally, in a system where the knowledge of the relevant facts is dispersed among many people, prices can

act to coordinate the separate actions of different people in the same way as subjective values help the individual to coordinate the parts of his plan. It is worth contemplating for a moment a very simple and commonplace instance of the action of the price system to see what precisely it accomplishes. Assume that somewhere in the world a new opportunity for the use of some raw material, say tin, has arisen, or that one of the sources of supply of tin has been eliminated.

All that the users of tin need to know is that some of the tin they used to consume is now more profitably employed elsewhere, and that in consequence they must economize tin. There is no need for the great majority of them even to know where the more urgent need has arisen, or in favor of what other needs they ought to husband the supply. If only some of them know directly of the new demand, and switch resources over to it, and if the people who are aware of the new gap thus created in turn fill it from still other sources, the effect will rapidly spread throughout the whole economic system and influence not only all the uses of tin but also those of its substitutes and the substitutes of these substitutes, the supply of all the things made of tin, and their substitutes, and so on; and all this without the great majority of those instrumental in bringing about these substitutions knowing anything at all about the original cause of these changes. The whole acts as one market, not because any of its members survey the whole field, but because their limited individual fields of vision sufficiently overlap so that through many intermediaries the relevant information is communicated to all. The mere fact that there is one price for any commodity—or rather that local prices are connected in a manner determined by the cost of transport, etc.—brings about the solution

which (it is just conceptually possible) might have been arrived at by one single mind possessing all the information
which is in fact dispersed among all the people involved in
the process.

The marvel is that in a case like that of a scarcity of one
raw material, without an order being issued, without more
than perhaps a handful of people knowing the cause, tens
of thousands of people whose identity could not be ascer-
tained by months of investigation, are made to use the material or its products more sparingly; i.e., they move in the
right direction.

This is an excellent statement of the crucial idea behind One
Lesson economics, showing how market prices signal opportunity costs. But Hayek stops his analysis there. Although he says,
"The price system is just one of those formations which man
has learned to use after he had stumbled upon it without understanding it," Hayek shows little interest in exploring alternative
ways in which human societies manage the problems and opportunities associated with information. We will examine this
point further in chapter 11.

3.2.1. Information Economics and Robinson Crusoe

Robinson Crusoe is, as we have seen, a stock character in economics textbooks, engaged first in the production of food and
clothing for his own use and then in trade with Friday. But the
textbooks rarely ask how Crusoe manages the problem of production. The simple answer, and the one that will occur first to
an economist who bothers to read the original story by Daniel
Defoe, is that Crusoe has the necessary inputs: labor (his own),
land (the natural resources of the island), and capital (tools and
raw materials that he salvages from the shipwreck).

Reading on, it becomes apparent that Crusoe has something far more important: information. He knows, to begin with, how to build a raft and a simple house and how to light a fire. Although he begins by relying on food retrieved from the ship and hunting wild game, he soon commences agriculture.

Crusoe has the technological knowledge that might be expected of a seventeenth-century European sailor. He knows the basics of sowing and harvesting crops and of domesticating animals such as dogs and goats. He does not know how to mill grain, bake bread, or make pottery or metal tools. However, he knows these things are possible and sets himself, successfully, to work out how they are done. As a result, his standard of living is soon higher than that of the indigenous inhabitants of the region, who lack this knowledge.[6]

Defoe's Crusoe does not trade with Friday, but rather provides him with information so that they can work together. As would be expected by the readers of the day, the relationship between the two is that of master and servant, a status justified by the fact that Crusoe has rescued Friday from enemies who were about to kill and eat him. He teaches Friday about agriculture, and thereby increases Friday's productivity.[7] In Defoe's story, though not in the economists' version, information is more important than trade in generating free lunches for Crusoe and Friday.

3.3. Uncertainty

Uncertainty is, in a sense, the flip side of information. In a situation of uncertainty, we face a number of possibilities, and we have insufficient information to determine which one will be

---

[6] Defoe's account is based on the real-life experience of Alexander Selkirk.

[7] As well as imparting the elements of Christianity.

realized. The logic of opportunity cost applies here, as it does in choices over time. To take a simple example, suppose I decide to go out for a walk, and think about the possibility of a rainstorm. I can take an umbrella and stay dry. The opportunity cost of this choice, compared to the risk of getting wet, is the more enjoyable walk I would have, in the event of sunny weather, without the encumbrance of the umbrella.

For some, but not all, uncertain events, it is possible to determine an objective probability, on which most people will agree. Most obviously, provided they are "fair," gambling devices like dice and roulette have known odds of ending on any given number. More important, many kinds of events that are uncertain in individual cases, such as the risk of a house catching fire, can be assigned objective probabilities by analyzing a large enough number of cases. It is common to use the term "risk" to describe these cases, leaving uncertainty to cover the more general case when probabilities may be subjective or even impossible to determine.

Insurance markets provide a way to manage risk. If I insure my house against fire, I gain the benefit of a net payout in the event that the house burns, at the opportunity cost of a premium paid in advance. The premium (a particular kind of market price) charged in a competitive insurance market will depend on the risk of the insured event happening. Commonly, the premium will vary depending on the structure of the house and the protection measures (such as alarms and sprinkler systems) that are in place. Insurance premiums are another illustration of Lesson One. The premium gives me information about the opportunity costs associated with the various possible outcomes of different choices regarding the risk of fire.

At least in the idealized form found in most textbooks, financial markets provide the same kinds of opportunities for trading between different possible future events. For example, speculative stocks will yield a high payoff in boom conditions but may become worthless in recessions. "Countercyclical" stocks, such as those of companies offering cheap entertainment, are highly valued by risk-averse investors because they perform well during recessions, providing income when it is most needed.[8] Government bonds provide a fixed payoff regardless of economic conditions. There is a whole branch of financial economics devoted to calculating the appropriate price of such assets and to inferring the opportunity costs of the contingent payments the assets will yield.

In principle, then, Lesson One applies to choices involving uncertainty, as it does to choices over time. In practice, as we will see in the second half of this book, things are much more complex. The failure of financial markets to perform the role allotted to them by economic theory is one of the most important reasons why economics needs Lesson Two as well as Lesson One.

Further Reading

Homer and Sylla (2005) provide a detailed history of interest rates. For critical counterpoints, try Felix Martin's *Money: The Unauthorized Biography* (2015) and David Graeber's *Debt: The First 5,000 Years* (2011).

The story of the rise of agriculture has been told many times, typically from a "progressivist" perspective, in which it is part of a process that has seen humanity enjoy steadily improving living standards, the development of science and culture and political

---

[8] The classic example was that of movies during the Depression of the 1930s. Adjusted for inflation, *Gone with the Wind*, released in 1939, was the highest-grossing movie of all time, even though the US population was much smaller than today, and the unemployment rate exceeded 15 percent.

democracy, culminating either in socialism (Wells 1921) or market liberalism (Fukuyama 1992), depending on the trends of the times and the beliefs of the writer.

As alternatives to this optimistic view, it is worth reading Jared Diamond's (1987) description of agriculture as the "Worst mistake in the history of the human race," essentially because it allowed denser populations, resulting in harder work, more disease, and unhappier populations than those of the hunter-gatherers displaced by agriculture.

Keynes's definition of the "wheat rate of interest" was presented in his classic *General Theory of Employment, Interest and Money* (Keynes 1936). Hazlitt's attempted rebuttal is derived from Hazlitt (1959), a page-by-page critique of Keynes.

There's a huge literature on the equity premium puzzle, but most of it is only of interest to economists who like solving puzzles. I've worked on the topic with Simon Grant, trying to explain what the equity premium means for resource allocation and implicitly drawing on an opportunity perspective. The most readable exposition of our analysis is Grant and Quiggin (2005).

To get some perspective on the issue, it's useful to look at the way interest rates, and the differentials between high-risk and low-risk rates, have fluctuated over time. The Federal Reserve Economic Database (FRED) maintained by the Federal Reserve Bank of St. Louis (2017) is an excellent source of data on this and many other topics.

Hayek's discussion of information harks back to the "socialist calculation debate," which began with Mises's (1920) assertion that a socialist economy could not possibly function because it would contain no meaningful pricing system. Hayek (1938) expanded this argument, responding to the contrary view, put forth by Lange (1936, 1937), that a system of planning in which prices were used to represent opportunity costs was consistent with collective ownership of productive resources.

Stiglitz (1996) provides an overview of the debate in the light of the experience of the twentieth century.

Lev-Ram (2008) discusses the countercyclical nature of moviegoing.

Unfortunately, I'm not aware of a good, simple introduction to the economics of uncertainty that captures opportunity cost in a way I could recommend.

LESSON ONE

■

PART II

Applications

> It is the good fortune of the affluent country that the opportunity cost of economic discussion is low and hence it can afford all kinds.
>
> —John Kenneth Galbraith, *Economics, Peace,*
> *and Laughter* (1971)

The economic analysis showing how market equilibrium prices reflect the opportunity costs facing producers and consumers is elegant and, for a certain kind of mind, convincing.

For most of us, however, it's more useful to see how the logic of prices and opportunity costs works in particular cases, sometimes in ways that conflict with strongly held intuitions. This will also give us more insight into the ways in which prices can fail to reflect opportunity costs for society as a whole, some of which we will examine in Lesson Two.

In this section, we will look at three aspects of Lesson One.

In chapter 4, we will begin with a simple example that illustrates some of the tricks and traps in opportunity cost reasoning. We will then see how the logic of opportunity costs works in various markets, including those for air travel, college education, and advertising.

In chapter 5, we will look at implications for government policy. An understanding of opportunity cost shows why policies with a good deal of political appeal (to both the left and the right of politics) don't work as intended. These include price and rent control, food stamps and other policies designed to control how the poor spend their money, toll roads, and closed seasons in fisheries. A crucial point, not understood by most One Lesson economists, is that government policies create a variety of property rights and override existing, often informal, rights.

In chapter 6, we will examine the surprisingly durable idea that the destruction caused by wars and natural disasters is economically beneficial. Hazlitt rightly criticizes this idea in *Economics in One Lesson*. Although he overstates his case in some respects, a careful consideration reinforces the main conclusion. The idea of opportunity cost as "that which is not seen" provides a corrective against any attempt to minimize the costs of destruction.

CHAPTER 4

■

Lesson One: How Opportunity Cost Works in Markets

The problem with opportunity cost is that opportunity cost is divided among many, many things.
—Dan Ariely, interviewed by Kristen Doerer, PBS (2016)

4.1. Tricks and Traps

One way to sharpen thinking about opportunity costs is to try out some examples. Here's one that allegedly fooled a lot of professional economists.

> You won a free ticket (which has no resale value) to see an Eric Clapton concert. Bob Dylan is performing on the same night and is your next-best alternative activity. Tickets to see Dylan cost $40. On any given day, you would be willing to pay up to $50 to see Dylan. Assume there are no other costs of seeing either performer. Based on this information, what is the opportunity cost of seeing Eric Clapton? (a) $0, (b) $10, (c) $40, or (d) $50.

Recall the definition of opportunity cost:

The opportunity cost of anything of value is what you must give up to get it.

In this example, the opportunity cost of seeing Clapton is the best available alternative, namely, going to see Dylan. What is the value of this alternative? Based on the information presented in the question, a ticket to the Dylan concert sells for $40 but is worth $50 to you. So, by attending the Dylan concert you would obtain a net benefit of $10. This is the opportunity cost of going to see Clapton. So, the correct answer is (b).

When two hundred professional economists were asked this question during the annual conference of the American Economic Association, their answers were virtually random. Only 22 percent chose the correct answer (b). Some defenders of the profession have come up with convoluted defenses of their colleagues, amounting to arbitrary redefinitions of the concept of opportunity cost.[1] It seems far more likely, however, that the conditions under which the question was asked were stressful and conducive to error.[2]

Among the incorrect answers to the question above, the most intuitively appealing is probably (a). Since the Clapton ticket is stated to be free, it might reasonably be concluded that the cost of going to see the concert is zero. This, in turn, would suggest that, unless you absolutely dislike Clapton, you should go. But the logic of opportunity cost shows that this reasoning is

---

[1] On reflection, it seems far less embarrassing to admit that economists sometimes make mistakes than it is to claim, not only that the concept of opportunity cost can be defined any way you like, but that no one has noticed this until now.

[2] One subject recalls, "I was on the job market and had gone to the 4th floor of the hotel to check on where my interviews were going to be. As you might imagine, I was incredibly stressed out and distracted. I was then approached by somebody who wanted me to fill out this form."

incorrect. If, for example, the value to you of the Clapton ticket is $5, you are better off throwing it away and going to see Dylan.

What if you had paid $5 for a (nonrefundable) ticket to see Clapton when the opportunity to attend the Dylan concert came up? This is an example of "sunk costs" discussed in section 1.2.1. The money spent on the Clapton ticket is gone, whichever choice you make. So, the opportunity cost of going to the Clapton concert is $10, just as if the ticket was originally free.

4.2. Airfares

There was a time when air travel was simple and comfortable, but invariably expensive. For 40 years from the 1930s onward, the Civil Aeronautics Board (CAB), a US government authority, regulated all domestic interstate air transport routes as a public utility, setting fares, routes, and schedules. If you wanted to fly from, say, New York to Los Angeles, you would do so on an airline authorized to serve that route and pay a fare that would be the same whenever and however you booked it, except for the distinction between economy (coach) class and first class (now largely replaced by business class). Nearly all fares were flexible, allowing passengers to cancel or reschedule their flights whenever they wanted.

The Airline Deregulation Act of 1978, introduced by the Carter administration, did away with the CAB and allowed airlines to set their own schedules, fly whatever routes they wished, and charge whatever fares customers were willing to pay.

Airline deregulation was, arguably, the biggest single success of One Lesson economics. New airlines entered the market and provided stiff competition for the established airlines, which were accustomed to an easy life in a regulated market. Airfares fell, particularly for price-sensitive travelers such as tourists.

Large numbers of people traveled by air for the first time—and kept on doing so.

Deregulation was accompanied by many changes, including the replacement of "point to point" networks, in which most journeys were nonstop, by "hub and spoke" networks, where travelers typically flew from their starting point to the airline's central hub, changed planes, and flew on to their destination. The most notable example was Hartsfield-Jackson Airport in Atlanta, which grew from a relatively small regional airport to the busiest in the world—the result of being chosen as the hub for Delta Airlines.

But the single biggest change was the disappearance of the standard airfare. Instead of offering a choice between two fares, economy and first class, airlines offered fares that varied from day to day and even from hour to hour. Mostly these fares were lower than the old economy fares, but sometimes, particularly when flights were nearly full, they were substantially higher.

How can we make sense of this? Understanding the opportunity costs faced by airlines and travelers makes everything clear.

From the airline's point of view, opportunity cost bites twice. The first is when the airline decides whether or not to fly a particular service on a given route. The opportunity cost of doing so is that the plane and crew cannot be used for some other route. So, the airline will only want to offer the service if it is more profitable than the alternatives.[3]

Once the decision to fly has been made, the opportunity cost of a seat on the plane is close to zero. Each additional passenger must be checked in, have baggage handled, and so forth, but the main costs of the flight (the pilots and crew, the cost of

---

[3] In the long run, the airline can operate more or fewer planes, and hire or fire workers. But in the time frame in which scheduling decisions are made, we can assume that the alternative option is to fly another route.

operating the plane, and so on) are the same or (in the case of fuel) not much different whether the plane flies full or empty.

It follows that, rather than travel with an empty seat, the airline would do better to sell it for the marginal cost of serving an additional customer. But this marginal cost is far below the average cost per passenger of providing the service, that is, the opportunity cost of an alternative service divided by the number of passengers. So, the airline needs to charge at least some customers more than the average cost, and therefore much more than the marginal cost, if they are to justify the decision to offer the service.

The key to achieving this goal is to identify those passengers willing to pay the most and charge them a high price. Business travelers often need to travel on relatively short notice (a few weeks is typical) and do not pay the fare themselves. So, airlines charge a higher premium for business class than is needed to cover the extra costs of a business class seat and increase their fares in the few weeks before the flight departs.

In the last few days before a flight departs, the airline will know whether they are likely to have empty seats (in which case the fare will fall) or not (in which case the fare will rise rapidly).

A final element of this process is overbooking, the cause of a lot of ill feeling and, in 2017, a spectacular incident in which a passenger was forcibly removed from a plane and seriously injured in the process. On nearly all flights, some passengers are "no-shows" who don't turn up at the airport. As we've seen, the airlines want to avoid flying with empty seats, so they sell more tickets than there are seats on the plane. If too many passengers turn up, they attempt to buy seats back by offering concessions to passengers who are willing to take a later flight.[4]

---

[4] Until the recent incidents, airlines capped the amount they were willing to pay, and gave priority to their own staff. This led to ticketed passengers being

Now let's look at things from the passenger's viewpoint. The opportunity cost of buying a particular ticket may be, but mostly is not, the monetary cost. If the best alternative option is to forgo travel and spend the money on something else, then the monetary cost is a good measure of the opportunity cost. But most of the time that's not the case; people want to get from A to B and the only question is how. In this case, the best alternative is to make the trip on another flight, or perhaps to travel by road or rail.

In this situation, it makes sense for intending passengers to spend a fair bit of time searching for alternatives to get the lowest possible fare, and to ensure that they are as flexible as possible in terms of the time and date of their travel. All of this searching involves costs, which are part of the opportunity cost of travel.

Technology plays a paradoxical role here. The ease of searching for fares on the Internet reduces the costs to passengers of searching for the cheapest fare. However, this makes it harder for airlines to cover their costs, so they invest in even more powerful "yield management" software to improve their capacity to discriminate.

On the whole, air travelers have benefited from deregulation. However, not everyone has gained. As we've already seen, business passengers pay more under a deregulated system, and the costs of business travel are part of the opportunity cost of producing goods and services. As Lesson One tells us, prices in competitive markets reflect opportunity costs. So, more costly business travel means higher prices for goods and services in general. People who don't travel by air but pay the higher prices resulting from deregulation are worse off.

---

denied boarding or being forcibly removed, producing a public relations disaster. These policies might never have been adopted if more attention had been paid to opportunity cost reasoning.

The biggest losers, however, have been airline workers. Deregulation allowed new entrants to the industry without union contracts. Worse, many of the incumbent firms went through bankruptcy procedures that enabled them to break their contracts. As a result, whereas airline workers without specialized technical skills were once highly paid, they now earn little more than ground-based workers in comparable jobs. For example, many flight attendants make only a little more than servers in restaurants.

There are too many complexities in airline pricing to be dealt with in this short section. What we have seen here is that the seeming mysteries can be resolved by thinking carefully about opportunity cost.

4.3. The Cost of (Not) Going to College

The rising cost of university tuition is a big problem in the United States and many other countries. Even after allowing for grant aid and tax benefits, the average cost of in-state tuition at a public four-year university has risen by nearly 60 percent, in real terms, since 1990.

Moreover, in-state college placements have become increasingly inaccessible, as colleges have sought to improve their financial position by enrolling interstate and international students, who pay more tuition and receive less aid. In California, long a trendsetter in such matters, the University of California system announced a cap on the number of in-state students in 2015. This decision cemented a long-term trend in which the increase in enrollment over the past 20 years has consisted entirely of interstate and international students.

Meanwhile, the rewards of a college education are not what they once were. The median salary for a new college graduate has fallen since the economic crisis of 2008, and is now lower, in inflation-adjusted terms, than it was in 1970.

On the other hand, the struggle to get into "good" colleges and universities has never been tougher. Harvard University, with standard tuition and boarding fees in excess of $60,000 per year, had nearly twenty applicants for every slot in 2013. At least one hundred US universities had three or more applicants for every slot.

So, we have what looks like a paradox. Young people are keener than ever to pay more and more for an education that rewards them less and less. This seeming paradox can be explained by thinking in terms of opportunity cost.

The opportunity forgone by attending college consists not only of the tuition fee but also of the returns from the alternative option of entering the workforce with a high school diploma. Historically, for the great majority of students, the wages forgone by attending university have represented a substantially greater opportunity cost than the monetary cost of tuition fees. This is another illustration of Lesson One.

And, while the labor market for college graduates is not as attractive as it once was, the alternative of taking a job straight after high school has become less and less attractive over the years. Real wages for male high school graduates in the United States have been falling ever since the 1970s, with only a brief recovery in the 1990s. For women, wages have risen only marginally, from levels that were very low to begin with.

And that's assuming you can get a job. Workers without college degrees have substantially lower employment rates than those with degrees, and this gap widens in periods of high unemployment. So, even though the monetary cost of a college degree has risen sharply, the opportunity cost has not increased nearly as much. This helps to explain why the demand for college places has been largely unaffected by increasing tuition fees.

Education is about more than getting a job. Particularly in the elite colleges that dominate the public discussion of education, higher education is seen as a "transformative experience" and therefore as an essential part of growing up as a member of the educated elite. More prosaically, elite education is a source of networks, contacts, and partners, in a society where these are increasingly important. The opportunity cost of forgoing education includes the loss of such potential networks and the opportunities for upward social mobility (or avoiding downward mobility) that they offer.

To sum up, even though the monetary cost of college education has risen steeply, the opportunity cost of not going to college has risen even more. So, there is no paradox in the combination of ever-higher fees and ever-fiercer competition for places.

4.4. An Exception That Proves the Rule: The Boom and Bust in Law Schools

The general statement that the opportunity cost of getting an education is less than the opportunity cost of not getting one isn't true for all kinds of college degrees. The most striking case is that of law schools, which enjoyed a decades-long boom beginning in the 1970s. By 2010, enrollments had risen to more than 145,000, an increase of nearly 50 percent since the early 1970s.

But the demand for practicing lawyers had not risen nearly as fast. Only 68.4 percent of 2010 graduates were able to find a job requiring bar passage, the lowest percentage since the National Association of Legal Professionals began collecting statistics.

Of course, not everyone who earns a law degree wants to be a lawyer. However, for those graduates who did not become lawyers, the opportunity cost of their law degree was rising fast. Tuition

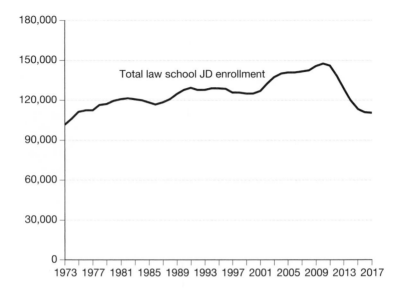

Figure 4.1. Enrollments in law schools. *Source*: http://excessofdemocracy.com
/blog/2017/12/2017-law-school-enrollment-jd-enrollment-flat-nearly-1-in-7
-are-not-in-the-jd-program.

fees for law degrees rose even faster than for college degrees in general. Moreover, it is arguable that the cost of delaying entry to the labor market is even greater when conditions are chronically slack, as they have been since the 2008 economic crisis. A graduate who enters the labor market straight out of college has three more years of work experience than one who goes on to law school.

In response to the declining benefits, and increasing opportunity costs, of going to law school, enrollments plummeted, dropping back to the 1970s level, as shown in figure 4.1. Law schools have responded by cutting or freezing tuition fees, and by offering more scholarships to students with high incoming grades, who can be expected to boost the school's reputation in the future.

However, the process of adjustment is very slow. For those who have already embarked on a law degree, much of the cost is "sunk."

So they stayed on to complete their degrees, with the result that the entering class of 2010–2011, the largest on record, entered a depressed job market in the wake of the Global Financial Crisis. Unsurprisingly, employment outcomes worsened even further, with only 57 percent of 2013 graduates finding jobs as lawyers.

As the adjustment continues, the number of new applicants will continue to fall until the benefits of attending law school come back into balance with the opportunity cost. That will require a combination of better employment outcomes, lower tuition charges, and, perhaps, a decline in the alternative employment opportunities for recent graduates.

4.5. TANSTAAFL: What about "Free" TV, Radio, and Internet Content?

We saw in section 2.1 that the "free lunch" provided by saloons wasn't really free in terms of opportunity cost. Rather, consuming the lunch involves forgoing the opportunity of buying cheaper beer at a saloon where lunch is charged separately.

The same point applies to "free" services provided by governments and financed by taxation revenue. The opportunity cost is the private expenditure forgone to pay taxes. This is the point being made by drivers with TANSTAAFL bumper stickers, even if many of them might be unhappy about paying to use "free" public roads.

There are, however, lots of other examples of services provided, apparently free of charge, by for-profit corporations. These include "free-to-air" radio and TV broadcasts, Internet services like Google, Facebook, and Twitter, and sponsorship for sporting and cultural events.

Although there is no monetary cost, TV and radio stations, much like Google and Facebook, bundle their free offerings with advertising, which comes as part of the package. Corporate sponsorship is based on the perception that it will create a favorable impression of the company concerned, which is a kind of advertising. How does our analysis apply to advertising?

In thinking about advertising in TV and similar media, we can easily dispense with the claim sometimes put forward by industry advocates, that such advertising provides consumers with useful information. If this were true, firms would not need to pay TV networks or Internet companies to broadcast the ads.

As is shown by the sales of specialist magazines of all kinds, consumers are willing to pay for useful information about consumer products. But no one will willingly consume ordinary ads unless they are packaged with a program they want to watch, or a webpage they want to view.

In fact, the original free lunch provides a much better analogy. Eating a meal or snack, particularly a salty one, increases the desirability of a cold drink, and the bar is there to provide it. Similarly, advertisements work because watching an ad increases the desirability of buying the associated product. This may be because the ad attaches desirable qualities (such as sophistication or sex appeal) to the product, or because it engenders dissatisfaction with the alternatives we are currently consuming.

In terms of opportunity cost, it does not matter whether an ad works positively or negatively. Either way, the opportunity cost of alternative products is increased relative to the value of the product being advertised. In the standard terminology of economics, a successful ad is complementary (in consumption) with the product being advertised.

In terms of our happiness, though, there's a big difference. The net effect of advertising is almost certainly to reduce our satisfaction with the things we buy, because most of the ads we see are designed to make us switch to something else. And of course, the things that are not advertised, such as quiet leisure time with family and friends, where no goods and services are required and no money is spent, are downgraded even further.

Market prices tell us about the opportunity costs we face, although the cost, like that of the original free lunch, is hidden. We can choose to watch the ads (and the programs with which they are bundled) and buy the advertised "brand name" products. Alternatively, we can avoid the ads and buy cheaper alternatives, which don't include the cost of advertising.

The third possibility is that of watching the ads but buying the cheaper products anyway. If ads work as they are supposed to, this should induce a feeling similar to that of eating salty bar snacks but not buying a drink to go with them. That is, we should feel less satisfied with our choice than if we had not viewed the ads for the brand name product, perhaps so much so that we change our minds and buy the advertised product instead.

Many readers (myself included) will probably judge that they are too strong-minded to be swayed by advertising, particularly the uninformative puffery that we get from mass media. But the continued market dominance of advertised name brands suggests that this is an illusion, similar to the one that leads around 80 percent of us to believe we are better than average drivers.

One exception to the analysis presented above is when we are willing to pay to see appropriately targeted ads. This is probably the case for special interest magazines, which contain lots of ads and sell for a price that seems high compared to the relatively limited content to be found in the articles.

Opportunity cost is as relevant to advertisers as it is to consumers. In particular, opportunity cost explains why some kinds of goods and services are commonly bundled with advertising, while others are not. The opportunity cost of producing a TV show or an attractive website can be substantial. But once a given program or website has been produced, the opportunity cost of allowing access to it is small (often less than the cost of restricting access).

In these circumstances, bundling the program with advertising may be the only way to cover the fixed costs of production. If so, the availability of the package as a whole makes us better off compared to the alternative.[5]

The problem is more complicated when there are alternatives, such as public funding for broadcasting, which might be financed (as it is in the case of the British Broadcasting Corporation) by a license fee for television sets. Choice is maximized when both methods of funding are available, but as a matter of political practice, advertising-funded commercial broadcasters will lobby to have publicly funded alternatives shut down or be forced to take ads. The Internet has shown the power, and the limitations, of a third alternative, that of voluntary provision by individuals (as with blogs) or by large cooperative groups (as with Wikipedia).

Finally, it's worth considering the case when we are forced to consume the advertising whether we want to or not, and without receiving any benefit. The most obvious example is that of highway billboard advertising, as distinct from informative signs regarding the services available at a given exit.

The case where the right to put up a billboard is controlled by (for example) a highway authority, and advertisers have to pay, is essentially the same as that of "free" TV and radio. Road users pay part of the cost of providing the highway by consuming ads.[6]

---

[5] At least on the (strong) assumption that we carefully consider the hidden cost of the "free lunch" we are being offered.

[6] Following the argument earlier in this section, consumers are worse off being forced to see the ad, then voluntarily buying the advertised product, than if they had chosen without being exposed to advertising.

By contrast, in the case where neighboring property owners can display billboards, neither the road users nor the providers get any benefit. In effect, the owner of the billboard is imposing a cost without any intervening market transaction. In the technical jargon of economics, this is a "negative externality." We'll consider this further in chapter 10.

Further Reading

The quote from Ariely (2016) was found at AZQuotes. The survey of economists' understanding of opportunity cost was reported by Ferraro and Taylor (2005). The tired job seeker quoted in footnote 2 made a comment at the Marginal Revolution blog (JC 2005). I found the response by Potter and Sanders (2012) unsatisfactory, but those interested may wish to follow it up.

Most accounts of airline deregulation have been celebratory, focusing on the lower fares paid by passengers with the flexibility to search for them. Thompson (2013) is a typical example. Closer examination reveals that these gains are offset, at least in part, by the opportunity costs discussed in section 4.2 (Richards 2007). I reached a similar conclusion in my own analysis of airline deregulation in Australia (Quiggin 1996). Poole (2015) gives information on flight attendants' wages.

In his most famous book, *The Affluent Society*, John Kenneth Galbraith (1958) did a good deal to establish the conventional wisdom[7] about advertising, namely that it was used to manufacture demand for goods and services people would otherwise not want. A more sensational presentation of this view was Vance Packard's (1957) *The Hidden Persuaders*.

---

[7] A term coined by Galbraith himself.

The analysis of advertising as a complementary good was put forward by Becker and Murphy (1993). Becker and Murphy note that advertising may be either a good or a "bad," but don't apply the obvious test: if advertising is a good, people will be willing to pay to consume it. The result is that their paper has often been seen as a refutation of Galbraith. In fact, as I pointed out in a blog post (Quiggin 2006a), TV, radio, and Internet audiences have to be paid, with free content, to look at ads, implying that ads themselves are undesirable.

One reason most people consider themselves above average, and, in particular, immune to the blandishments of advertisers is that the least competent in any cognitive activity are also most likely to over-estimate their own abilities. This is called the Dunning-Kruger effect, and was first shown in the classic study by Kruger and Dunning (1999).

Evidence on the costs and benefits of attending college is provided by College Board (2016), Harvard University (2016), and US News and World Report (2015). Kitroeff (2015) and Olson (2014, 2017) look at the case of law school.

CHAPTER 5

■

Lesson One and Economic Policy

In many cases rent control appears to be the most efficient technique presently known to destroy a city—except for bombing.

—Assar Lindbeck, *The Political Economy of the New Left: An Outsider's View* (1972), p. 39

Lesson One is a powerful tool for critical analysis of economic policy. All too often, superficially appealing policies fail because their design does not take account of opportunity costs and the role of prices in signaling those costs. Conversely, many policies may be improved by making prices explicit. In this chapter, we will examine a variety of examples.

5.1. Why Price Control Doesn't (Usually) Work

When the price of some important commodity or service rises rapidly, governments face pressure to do something about it. A variety of options are commonly considered.

Governments can, and often do, subsidize the supply of goods seen as vital, including food and fuel. Such policies are popular, often cost relatively little at first, and are politically hard to remove. But who benefits and what are the opportunity costs?

Particularly in less developed countries, such subsidies usually benefit urban dwellers, and particularly the middle class, who tend to have more political influence than the rural poor. Subsistence farmers do not benefit from food subsidies. If subsidized food is imported, with the result that the domestic price falls, farmers producing for the local market are also likely losers. Fuel subsidies generally benefit those on higher incomes, who use more energy. As with food, this effect is particularly marked in less developed countries where the rural poor may rely on collecting wood or dung for fuel, and on oxen, or their own effort, for energy inputs to food production.

The opportunity costs of food and fuel subsidies are not hard to find. Government revenue allocated to subsidies cannot be spent on services like health and education, or on income support for the poor. Even where funding for subsidies is notionally derived from cutting wasteful or unproductive expenditure, the true opportunity cost is the best use to which the funds released in this way could have been put.

Where governments want to cut prices but lack the resources to subsidize consumers, the simplest, and seemingly least costly, response is to legislate to fix the price at a "fair" level. Such policies have been tried many times and can be reasonably effective in preventing price increases resulting from temporary shortages ("gouging"). In wartime, the constraints against "profiteering" are stronger, and controls can be maintained for years on end. But attempts to maintain price controls over longer periods have mostly failed.

A classic example, discussed by many economists, is that of rent control in New York City. Controls were introduced during World War II and have been maintained with various changes ever since. The experience of New York City has shown that comprehensive rent controls can't be sustained for long without producing severe housing shortages. Once comprehensive controls are in place, construction of new rental housing grinds to a halt, and landlords try to spend as little as possible on maintenance.

When shortages become acute, the typical solution is what is often called "grandfathering." Rent control is enforced over existing housing units, but builders of new units are allowed to charge whatever the market will bear. Since rent-controlled units are effectively off the market, the market rent will be higher than would be the case in the absence of rent control.

The result is to create two classes of tenants.[1] Sitting tenants in rent-controlled units continue to benefit, but those entering the market pay more than the pre-control rent (which, we should recall, was regarded as being so unaffordable as to constitute an emergency). Eventually, as is happening in New York City now, the rent-controlled tenants die or move away, and the system breaks down altogether.

The problem with price controls is simple when we think in terms of opportunity cost. If prices are fixed by law, they cannot tell us anything about the true opportunity cost of goods and services. Nevertheless, the logic of opportunity costs still applies to producers, including landlords, and consumers, including tenants.

Producers will supply a good if the price they receive is more than the opportunity cost. If the price is fixed at a low level, then producers will supply only small amounts, or none at all. Similarly, consumers will be willing to buy more of a good if the opportunity cost is less than its value to them. The opportunity cost consists of the price, along with any other costs involved in

---

[1] New York City has three classes of tenants. Rent control applies to around 20,000 tenants of pre-1947 apartments who have been in place since 1971. Rent stabilization, a system under which rent increases are regulated, applies to tenants of apartments built between 1947 and 1973. Tenants of newer apartments pay the market rate.

obtaining the good. If the price is fixed at a low level, and the good is freely available, they will choose to consume a lot.

But there is a contradiction here. If the price is fixed at a low level, consumers will demand a lot, and firms will offer very little. So, the good will not be freely available. One possible outcome is that consumers will spend time searching for supplies or standing in line. The opportunity cost of the time they spend will make up the difference between the fixed price and the value of the good to the consumers concerned.

Another possibility is that formal or informal systems of rationing will be developed. For example, the government may estimate the needs of the average person (with some allowance for children) and issue each household a corresponding number of ration coupons, allowing them to purchase goods at the legal fixed price. Inevitably, once such a system has been in place for a while, a black market (or quasi-legal "gray market") will develop, as in the systems of ticket scalping for sporting and music events. So, for a household, the opportunity cost of a good bought within the official system will be the legal price, plus whatever they could have obtained, in cash or favors, for passing the ration coupon to someone else. For someone buying black-market ration coupons, the cost of the good again includes the legal price and the cost of the coupon, as well as the risk and difficulty associated with a black-market transaction.

If price controls are effective, and ration coupons are freely traded, the opportunity cost for consumers (the sum of the official price and the coupon price) must be higher than the price that would have emerged in the absence of control. That's because producers will supply less of the good than in the absence of controls. The logic of marginal cost and benefit implies that the opportunity cost of the marginal item for consumers must therefore be higher under price control.

Price control with rationing produces both winners and losers. The biggest winners are those consumers and households who would not have consumed any more than the rationed allowance at the market price. They get the same amount of the good, at a lower price, and perhaps get some extra benefit from selling surplus coupons.

The most obvious losers from price controls are the suppliers of the goods and services subject to controls. In the case of food, this group includes farmers, farm workers, those engaged in food processing (flour millers, butchers, and so on) as well as a wide variety of people (sometimes described as "middlemen") engaged in transport, wholesale and retail trade, and so on.

Another group of losers are consumers who would have willingly paid more, at the market price, for a higher quantity than they end up consuming under rationing. They must either do without goods they would willingly pay for or pay both the fixed price and the cost of illegally acquiring extra coupons.

Sometimes, the gainers from price controls are, or are seen as, more deserving than the losers. From a social point of view, however, it is usually better to redistribute income directly than to attempt to stop price increases through controls or to offset them using subsidies. As we will argue in the next section, if you want to help poor people, give them money.[2]

5.2. To Help Poor People, Give Them Money

The problem of poverty is huge, in rich and poor countries alike. Around the world, nearly a billion people live in extreme poverty, living on less than US$1.50 a day. Even in the United

---

[2] This way of posing the problem raises the question: what about minimum wages? On the one hand, as Hazlitt stresses, minimum wages are a kind of price control. On the other hand, since they raise the incomes of the poorest group of workers, increasing their ability to purchase all kinds of goods and services, minimum wages will almost always be a superior alternative to price controls. We will study this further in chapter 12.

States, by many measures the wealthiest country in the world, the US Department of Agriculture estimates that 12.3 percent of the population experience food insecurity, defined as being "uncertain of having, or unable to acquire, enough food to meet the needs of all their members because they had insufficient money or other resources for food."

Faced with images of the hunger and suffering caused by famines and extreme poverty, a natural and intuitive reaction is to send food. This reaction is often politically appealing in countries that happen to have large stockpiles of food, either because of unforeseen declines in market demand or because of government policies such as price supports for farmers.

On the other hand, many advocates of development aid dismiss food aid as a short-term "Band-Aid" and argue that the aim of aid should be to provide the "right" kind of assistance, as measured by subsequent economic growth. Advocates of aid initially focused on economic infrastructure and industrial development and have more recently turned their attention to health and education.

Similar debates have played out in the United States. The Supplemental Nutrition Assistance Program (SNAP), better known as food stamps, has played a central role in US programs to assist low-income households since it was introduced in 1964. With cuts in other welfare programs, its importance has increased over time. On the other hand, as with international food aid, SNAP is regularly derided as a Band-Aid approach. Liberals frequently point to education as the way to provide real opportunities for the poor.

Which of these approaches is right? Much of the time, neither. While support for health and education has a better track record than food aid, there is a growing body of evidence to say that, in both poor countries and rich ones, the best way to help people is to give them money.

To see why this should be so, ask: What would a desperately poor family do with some extra money? They might use it to stave off immediate disaster, buying urgently needed food or medical attention for sick children. On the other hand, they could put the money toward school fees for the children or save up for a piece of capital equipment like a sewing machine or mobile phone that would increase the family's earning power.

The poor family is faced with the reality of opportunity cost. Improved living standards in the future come at the cost of present suffering, perhaps even starvation and death. Whether or not their judgments are the same as we would make, they are in the best possible position to make them.

This is a straightforward application of Lesson One.

Market prices reflect (and determine) the opportunity costs faced by consumers and producers.

Exactly the same points apply in rich countries. Giving poor people assistance in kind, such as food stamps and subsidized housing, has a lot of political appeal. Not only does it meet an apparent need, but it also appears to reduce the chance that the recipients will waste their extra income on luxuries, including alcohol and tobacco. In addition, as in the case of the US food stamps program, it may also be possible to form a political coalition with producer interests, represented in this case by the farm lobby.

Thinking in terms of opportunity cost, however, we can see that aid in kind almost inevitably results in waste. The opportunity cost of subsidized housing is the low rent paid for the house, while the opportunity cost of moving usually includes going to the back of the line. Having secured subsidized housing, people will stay there even if the house no longer suits their needs, because it is too big, too small, or too far away from a new job.

The same kinds of problems occur with food stamps. Families poor enough to qualify for food stamps face many hard choices. They might, for example, need urgent medical or dental care, or be faced with eviction if they don't make a rent payment.

Much of the time, food stamps cover only part of a family's food budget, so they are really just like cash. Families can meet some of their food bills with stamps, then use the money they save to meet other needs. The opportunity cost of spending more on food is the alternative that can't be afforded.

But it's precisely when people need money most, to the point where they are prepared to live on a restricted diet, that the limits of food stamps start to bite. If poor families were given money, they could choose to pay the rent bill even if it meant living on rice and beans. That's a hard choice, but it might be the best one available.

Unsurprisingly, then, poor people often try to exchange some of their food stamps for money. This is denounced as "fraud" and used as a reason for cutting food stamps even further.

It is market prices that determine the opportunity costs of goods and services for individuals and families. When people choose how to spend additional money, the opportunity cost of one choice is the alternative that could be bought for the same amount.

The idea that poor people don't understand this is patronizing and wrong. The tighter the constraints on your budget, the more important it is to pay attention to them. Poor people often have limited access to markets, including supermarkets and basic financial markets such as bank accounts. They face complex and variable prices as a result. Nevertheless, many of them manage to find highly creative ways of stretching a limited budget to meet their needs. Additional constraints, in the form of payments that can only be spent in particular places and on particular goods, are the last thing they need.

These arguments have been going on for many years, but resolving them has proved difficult, since there are usually many different factors that determine good or bad outcomes for poor families. In recent years, however, a combination of improved statistical techniques and careful studies of experimental pilot programs have allowed an assessment of the evidence to emerge. Overwhelmingly, it supports the view that giving people money is more effective than most, if not all, forms of tied assistance in improving well-being and life outcomes.

If the best way to help the poor is to give them money, what is the best way of doing that? In a market economy there are two possible answers. The one that has been discussed most is redistribution; that is, using the taxation and welfare systems to transfer some market income from the rich to the poor. More difficult, but arguably more effective, is to change the structure of markets and property rights to produce a less unequal distribution of market income—this is sometimes called "predistribution." We will examine these issues in chapter 11.

5.2.1. Has Foreign Aid Failed?

The question of how we can most effectively help poor people is central both to social welfare policy at home and to decisions on how, if at all, to provide aid to poor people overseas.

The idea that we should simply give more money to the poor contrasts sharply with the belief, widespread even among economists, that historical experience shows that aid does not work. Most of these arguments have ignored the question of how much aid individuals and households receive, and what they would do with it if they were free to make their own choices.

Looking at the first question, it's often claimed that aid has been given on such a lavish scale that, if it were effective, the benefits ought to be obvious. The most prominent proponent of these claims is William Easterley, who said in 2006, "The evidence is stark: $568 billion spent on aid to Africa, and yet the typical African country is no richer today than 40 years ago."[3]

Here's a rough calculation. Easterley's estimates were made in the early 2000s, about 50 years after the "Winds of Change" that produced African independence. That is, the massive total of $568 billion amounts to about $11 billion a year. That has increased somewhat over time, at least in dollar terms, so the annual flow now is about $15 billion. The population of Africa is around a billion, so on average, that's about $15 per person per year.

Ideally, though not in reality, the money would be targeted to the poorest, the hundreds of millions living on $2 per day or less. Even so, the benefit could not be more than a dollar a week for every poor person. Does Easterley (or anyone repeating claims like this) really think that an extra dollar a week is enough to lift a family out of poverty?

Leaving this point aside for a moment, how would we expect, or want, aid to be used? Easterley's observation that the typical African country is no richer than it was decades ago implies that aid should have been invested to promote economic growth. That sounds plausible at first, but it ignores opportunity cost. Money invested to promote economic growth, and thereby increase income in the future, can't be used to relieve desperate poverty today.

Thinking about the opportunity costs of different uses of aid helps us to understand this seemingly endless debate. Put yourself in the position of a desperately poor African family, to the extent that such an imaginative exercise is even possible for

---

[3] Easterley has somewhat modified his views in recent years, accepting the argument presented here that aid is insufficient to lift whole countries out of poverty, but agreeing that well-designed programs may have substantial net benefits.

those of us living a (comparatively) privileged Western lifestyle. Given a few extra dollars a week, how would you spend it?

Perhaps, with exceptional discipline, you might be able to save the money to buy, say, a used sewing machine, or put it aside for school fees for your children.[4] But the opportunity cost of your investment would be to see your family ill-fed, and perhaps missing out on much-needed medical care.

There is no "right" choice here. But those facing such hard choices are better placed to make them than a well-off observer in a faraway country.

By contrast, Easterley, like much of the literature evaluating foreign aid, takes it for granted that the sole purpose of aid is to promote income growth, rather than to relieve current suffering.

Even in its own terms, the argument doesn't stand up. If the recipients of aid chose to invest all of it, the amount when expressed in terms of dollars per person is so tiny that it would be absurd to expect big payoffs in terms of economic growth.

We can illustrate this by example. Suppose that an African family chose to invest its $15 per person in farm equipment or a sewing machine and managed to get a net return of 10 percent per year. That's more than the average return on investment realized by major corporations in developed countries. The net return would be $1.50 per year, or one day's worth of poverty line income. Expressed as an addition to the rate of growth, it would amount to less than half a percentage point.

Admittedly, if governments are willing to hold living standards down to destitution levels for decades or more, and use all of the surplus income for investment, it's possible to generate high rates of economic growth, at least for a time. The Soviet Union did this under Stalin, and a number of less developed countries have tried to follow the Soviet model, with limited

---

[4] School education is rarely free in poor countries.

success. But even where the Soviet model worked in its own terms, the opportunity cost of higher output in the future was immense suffering in the present.

The idea that development aid is a proven failure has found a receptive audience among governments eager to cut their spending. But some simple arithmetic and an understanding of opportunity costs show that it is wrong. In foreign aid, as in domestic policy, the best way to help people is to give them money.

This simple point is gradually being appreciated by policymakers. A number of experimental programs have shown that poor people make better use of direct cash transfers than is achieved when governments or aid agencies decide what they should be given.

5.3. Road Pricing

For much of the twentieth century, the road was a symbol of freedom, at the center of cultural productions as diverse as Jack Kerouac's *On the Road*, Thornton Wilder's *The Happy Journey to Trenton and Camden*, and the vast Hollywood output of road movies. But roads are not free. The costs of road construction and maintenance represent a major share of the budget at all levels of government (local, state and national) and attract a fair amount of attention. Even larger, but more rarely considered, are the opportunity costs of the road network.

The capital tied up in roads represents a large share of the stock of investments owned by governments. This capital investment comes at the expense of alternatives like schools, hospitals, and, most notably, public transport systems. The opportunity cost of land dedicated to roads is larger still.

Turning from roads to vehicles, road users impose costs on one another in the form of traffic congestion and crash risks, as well as the general annoyance that has given rise to the term "road rage." These costs aren't symmetrical; big vehicles and fast drivers contribute more to crash risks, while slow vehicles may cause more congestion. A whole book could be written (and probably/inevitably has been) on the conflicts between motorists and cyclists. Finally, road users impose costs on others through noise, air pollution, and the crash risk faced by pedestrians and other non-motorists. We'll discuss these "external costs" in more detail in chapter 10.

We pay for roads in many different ways: gas taxes, tolls, vehicle registration charges, and through general government revenue. Typically, these systems have evolved through historical processes driven by the exigencies of funding, with little or no underlying rationale. As a result, a road built during a period of relatively flush public funding may be a freeway, while another one nearby may be subject to tolling. Some jurisdictions tax gasoline, while others levy charges on vehicles. These prices usually bear little or no relationship to opportunity costs, a fact that helps to explain why driving is so often a source of frustration and sociopolitical dispute.

At present, the most common approach to road pricing involves the use of tolls to finance the construction of a new road. This is commonly undertaken through a "public–private partnership" (PPP), also called a "Build Own Operate Transfer" (BOOT) scheme, in which a private sector consortium agrees to construct the road in return for the right to collect tolls for a set period, typically around 25 to 30 years. At the end of this period, the road returns to public ownership and the toll is removed. Meanwhile, alternative routes, typically through residential streets, remain untolled.

It would be hard to design a pricing scheme more directly contrary to the lessons of opportunity cost. When a road is brand new, and uncongested, the opportunity cost of an additional driver using the road is almost zero. The relatively small number of drivers means that none of them are slowed down by the traffic flow they all generate. The fact that the road is of recent construction normally means that it does not pass through residential areas, where residents would be affected by noise and accident risk.[5] The physical capacity of the road itself to bear traffic without incurring damage is the best it will ever be. If prices were set equal to opportunity costs, the road would be untolled.

Fast forward 25 or 30 years to the day the toll is removed. By now, traffic on the road is heavy much of the time, and the removal of the toll will only make this worse. The availability of the road will have encouraged development of residential and business areas in its vicinity. Finally, even with careful maintenance (by no means assured), the road will be old and more easily damaged by heavy vehicles and traffic in general.

In addition to failing Lesson One, the standard system of road pricing is arbitrary and unfair. The question of whether a road will be tolled or free is almost entirely one of historical accident. If a community has always been well served by good roads, perhaps because its residents are well-off and politically influential, motorists traveling there pay nothing. Similarly, if the government's budget is flush in the year a road project comes up, it may be provided for free. But, when budgets are tight, and new roads are needed, tolls are imposed.

Some cities have done a better job than most in putting prices in line with opportunity cost. The most striking example is that of London, which introduced a "congestion charge" in 2003. The mayor who introduced the change was a member of the Labour Party, Ken Livingstone, often referred to as "Red Ken"

---

[5] Some houses have been demolished to allow its construction, but this is a "sunk cost."

because of his left-wing views. However, the originator of the idea was the famous Chicago economist Milton Friedman. The London experiment is generally regarded as successful. It has reduced traffic on London roads when, in the absence of a charge, the number of vehicles would almost certainly have increased. Since the charge was introduced, numerous measures have been taken to improve safety and amenity for pedestrians. Because the number of cars has been reduced, it has been possible to do this without increasing travel times for motorists.

Despite the apparent success of the congestion charge, very few cities have followed London's example. In large measure, this reflects the failure of policymakers and the public at large to understand the lessons of opportunity costs. People are unwilling to pay for something that was once "free," even though as members of society we all bear the costs of congested roads.

Failures of understanding cannot fully explain this outcome, however. Charges have been introduced for a wide variety of public services that were formerly not priced, and the public has mostly accepted the change, willingly or otherwise.

The crucial difference with congestion pricing is that the people most directly affected are those who drive to work in the central business district of cities, such as businesspeople with access to office parking. These are among the people most likely to come into contact, on a regular basis, with the members of the state or local governments that commonly make decisions on road pricing. In Bastiat's terms, their hostility to paying for access to the city will be highly visible, while the opportunity costs of free access are "that which is not seen."

There is probably no way to bring the prices paid by road users completely into line with the opportunity costs they generate. Nevertheless, it would be hard to do worse than the pricing systems commonly used in relation to toll road projects around the world. Increased use of road pricing, based on congestion and externality cost rather than historical cost accounting, would certainly help.

5.4. Fish and Tradable Quota

Fisheries provide another example of the importance of opportunity costs, and what prices and markets can tell us about them.

The proverbial advice "there's plenty more fish in the sea" reflected what seemed, until modern times, to be an inexhaustible abundance. The vastness of the oceans, the proverbial difficulty of catching fish, and the reproductive capacity of most fish species made it seem that, no matter how many fish might be caught in one season, there would be just as many to catch in the next.

The industrialization of fishing in the late nineteenth century changed all that. Steam-powered vessels could travel farther and were independent of wind and currents. The development of factory ships allowed catches to be processed on board, so that voyages could be longer. These were followed in the twentieth century by new trawling techniques, longline fishing, electronic navigation, and radar and sonar systems. Catch rates soared and then, predictably, crashed.

With the slow reproduction rates typical of mammals, and the misfortune of being valuable sources of lighting oil, whales were among the first species to be hunted to the edge of extinction. The right whale (supposedly so-called because it was the "right" whale to catch) was almost extinct by the 1930s, with the result that hunting right whales was banned worldwide in 1937. Even so, nearly 70 years later both the North Atlantic and North Pacific right whales are critically endangered, with populations still in the hundreds.

Fish species soon followed. The decline of the Atlantic northwest cod fishery was typical. Catches rose steadily over the first half of the twentieth century, reaching a peak in the 1960s. Then came a sharp decline, as stocks crashed. This decline did not, at least initially, produce a decline in fishing effort. Rather, efforts were intensified in an attempt to maintain declining incomes.

By 1992, catches had fallen almost to zero, and it was estimated that only 1 percent of the original stock remained. The Canadian government imposed a moratorium, originally intended to be temporary. As with the right whales, however, the damage was too severe to be remedied by a temporary respite. More than 20 years later the moratorium is still in place. There are some limited signs of recovery in fish populations, but the resumption of commercial fishing is still a long way off. The same story has been repeated in fisheries all around the world with minor variations.

Thinking in terms of opportunity cost makes the reason clear. If a landowner fells a tree and sells the timber, the opportunity cost includes the return that might have been gained by letting the tree grow for another year. But catching a fish has no such opportunity cost for the fisher. Left in the sea, it might have grown and reproduced, increasing future catches. But for any individual fisher, thinking about whether to cast the net one more time, fish that are not caught now are gone forever.

Some other fisher might catch them in the future, but that is not part of the individual's opportunity cost. The opportunity cost for an individual fisher includes the time and effort spent fishing, the cost of boats, fuel, nets, and so forth, but not the impact on the fishing stock.

In these circumstances, once technology advances far enough to permit it, overfishing is virtually inevitable. A wide range of responses has been tried in an attempt to prevent overfishing: the number of boats in a fishery has been limited, the gear they can use has been restricted, and allowable fishing seasons have been shortened.

These measures have almost invariably proved ineffective. If the number of boats is limited, fishers buy bigger boats. If gear restrictions are imposed, new types of gear are developed to evade them.

If the open season is limited, effort is increased, and boats put to sea in good weather or bad, with the result that overfishing continues. The response is commonly to shorten the season still further. As Laurence White of New York University's Stern School of Business observes:

> [T]hese input limitations—especially the limits on the number of calendar days for fishing—have led to "fishing derbies" or "races for the fish," in which fishermen try feverishly to maximize the amount of fish harvesting that they can accomplish within the limited time period available to them.
>
> The contraction of the Alaska halibut season is a "poster child" for this process. From an open season of over 150 days in the early 1970s, the season length shrank to only 47 days by 1977 and then collapsed to an average of only 2–3 days per year between 1980 and 1994. Similarly, the collapse of the surf clam fishery in the Mid-Atlantic region caused a progressive shortening of allowable fishing time until, in 1990, a surf clam vessel was permitted to fish only 6 hours every other week.

Even this is not the most extreme case. The spawn of Alaska herring is highly valued for its use in sushi. During the harvesting season in 2017, fishers took 3 hours and 20 minutes to catch half the year's quota. A second opening lasting only 15 minutes exhausted the rest. Some fishers who had trouble starting their boats missed the entire event.

5.4.1. Private and Common Property in Fisheries

To sum up, any attempt to control overfishing by limiting effort has ultimately collapsed into absurdity. The only measure that has consistently been shown to work is the creation of property rights. Three main systems of property rights have been employed.

First, there is privatization, where an entire fishery may be handed over to a single private owner, typically a corporation. The owner has control over the number of boats that are used, the number of fish that are caught, and so on, bears the costs of managing the fishery, and receives all the net return from fishing. This is the solution seen as "ideal" by some One Lesson economists.[6]

The second option, and the most common in practice, is a system of individual catch quotas. These are limits on the number of fish that an individual fisher can catch, combined with exclusion from the fishery of anyone who does not hold a quota. Typically, the total allowable catch is determined, then divided up in the form of individual transferable quotas (ITQs). Each of the fishers is assigned a quota that they can catch. If they want to catch more fish, or if a new boat wants to enter, they must buy the quota from someone willing to sell.

Finally, where the industry is organized in a cooperative fashion, an aggregate quota may be determined for the season and allocated among a group of fishers in the industry by mutual agreement. Again, those outside the group are excluded. In this way, the group members acquire common property rights over the fishery in question.

---

[6] Notably including H. Scott Gordon, widely regarded as the founder of fisheries economics, and Garret Hardin, the ecologist who popularized the phrase "tragedy of the commons."

Common property rights have existed in various forms throughout history, mostly coexisting with private property rights. In common-property fisheries for example, it is usual for the boats and gear to be owned by individual fishers, and for the fish, once caught, to be the property of whoever catches them. A similar mix of private and common property is found in an apartment complex organized as a condominium (the term is derived from the Latin for "shared property").

Unfortunately, One Lesson economists routinely treat common property as a synonym for "no property." The most notable example is Garret Hardin, whose persuasive, but historically inaccurate, article "The Tragedy of the Commons" was highly influential from the 1970s onward.[7] After giving a historically inaccurate account of the common grazing system that prevailed in much of England until the eighteenth century, Hardin says,

> Therein is the tragedy. Each man is locked into a system that compels him to increase his herd without limit—in a world that is limited. Ruin is the destination toward which all men rush, each pursuing his own best interest in a society that believes in the freedom of the commons. Freedom in a commons brings ruin to all. (Hardin 1968)

Hardin's article, leading to the conclusion that the inherent logic of the commons remorselessly generates tragedy, made the case for privatization, but glossed over the historical reality that common-property institutions have worked well in many contexts and over long periods.

---

[7] Although Hardin was an ecologist by training and profession, he was also an enthusiastic advocate of One Lesson economics, as well as various forms of eugenics and mandatory population control.

Many economists have criticized Hardin, some in quite acerbic tones. The sharpest response was that of Partha Dasgupta, who observed, "It would be difficult to locate another passage of comparable length and fame containing as many errors as the one above."

The most detailed and influential refutation was that of political scientist Elinor Ostrom. Ostrom's study of the workings of common-property institutions combined deep economic insight with a detailed analysis of the formal and informal institutions involved in managing common property. She was awarded the Nobel Memorial Prize in Economics for her work. She is, so far, the only woman, and one of a handful of non-economists, to receive this award.

Whether individual or collective, the choice of setting a quota for a season forces fishers to confront the problem of opportunity cost. A higher catch in the current season means a smaller stock, which will make fishing more costly in future seasons. If the catch exceeds the maximum sustainable yield, then future catches must decline, regardless of effort.

The appropriate point at which to set the aggregate catch quota is that at which the value of any further increase in the catch is equal to the cost of catching the fish plus the opportunity cost (incurred in the future) of reduced stocks.

The determination of an aggregate quota leaves open the question of how fishers, boats, and fishing time will be organized to catch the allowable number of fish. In this respect, the different systems of property rights vary with respect to the role played by markets and prices in determining the opportunity costs.

The role of markets and prices is largest and most evident in a system of ITQs. Here, decisions by individual fishers to catch their quota have an obvious opportunity cost: the value they could realize by selling the quota and using their labor and capital somewhere else.

By contrast, in a fully privatized fishery, individual fishers are employees or contract workers for the owner of the fishery. Decisions about who will fish, and when and where they will fish, are made by managers rather than individual fishers.

Under common-property systems, mutual agreement takes the place of market transactions. These examples show that, while market prices tell us about opportunity cost, they are not always and everywhere the best way of transmitting this information.

The effect of introducing quotas is to create new property rights. The introduction of transferable quotas, with appropriate institutional arrangements, may result in the emergence of markets where none existed before. However, the creation of property rights, including the creation of property rights over fisheries, is a politically fraught and philosophically controversial process.

Formal property rights, by their nature, supersede expectations and social judgments about who has the right to use a socially valuable asset like a fishery and how they can use it. When an asset previously open to all is made the subject of property rights, rights of access that were formerly taken for granted are withdrawn or strictly circumscribed. Those who are expropriated in this process may or may not receive some compensation. But even where compensation is paid, it is commonly insufficient to offset a feeling of injustice.

The conflict is even greater when, as is often the case with local fisheries, an informal system of common-property management has emerged. Property rights systems established by national or state governments, which are typically neutral as between citizens of the entire jurisdiction, commonly conflict with established social norms among existing fishers. These norms, which typically stress local ownership and controls, are strongly held, but may be challenged by "outsiders," excluded from access.

In the case of fisheries regulation, the inherent conflict is sharpened by the fact that formal property rights are typically not introduced until well after the actual catch rate has reached unsustainably high levels and begun to decline.

Fishers have built their way of life, and invested large amounts of capital, based on the assumption that large catches could be maintained indefinitely. The process of reducing catches to a sustainable level involves sharp and often painful adjustments, such as a reduction in the number of boats and fishers in a given fishery. This adjustment, taking place in combination with changes in property rights, frequently gives rise to conflict.

5.4.2. The Creation of Property Rights

The process of creating new property rights and markets raises a variety of philosophical concerns. As the discussion above indicates, the creation of new formal property rights has an opportunity cost, namely, the loss of old, informal rights.[8] Particularly in the case of full privatization, the redistribution that takes place commonly benefits the rich and politically powerful at the expense of everyone else.

Unsurprisingly then, critics of markets and property rights are hostile to proposals for their extension. The difficulties are least in the case where existing common-property institutions are formalized, but even here the issue of opportunity cost cannot be avoided: common property for some means exclusion for others.

Philosophical difficulties with the creation of new property rights are not confined to critics of the market system. One Lesson economists like Hazlitt are often unwilling to confront the

---

[8] We will discuss this further in Lesson Two.

fact that formal property rights and the markets in which they are traded are creations of government and the legal system.

The result is a great deal of inconsistency, depending in part on which groups in the community benefit or lose from a given change in property rights. For example, the propertarian Cato Institute has enthusiastically backed transferable quotas in fisheries but has opposed the conceptually identical policy of tradeable permits for greenhouse gas emissions.[9]

Consideration of both Lesson One and Lesson Two suggests that any proposal for expanding the role of property rights must be subject to careful scrutiny. But, at least in the case of fisheries, some form of property, which may be individual, common, or corporate, seems to be essential.

5.5. A License to Print Money: Property Rights and Telecommunications Spectrum

The discovery of radio waves at the end of the nineteenth century gave humanity access to a new form of communication. For the first time, it was possible to transmit signals (initially in Morse code, and then ordinary sound) over large distances without the use of wires.

Initially, this technology was freely available to anyone with the necessary technical apparatus to send and receive signals. However, it soon became apparent that, here as elsewhere, the logic of opportunity cost was critical.

Radio signals sent on the same or nearby frequencies interfere with one another, producing the annoying noise we know as static. As radio stations proliferated in the early twentieth century, the problem became more and more severe. The use of

[9] Like other propertarians, Cato describes its position as "libertarian."

a frequency by one station had the opportunity cost of making it unavailable for others.

The US government's response was the Radio Act of 1927, which established the Federal Radio Commission, later renamed the Federal Communications Commission (FCC), with its authority extended to cover television and other telecommunications technologies. The Commission was empowered to license broadcasters, determining the frequency they could use, and the permissible geographical coverage and signal strength.

In determining who should receive licenses, the FCC was, and still is, required to take account of "the public interest." Despite being in operation for nearly a century, the public interest criterion remains vague and undefined. One aspect, which has gradually eroded over time, was the imposition of constraints on coarse language and sexual content that were tighter for broadcast media than for competitors such as cable TV.

A more important implication of the public interest criterion was the "Fairness Doctrine," which prevailed between 1949 and 1987. This doctrine required the holders of broadcast licenses both to present controversial issues of public importance and to do so in a manner that was—in the Commission's view—honest, equitable, and balanced. In practice, this usually meant presenting "both sides" of issues that were the subject of partisan debate between the Republican and Democratic parties, while maintaining what aimed to be a neutral and objective position. This approach has been described by Rosen (2010) as the "view from nowhere." While providing an appearance of objectivity, it effectively excluded dissenting viewpoints on issues where the two major political parties were in agreement.

The abandonment of the Fairness Doctrine led to the rise of openly partisan broadcasters like Fox on the political right and, later, MSNBC on the left. With the end of the Fairness Doctrine and increased general tolerance for coarse language and sexual content in the media as a whole, the public interest criterion has become virtually insignificant in practice.

The real point of the public interest criterion, from its inception, has been that it justifies allocating property rights over sections of the electromagnetic spectrum to private owners, who could exclude all others from the broadcasting spectrum. Such rights were commonly described as "a license to print money." Indeed, this description can be applied to any situation where the state creates enforceable property rights and gives them away to particular people or corporations.

What is the alternative? Technological progress makes it possible to use bandwidth more efficiently, with the result that some of the spectrum is free to be used for new purposes. Increasingly in recent years, rather than giving this spectrum away, governments have auctioned it. In 2015, the FCC raised $45 billion for auctions of "mid-band" spectrum, between 1700 MHz and 2100 MHz. This type of spectrum is not considered as valuable as low-band spectrum, such as the TV broadcast spectrum, because signals travel shorter distances than over lower frequency spectrum.

Unsurprisingly, the private owners of spectrums given away in the past have taken advantage of the same possibilities. An auction of broadcast spectrums relinquished by private TV stations, concluded in 2017, yielded a total of nearly $20 billion, of which the stations received $12 billion, with the rest going to the US Treasury. The prices realized in these auctions give an indication of the opportunity cost of the old policy of free allocation.

It isn't necessary to auction the entire spectrum, even after reserving bandwidth for vital public needs such as police and emergency services. Some space can be made for broadcasters who take the "public interest" idea seriously, rather than as a fig leaf for profit-driven programming. But, inevitably in a market economy, most of the spectrum is going to be allocated to commercial services. Those who acquire the right to use a spectrum in this way should compensate society for the opportunity cost of the scarce and valuable services that they have been allocated.

5.6. Concluding Comments

This chapter has covered a range of disparate issues. The unifying theme is that of Lesson One. Prices tell us about opportunity costs, and trying to make public policy by regulating prices or allocating scarce goods and services by fiat rarely works well. One Lesson economists draw the conclusion that governments should do nothing. But a more careful examination of the issues discussed here suggests a different conclusion, which we will discuss in Lesson Two: if you want to fix social problems, fix the allocation of property rights.

Further Reading

The Furman Center (2012) gives details on rent control and rent stabilization in New York City. Crouch (2015) describes similar problems in Stockholm. Evidence on fuel and food subsidies is provided by del Granado et al. (2012), Pinstrup-Anderson (1988), and Bacon, Ley, and Kojima (2010).

Recent studies showing that cash assistance yields better outcomes than other forms of aid to poor people in developing countries include Haushofer and Shapiro (2013), Staunton and Collins (2013), and Davala et al. (2015). Goldstein (2013) and Kenny (2015) provide easily readable summaries.

In developed countries, the evidence in support of unconditional cash payments has led to renewed interest in ideas such as Universal Basic Income and the Negative Income Tax. Widerquist (2005) looks at experiments on Negative Income Tax. Rensin and Shor (2014) present some additional evidence in the context of a polemic against the idea that education, rather than income redistribution, is the key to a more equal society.

The arguments of Easterley (2006) have become, in the words of J. K. Galbraith (1958), "conventional wisdom," but that does not make them correct.

Friedman's essay on road pricing was first written in 1951 but was not published until long afterward. The most accessible version is Friedman and Boorstin (1951). Some background on the London congestion pricing scheme is given by Beckett (2003) and Timms (2013). I've written extensively on the problems of PPP and BOOT schemes, beginning with my book, *Great Expectations* (Quiggin 1996), and most recently in Quiggin (2014).

Dolin (2008) is a readable history of the US whaling industry. The review by White (2006) provides background to the problems of US fisheries. The quoted passages are from pp. 71–72 and pp. 304–7.

Garret Hardin (1968), whose persuasive, but historically inaccurate, article "The Tragedy of the Commons" was highly influential from the 1970s onward, popularized the mistaken idea that common property is the same as "no property." A more accurate understanding of common property emerged from the 1970s with the work of Ciriacy-Wantrup and Bishop (1975) and Dahlman (1980). I wrote my master's thesis on this topic, and developed my ideas in Quiggin (1988, 1995). The most important contribution to the systematic study of common-property institutions has been that of Elinor Ostrom (1990).

For Hayek's association with the Pinochet dictatorship, see Farrant, McPhail, and Berger (2012). Hayek's interaction with Thatcher is discussed by Corey Robin (2013a) in chapter 2 of his excellent book, *The Reactionary Mind*, with further documentation in Robin (2013b).

For the public interest and fairness doctrines in US broadcasting policy, see Ruane (2011) and Brotman (2017). Rosen's (2010) critique of the "view from nowhere" is part of a more extensive critique of US media, presented at his blog, pressthink .org. Reardon (2015) and Johnson (2017) report on the outcome of FCC auctions.

Other references are Cohan and Hark (1997), Dasgupta (1982), Fry (2017), Gordon (1954), Kerouac (1957), and Wilder (1931).

CHAPTER 6

∎

The Opportunity Cost
of Destruction

> Every gun that is made, every warship launched, every rocket
> fired, signifies in the final sense a theft from those who hun-
> ger and are not fed, those who are cold and are not clothed.
> —Dwight Eisenhower, Final Address, 1961

> Enter through the narrow gate. For wide is the gate and broad is
> the road that leads to destruction, and many enter throught it.
> —Matthew 7:13, New International Version

Careful consideration of Lesson One enables us to refute an
idea that is popular among both admirers and critics of markets,
namely that waste and destruction, such as that caused by war,
are economically beneficial. Hazlitt's critique of this idea is one
of the strongest parts of his book.

After describing his lesson in general terms, Hazlitt begins
the main part of his book with a parable, taken from Bastiat,
about a broken window that requires repair, and the tempting
idea that random destruction may, by "creating work," be beneficial. As Bastiat observes, this idea fails to take account of the
opportunity cost of the resources used in the repair work.

Hazlitt extends this simple parable to a real-life policy issue,
of vital importance at the time he was writing (1946). This is the

question of whether the need to repair the destruction caused by war, and to meet the demand for consumer goods and services that was suppressed under wartime conditions, will stimulate economic activity and ensure prosperity. Hazlitt argues that it will not.

In this chapter, I will develop Hazlitt's key points a little further, spelling out the role of opportunity cost in the analysis, and extending the argument to cover natural disasters.

I'll show that Hazlitt and Bastiat are mostly correct: in most cases, natural disasters are also economic disasters. What is true of natural disasters is even more true of the disasters we inflict on ourselves and others. Of these human-made calamities, the greatest is war.

On the other hand, spelling out the argument also draws attention to its limits. Most important, the "broken window" parable, based on Lesson One, assumes that the economy is operating at full employment. To understand the implications of unemployment, we need Lesson Two. We'll look at this in more detail in chapter 8.

6.1. The Glazier's Fallacy

Bastiat's clearest single exposition of the idea of opportunity cost is his "parable of the broken window." Hazlitt presents the same idea (with acknowledgment to Bastiat) as "the glazier's fallacy."

> A young hoodlum, say, heaves a brick through the window of a baker's shop. The shopkeeper runs out furious, but the boy is gone. A crowd gathers, and begins to stare with quiet satisfaction at the gaping hole in the window and the shattered glass over the bread and pies. After a

while the crowd feels the need for philosophic reflection. And several of its members are almost certain to remind each other or the baker that, after all, the misfortune has its bright side. It will make business for some glazier. As they begin to think of this they elaborate upon it. How much does a new plate glass window cost? Fifty dollars? That will be quite a sum. After all, if windows were never broken, what would happen to the glass business? Then, of course, the thing is endless. The glazier will have $50 more to spend with other merchants, and these in turn will have $50 more to spend with still other merchants, and so ad infinitum. The smashed window will go on providing money and employment in ever-widening circles. The logical conclusion from all this would be, if the crowd drew it, that the little hoodlum who threw the brick, far from being a public menace, was a public benefactor.

Now let us take another look. The crowd is at least right in its first conclusion. This little act of vandalism will in the first instance mean more business for some glazier. The glazier will be no more unhappy to learn of the incident than an undertaker to learn of a death. But the shopkeeper will be out $50 that he was planning to spend for a new suit. Because he has had to replace a window, he will have to go without the suit (or some equivalent need or luxury). Instead of having a window and $50 he now has merely a window. Or, as he was planning to buy the suit that very afternoon, instead of having both a window and a suit he must be content with the window and no suit. If we think of him as a part of the community, the community has lost a new suit that might otherwise have come into being, and is just that much poorer.

The glazier's gain of business, in short, is merely the tailor's loss of business. No new "employment" has been added. The people in the crowd were thinking only of two parties to the transaction, the baker and the glazier. They had forgotten the potential third party involved, the tailor. They forgot him precisely because he will not now enter the scene. They will see the new window in the next day or two. They will never see the extra suit, precisely because it will never be made. They see only what is immediately visible to the eye.

This is mostly correct, but there are some important qualifications to be made. Hazlitt does not spell out all the steps in his argument, so we will do it for him.

The argument depends implicitly on the assumption that the economy is in a state of competitive equilibrium. In such a state, an increase in the production of one good, such as windows, can only come at an equal or greater opportunity cost, in this case a reduction in the production of suits. In this case, there is no net gain to set against the destruction of the window with which the story began.

Let's remind ourselves of the conditions of competitive equilibrium we discussed in section 2.4. The critical assumption in Hazlitt's version is (A) "Everyone faces the same market-determined prices for all goods and services, including labor of any given quality, and everyone can buy or sell as much as they want to at the prevailing prices."

Since, by assumption (A), both glaziers and tailors already have as much work as they want, an increase in one line of work, say, that of glazing, can only happen if glaziers are induced to work harder than they would like at current wages or if workers switch from other activities like tailoring, and take up glazing instead. Either way, there is no net gain. This is the core of Lesson One.

When it's spelled out this way, it's obvious that the argument depends on the assumption of full employment. On the other hand, the reaction of the crowd implies that unemployment is a problem that comes immediately to the minds of the onlookers. Under full employment conditions, a more likely reaction would be "there goes my chance of getting any work done on my windows." Anyone who has tried to get renovation or repair work done during a building boom is quickly made aware of this manifestation of opportunity cost.

The glazier's story is, of course, a parable. It helps us to understand the economic implications of the larger-scale destruction caused by natural disasters and, even more, by war.

6.2. The Economics of Natural Disasters

Natural disasters like floods, earthquakes, and hurricanes come seemingly out of nowhere, wreak intense havoc in a short period, and move on, leaving vast, and largely random, destruction in their wake. Productive economic activity is halted or disrupted, often for weeks or months after the initial impact has passed.

Reports of such events commonly provide estimates of the associated damage bill and the cost of lost production. The cost is partially covered by insurance claims and government disaster assistance, but inevitably much of it falls on the residents of the area hit by the disaster.

It is only natural for people, faced with such disasters, to seek some consolatory "silver lining," and one such consolation is the idea that natural disasters will create work and thereby stimulate the economy. Disasters certainly create work for emergency services, and for the workers needed to rebuild damaged houses and infrastructure.

The wages earned by these workers might be seen as an offset against the damage from the disaster. That would be true if they had nothing else to do. But, most of the time, such workers are not sitting idle and waiting for a disaster to happen.

Government budgets are chronically tight, so emergency services are routinely overstretched. Providing additional services to respond to a disaster comes with an opportunity cost, that of the more routine services that would ordinarily be provided.

Similarly, unless the disaster happens to coincide with a slump in the construction industry, rebuilding damaged houses comes at the expense of the new houses that would otherwise have been built. Natural disasters strike at random, and most of the time do not coincide with any requirement to create jobs in the construction sector. Moreover, there are many more useful ways of creating jobs. Expecting economic benefits from a natural disaster is like hoping that a car crash will fix your wheel alignment.

To sum up, in economic terms, disasters are, in most cases, just as bad as they appear at first sight. As with the example of the broken window, the economic activity generated by disaster repairs comes at the opportunity cost of productive activities that may be overlooked because they are never undertaken.

6.3. The Opportunity Cost of War

Even the worst natural disasters, destroying whole cities and causing thousands of deaths, pale into insignificance when compared to the disasters humans inflict on one another through war, revolution, and civil strife. Yet even more than with natural disasters, the idea that wartime destruction is economically beneficial was long taken for granted and remains influential.

As with natural disasters, this idea is mostly but not entirely false. Most of the time, the resources needed for war, or destroyed in the course of war, would otherwise be employed for more useful purposes. Attempts to undertake even a medium-sized war require either substantial increases in taxation, conscription, or, most commonly, inflation.

The classic recent example of this was the Vietnam War. US involvement in the war began in the early 1960s in the middle of the decades of full employment associated with Keynesian macroeconomic management. The war coincided with the Great Society programs, an ambitious expansion of social welfare and publicly provided health and education. Given that there were no free lunches to be had, Lesson One applied with full force. The additional resources had to come from somewhere, and the only source was private consumption and investment.

Because these implications weren't recognized, the resources required for the war and the expansion of social programs weren't mobilized through taxation but through inflation. Inflation reduced the value of private savings, and, at least initially, the real value of wages. As workers realized that their wages were buying less, they demanded more, which in turn led to further price inflation. The process eventually led to the imposition of price controls (section 5.1), which inevitably failed. The core problem was the attempt to extract additional resources from a fully employed economy. No stable set of prices can reflect the opportunity costs involved in such a policy, so inflation is inevitable. This is a necessary, if subtle, implication of Lesson One.

The Vietnam War was not unusual. Historically, wartime inflation has been the norm rather than the exception. The American Revolution was financed by inflated currency printed by the Continental Congress (hence the expression, "not worth a Continental"). Both sides in the Civil War, but especially the Confederates, relied on inflation.[1] The same was true of World War I and many others.

---

[1] Confederate dollar inflation peaked at an annual rate of 700 percent in 1864.

There is, however, one great, if often misunderstood, exception to this rule. In the decade before World War II, during the years of the Great Depression, as many as one in three workers had been idle. Starvation and misery had been widespread. By contrast, in the war years, even though millions of workers joined the armed forces and all surplus resources were being diverted to the war effort, standards of living improved for many previously unemployed families. Standards of nutrition improved for the population as a whole.

Once the war ended in 1945, resources were shifted from war production to domestic needs. Initially, there was a large unmet need for capital goods like houses and cars, for which production had been greatly curtailed during the war. But even when this backlog of investment was eliminated (and after allowing for underlying technological progress), production and living standards were maintained at levels far above those of the 1930s.

As Australia's *White Paper on Full Employment*, issued in 1945, put it:

> Despite the need for more houses, food, equipment and every other type of product, before the war not all those available for work were able to find employment or to feel a sense of security in their future. On the average during the twenty years between 1919 and 1939 more than one-tenth of the men and women desiring work were unemployed. In the worst period of the depression well over 25 percent were left in unproductive idleness. By contrast, during the war no financial or other obstacles have been allowed to prevent the need for extra production being satisfied to the limit of our resources.

The *White Paper* called for a government commitment to ensure full employment. In Australia, and throughout the developed world, governments abandoned the One Lesson economics that had produced the Great Depression and committed themselves to the achievement and maintenance of full employment. This commitment, sustained for more than 30 years, produced an era of broadly enjoyed prosperity unequaled either before or since.

The crucial lesson here is that, while war and destruction may produce economic benefits compared to a depression, much greater benefits can be obtained if the economy is managed so as to maintain full employment while using labor and resources for production rather than destruction.

Every crisis in the world brings forward a call for military intervention, often from people who regard "foreign aid" as a proven failure. The failure rate for these interventions is far higher than for ordinary foreign aid projects. Of the major US military interventions in the past 20 years (Kosovo, Somalia, Gulf War I, Afghanistan, Gulf War II, Libya, and Iraq/Syria) only Kosovo could be regarded as a clear success, and even there the outcome is a weak state bitterly divided between two hostile communities, kept apart by armed peacekeepers.[2]

But even when military action works as planned, it is hard to justify in terms of opportunity cost. The total figures are staggering. The Afghan and Iraq wars combined are estimated to have cost the United States between $4 trillion and $6 trillion in wartime expenditures and future medical bills for veterans. That's ten times the total amount of aid received by the whole of Africa since 1945, an amount regularly cited to show the futility of foreign aid. And it excludes the huge costs associated with death and injury to US personnel, not to mention civilian "collateral damage."

---

[2] Gulf War I succeeded in the terms originally set out, but, beginning with the incitement of the failed Shi'ite uprising, set in train the disastrous process that ultimately produced Gulf War II, and, another decade later, the war against ISIS.

Rather than attempt to apply opportunity cost calculations to such stupendous numbers, let's look at the opportunity cost of maintaining a single additional soldier in Afghanistan. The direct cost has been estimated at $2.1 million per soldier per year, though support costs and the need to provide for future medical care would almost certainly double this.

We could look at the opportunity cost in terms of alternative ways of providing aid to Afghanistan. The US development agency USAID provides around $70 million a year in educational and social services aid to Afghanistan, a sum that is claimed to enable one million additional children to enroll in school. Obviously there is plenty of room for more expenditure of this kind, in Afghanistan or elsewhere. A simple calculation shows that the opportunity cost of keeping thirty-five soldiers in the field is equal to school education for a million young people.

Most advocates of the war, faced with this kind of calculation, would say that the object of the war is not (primarily) to promote the welfare of Afghans but to protect Americans from the threat of terrorist attack. It might seem to be impossible to place a monetary value on such protection. However, it is at least possible to identify the opportunity cost, and the US government does so explicitly.

US government interventions aimed at protecting Americans from threats to their life and safety are typically approved only if the cost per life saved is less than the "Value of Statistical Life" for the agency concerned. In particular, this procedure applies to policies aimed at protecting Americans from terror attacks within the United States. In assessing a September 2007 Department of Homeland Security proposal to expand air travel security, the US Customs and Border Patrol estimated life-saving benefits using two separate life values: $3 million and $6 million.

No such analysis is applied to overseas military action. Nevertheless, the logic of opportunity cost applies, whether or not it is taken into account by planners. Each additional soldier deployed in Afghanistan comes at the cost of the alternative use that could be made of the required funding. Using the $6 million estimate cited above, the opportunity cost of the $6.3 million spent to deploy three additional soldiers is the funding of a domestic security program that would save one American life per year.

If the casualty rate for soldiers in the field were anything like one in three, the war would have ended long ago. Yet the same cost in lives, in the form of forgone opportunities to protect Americans at home, has been accepted with bipartisan support, because it is invisible, unless viewed through the lens of opportunity cost.

Bastiat's contrast between "that which is seen" and "that which is not seen" has never been more apposite.

6.3.1. Eisenhower and the Military-Industrial Complex

Dwight Eisenhower, Supreme Commander of the Allied Forces in Europe during World War II, was arguably America's greatest military commander, and served as president of the United States at the height of the Cold War with the Soviet Union. It is striking, then, that more than any US political leader before or since, Eisenhower showed an acute understanding of the limitations of military power and of the economic costs of military expenditure. He is perhaps best remembered for warning of the dangers of the "military-industrial complex" as a standing lobby for armaments spending.

Even more penetrating was his observation, in his Final Address, that

> Every gun that is made, every warship launched, every rocket fired, signifies in the final sense a theft from those

who hunger and are not fed, those who are cold and are not clothed.

The logic of opportunity cost has rarely been put more simply or sharply, particularly as it applies to military expenditure. Nearly 50 years after Eisenhower's death, the lesson he stated so simply and forcefully has not been learned.

6.4. Technological Benefits of War?

Despite, or perhaps because of, the obvious waste and destruction of war, it's often claimed that war has economic benefits, and even that it's necessary to the successful functioning of the economy. We've already looked at arguments based on the "blessings of destruction."

In this section, we'll look at another popular argument, namely, that war is a spur to research and development (R&D), and therefore to peacetime prosperity. It was recently revived by economist Tyler Cowen, who argued that slow economic growth has been due in part to the persistence and expectation of peace.[3] Like other advocates of this thesis, Cowen focuses on the example of World War II.

As in many other instances, World War II was exceptional. World War I produced some notable advances in the technology of death and destruction (poison gas, tanks, and submarine warfare to name a few), but little of any value beyond that. Other twentieth-century wars, with the exception of the Cold War, discussed below, have been too small in their scale to have

---

[3] https://www.nytimes.com/2014/06/14/upshot/the-lack-of-major-wars
-may-be-hurting-economic-growth.html.

much impact on the technological development of the world as a whole.

World War II was different, at least on the face of it. Penicillin, nuclear energy, computers, and jet aircraft are examples of technologies that were developed, or advanced rapidly, during World War II and played a major role in postwar prosperity.

In all of these cases, the underlying research had been commenced in the 1920s and 1930s. Following the fortuitous discovery of the antimicrobial properties of penicillin by Alexander Fleming in 1928, Howard Florey and Ernst Chain began work in 1939 to understand its therapeutic action and chemical composition. Frank Whittle patented the turbojet in 1930 and built the first prototype in 1937. Turing's fundamental work on computability was also undertaken in the 1930s. Atomic fission was first demonstrated in 1938, the culmination of decades of research. In August 1939, a group of physicists including Albert Einstein wrote to President Franklin D. Roosevelt warning that this discovery raised the possibility of an atomic bomb.

The outbreak of war led to a massive push to apply these and other research discoveries on an industrial scale, producing millions of doses of penicillin, hundreds of thousands of airplanes, including the first jet fighters, and of course the atomic bomb. ENIAC, the first electronic general-purpose computer, was commissioned to compute artillery tables, but did not appear until 1946, when it was used for computations to produce the first hydrogen bomb.

Opportunity cost reasoning leads us to ask what was forgone to release the resources. In large part, the answer is "research of the kind that made these developments possible." War gives great urgency to the "D" part of R&D, at the expense of "R." This can produce some impressive short-run payoffs, such as those described above.

On the other hand, the need for immediate results can lead to losses in the long run. This is evident, for example, in the case of computing. Overall, it seems likely that World War II delayed the development of modern digital computers. The urgent demand for computational power to be delivered as soon as possible meant that designs remained close to those of older analog computing devices.

Much harder to measure, but almost certainly more significant, is the loss arising when scientists are shifted from fundamental research to activities more directly relevant to the war effort, much of it with very little value beyond the immediate needs of the military. Then there are the vast numbers of young scientists whose careers were interrupted because of military service.

For quite a few scientists, war service has been more than a career interruption. Harry Moseley, widely regarded as the greatest experimental physicist of the twentieth century, was killed at Gallipoli in 1915.[4] The great theoretical physicist Karl Schwarzschild died the following year. Losses in World War II include the mathematicians Jean Cavailles, shot by the Gestapo, and Wolfgang Doblin, who killed himself when faced with capture by the Germans. Another tragic and heroic story is that of the scientists of the Pavlovsk Experimental Station near Leningrad (now St. Petersburg), 12 of whom starved to death while protecting the station's seed bank during the siege of the city in 1941. Many more young scientists died before having any chance to contribute. One can think of the 50 percent fatality rate suffered by the class of 1914 at the École Normale Supérieure in Paris.

As the example of the Pavlovsk Experimental Station shows, scientific projects themselves were not immune from the destruction. The first programmable computer to be built was not ENIAC, but the Z1, designed by German Konrad Zuse. This

---

[4] Niels Bohr is supposed to have said that even if no one else had died, the death of Harry Moseley alone was enough to make the First World War an unbearable tragedy.

computer and its successors, the Z2 and Z3, were destroyed by Allied bombing raids, and Zuse's work was not resumed for years.

Yet again, the idea of opportunity cost as "that which is not seen" provides a corrective against any attempt to minimize the costs of destruction.

Further Reading

Fontevecchia (2012), writing in *Forbes* magazine, quotes Goldman Sachs as suggesting that Hurricane Sandy will be good for the economy. Numerous One Lesson economists, such as Skorup (2011), reproduce the standard Bastiat critique of the "broken window," without noticing that it depends on the assumption of full employment.

Passell (1995) gives a more balanced treatment, citing the classic textbook by Samuelson (1948) to argue, as I have, that the "silver linings" idea is at best a "quarter truth," valid only if the disaster coincides with high unemployment. I discuss some of the problems with using measures like GDP to assess the impact of disasters in Quiggin (2011a).

Australia's *White Paper on Full Employment* is Commonwealth of Australia (1945). It's discussed further in *Work for All* (Langmore and Quiggin 1994).

Eisenhower's "The Chance for Peace" (1953) and "Farewell Address" (1961) are well worth reading, particularly by comparison with the debased rhetoric of the current US president.

Information on the costs of war is derived from Harrison (2013), Crawford (2016), and US Agency for International Development (2017). Madia (2008) is the source for the value of life estimates.

Wikipedia provides biographies for the scientists mentioned in section 6.4. Vidal (2010) tells the story of the Pavlovsk

Experimental Station, and a more recent threat from real estate developers, which appears to have been staved off (REALS 2015). Prochasson (2010) gives information on the deaths of scientists and other intellectuals in World War I.

Arguments supporting the view that military expenditure provides a fiscal stimulus have been put forward by Barro (2001) and Feldstein (2009). The views of critics including Robert Higgs on the political right and Brad DeLong on the left are summarized by Zelveh (2009). Cowen's (2014) exposition of the case for technological benefits of war draws on Morris (2014).

LESSON TWO

■

PART I

Social Opportunity Costs

In Lesson One, we saw how prices in competitive markets reflect the opportunity costs faced by producers and consumers. In Lesson Two, we will see that many opportunity costs arising in the process of production and consumption aren't reflected, or aren't fully reflected, in market prices.

For many writers on economics, including Hazlitt, this is the beginning and end of the story. The conclusion they draw is that government action that moves economic outcomes away from an observed market equilibrium can make society worse off. In reality, however, markets don't work in the idealized fashion assumed in simplistic tracts like *Economics in One Lesson*.

To begin with, there is nothing special about the particular market equilibrium we observe at any given time. As we will show in chapter 7, there is an infinite range of possible allocations of property rights, each corresponding to different social choices, and each associated with a different competitive equilibrium. As property rights change continuously over time, so does the competitive equilibrium toward which market processes push the economy. So, we need to consider the fairness or otherwise of the distribution of property rights before we can say anything about the desirability of an equilibrium outcome.

Second, the actual outcome in a market economy differs greatly from the ideal competitive equilibrium. Markets for vital services like health and education work poorly or don't exist at all. Social and economic problems including unemployment, pollution, and monopoly are further examples where markets don't work in the way that Hazlitt assumes. This large class of problems is collectively known as "market failure." Although market failures are many and varied, all involve the failure of market prices to reflect opportunity costs.

One type of market failure, the cycle of boom and bust that gives rise to mass unemployment, is so severe and so pervasive that it has become the subject of a special branch of economics, called macroeconomics. The name, which refers to the study of the economy at an aggregate level, is distinguished from microeconomics, the study of individual prices and markets and the way that they interact in equilibrium.

The evidence from macroeconomics is that, for the economy as a whole, resources are not always allocated on the basis of opportunity cost. Rather, there are long periods of recession and depression where productive resources sit idle, so that their opportunity cost, in effect, is zero.

The various types of market failure, including macroeconomic failures and the inability of markets to resolve questions about the distribution of property rights, form the basis of Lesson Two:

> Market prices don't reflect all the opportunity costs we face as a society.

In this part of the book, we will look at Lesson Two in detail. In chapter 7 we examine how the logic of opportunity cost applies to the distribution of income and wealth. We will stress the point that systems of property rights are social constructions rather than part of the natural order and show how advocates of "natural rights" in property, beginning with Locke, have used this idea as a cover for exploitation and expropriation. We will also look at the idea of "Pareto optimality," central to One Lesson economics, and show how it is a misleading description of a "no free lunch" situation.

In chapter 8, we will consider how to interpret the classic macroeconomic problems of recession, unemployment, and inflation in terms of opportunity cost. The central theme will be the fact that recessions and mass unemployment are not rare disasters but are part of the normal working of a market system, unless these tendencies are offset by public policy. The fact of regular mass unemployment is, in itself, sufficient to invalidate the assumptions of One Lesson economics.

Turning to microeconomics, we will consider problems more commonly associated with the term "market failure." The first class of market failures, discussed in chapter 9, are those where markets are not fully competitive, including monopolies, oligopolies, and monopsonies. Next, in chapter 10, we consider externalities and pollution. Finally, in chapter 11, we examine problems associated with information, uncertainty, and financial markets.

CHAPTER 7

■

Property Rights and Income Distribution

There is no property in durable objects, such as lands or houses, when carefully examined in passing from hand to hand, but must, in some period, have been founded on fraud and injustice.

—David Hume, *Essays, Moral, Political, and Literary* (1742), Part II, Essay XII, of the Original Contract

The competitive equilibrium we talked about in Lesson One is not the unique product of spontaneous social processes. Rather, it depends on the allocation of property rights on which trade is based. Before we can trade in markets, we must determine who owns what. This determination is subject to the logic of opportunity cost, but can't be reduced to market transactions.

Presented with this problem in the abstract, most people would prefer an egalitarian initial allocation, leading to outcomes where everyone is better off than they were before entering into trade, and no one is much better off than anyone else. In reality, though, there is no starting point at which we get to make a once-for-all choice and no final equilibrium we can observe. Both property rights and economic outcomes are changing all the time, partly through market transactions, but also through births and deaths, taxes, crime, inventions, and changes in the laws applying to all of these processes.

People enter the world with endowments that are determined, in greater or lesser measure, by those of their parents. They have innate or acquired characteristics that may prove valuable, or harmful, to their chances of doing well in a given society. In some societies, for example, strength and a propensity for physical violence may lead to positions of power, in others to imprisonment and poverty. This process continues from birth to death. People experience good and bad luck over the course of their lives, as well as incurring the consequences of life choices that may or may not be wise.

Social decisions about property rights influence the allocation of opportunities between people in a given generation, and between generations. Again, there is no point at which a "once and for all" fair allocation can be settled, leaving everything to market exchange from then on. Every day, children are born, helplessly dependent on their parents, and, every day, people die, leaving assets of various kinds behind. Decisions made today supersede the wishes of the departed and constrain the opportunities of the young and of those yet to be born.

But such decisions must be made all the time, implicitly and explicitly, and the logic of opportunity cost applies to them. Rights allocated to one person or group cannot be allocated to another. The way in which this allocation takes place is the central topic of this chapter.

7.1. What Lesson Two Tells Us about Property Rights and Income Distribution

In any market economy, the outcome of interactions between individuals, families, businesses, and governments depends on the allocation of property rights and resources that determines the starting point for trade and employment. Those property rights include not only ownership of houses, factories, and so on, but also the set of rights and obligations created by taxation and welfare systems, and the legal framework within which economic activity takes place.

The range of possible allocations and institutions is vast, and so is the range of possible market outcomes they can generate. In fact, according to economic theory, any final outcome that is consistent with the technological possibilities available to society, and that takes full advantage of the possibilities for trade, can arise as the market outcome, given an appropriate allocation of property rights.

What this means is that the choice of any particular starting point for the allocation of property rights entails an opportunity cost, namely, forgoing all the alternative possibilities. Increasing the allocation of rights to one person or group will, in general, reduce what is available for everyone else, and this will be reflected in the market outcome.

7.2. Property Rights and Market Equilibrium

As we saw in section 2.4, the core of Lesson One is that, in a perfect competitive equilibrium, prices exactly match opportunity cost. There are no "free lunches" left. Any additional benefit that can be generated for anyone in the economy must be matched by an equal or greater opportunity cost. This opportunity cost may be borne by those who benefit from the change or by others.

For One Lesson economists like Hazlitt, that is all we need to know. On their reading of Lesson One, it tells us that once we are at a competitive equilibrium, it is impossible to improve on the outcome. In the technical jargon of economics, the competitive outcome is "Pareto-optimal," after the Italian economist Vilfredo Pareto, who first proposed this idea.[1] In a more grandiose piece of jargon, this theoretical finding is referred to as the First Fundamental Theorem of Welfare Economics.

One problem with this argument is that the conditions it requires are never satisfied in practice. They would be even further from reality if it weren't for extensive government action to reduce unemployment, restrict monopoly power, and bring prices closer to opportunity costs (more on this in chapters 8 and 9).

More important, there is nothing special about the particular market equilibrium we observe at any given time. There is an infinite range of possible allocations of property rights, and each one corresponds to a competitive equilibrium with no free lunches.

A more striking way of making this point is to observe that any allocation with no free lunches can emerge as a market equilibrium given a suitable starting position, that is, given a suitable allocation of property rights. Unsurprisingly, this result is called the Second Fundamental Theorem of Welfare Economics. As with the Laws of Thermodynamics and Motion, the Second Theorem is more interesting than the first.

Unfortunately, most mainstream discussion of the Second Theorem misses the central point. Rather than looking at the implications for the distribution of property rights, the mainstream literature has focused on the theoretical concept of "lump-sum" taxation, that is, taxes that redistribute income without any effect on the supply of labor and capital. If lump-sum taxation

---

[1] Pareto followed a surprisingly common process of political development, beginning as a free-market liberal and ending up as a supporter of Mussolini's fascist government. Another example is given by Hayek's support for the Chilean dictator Augusto Pinochet. The relationship between Pareto's political and economic theories is discussed in section 7.5.

were feasible, the distribution of property rights would not matter, since any problems could be fixed by redistributive taxation.[2] Whatever their theoretical attractions, however, lump-sum taxes are not feasible in practice. Discussion framed in these terms obscures the central role of property rights.

It is crucial, therefore, to think clearly about property rights and their implications for income distribution. To begin thinking about the topic, it's important to understand the property rights that currently exist and therefore represent the starting point for any analysis of possible changes.

7.3. The Starting Point

If we are going to consider changes in the distribution of income and wealth, what should we take as our starting point? There are various possibilities, many of which are of theoretical interest, but not of much practical use.

Hazlitt doesn't spell out the starting point for his analysis. However, his analysis is based on the implicit claim (spelled out in more detail by Bastiat) that there is a natural distribution of private property rights, and that this natural distribution exists prior to any government activity such as taxation and the payment of welfare benefits. This is nonsense. It is impossible to disentangle some subset of property rights and entitlements from the social and economic framework in which they are created and enforced.

The ordinary meaning of "property" refers to a specific kind of control over resources, most completely realized in freehold ownership of land and in private ownership of capital. In the idealized model that forms the basis of One Lesson thinking

---

[2] The distinction between predistribution (the allocation of property rights) and redistributive taxation is discussed further in chapters 12 and 13, respectively.

about property, all property is of this kind. The "natural" distribution of property implicit in Bastiat and Hazlitt is one in which restrictions currently associated with property in land and capital are removed, while rights that do not fit the idealized model of property ownership are erased.

Most of the time, we take the existing allocation of property rights for granted. This is, however, an example of exactly the fallacy pointed out by Bastiat, namely, that of focusing on what is seen and ignoring the unseen alternatives. All property rights began with a decision by governments to create and enforce someone's right to use a particular good, asset, or idea, and to regulate the way in which that right might, or might not, be transferred to others.

In some of the cases discussed earlier, such as those of telecommunications spectrum and fishing quotas, the rights were created relatively recently, and the process by which they were created is well documented. In somewhat older cases, such as that of the nineteenth-century innovations that created limited liability corporations, the history has been forgotten by all but a few specialists.

Going even further back, property rights in land are all ultimately derived from grants by a king or government, whose rights in turn were ultimately derived from seizure or conquest. Since land is finite, the decision to allocate property rights in land to one person or corporation implies an opportunity cost borne by those who might otherwise have owned the land.

For example, the famous Domesday Book, completed in 1086, represented the allocation of rights and obligations over all the land in England, following the victory of William the Conqueror over his Saxon predecessors. William's need to reward his Norman followers implied an opportunity cost, borne by the dispossessed Saxons, and by anyone else who might have been allocated land but wasn't. All of this land, along with the associated rights and obligations, has changed hands many times since then, and in many ways, but their foundation still lies in choices made by the state.

Property rights in land create a right for the owner to receive rent from those who occupy or farm the land. In the feudal system of Norman England, and well into the nineteenth century, rent on land was the basis of most great fortunes. What is true of rights in land is true of every newly created property right. All such rights create rents, paid to the owners by those who need access to their property.

In any society, people have views about what property rights are legitimate and, in particular, what they themselves are entitled to. These views may or may not match the property rights that actually prevail in that society. For example, workers commonly regard their jobs as belonging to them, in some sense. In some places, this perception is supported by laws prohibiting unfair dismissal. In the United States, by contrast, the doctrine of "employment at will" means that the job is the property of the employer.

One Lesson economists like Hazlitt want to pare down government to the minimum necessary to protect the property rights of which they approve. These include rights over land and houses, private sector financial assets, and personal possessions.

There are two main difficulties with this. First, One Lesson economists disagree among themselves as to which property rights should be maintained. For example, some One Lesson economists support the concept that the creators of ideas should have unlimited "intellectual property" in those ideas, while others believe that "information ought to be free."[3] Moreover, while One Lesson economists oppose "welfare" benefits paid out of tax

---

[3] The fine distinctions between the various One Lesson sects, such as Austrians, objectivists, and anarcho-capitalists, are too complex and tedious to be detailed here.

revenue, such as Social Security, there is no clear dividing line between these benefits and contractually obligatory payments such as pensions for public and private workers and contracts with private firms to supply public services.[4] Any attempt to define, on the basis of logical first principles, a "natural" set of property rights, independent of government, runs rapidly into quicksand.

The second problem is that any attempt to strip all rights and entitlements back to a minimal set corresponding to a naive notion of "private property" would not produce anything like the existing distribution of private property rights. Some kinds of private property would become much more valuable, and others much less so. An example can be seen in the mass privatizations that followed the end of communism in Russia and other countries in the former Soviet bloc. These processes greatly enriched a handful of oligarchs and greatly impoverished everyone else, leading, for most people, to the loss of the limited property rights they had under communism.

It is impossible to describe, with any accuracy, a proposed starting point based on such a radical change. We can't really say what the opportunity cost of shifting property rights from one person to another might be in such a situation. It makes sense, therefore, to start thinking about changes in the allocation of property rights with reference to our actual position rather than to some theoretical ideal.

In most modern societies, governments collect a substantial proportion of national income in taxation revenue. Some of this revenue is spent on the provision of public services and some on "transfer payments" such as Social Security, unemployment and disability insurance, and assistance to poor families.

---

[4] Social Security and Medicare are notionally set up as contributory funds. In reality, however, beneficiaries of these programs receive substantially more than they contribute, even allowing for investment returns.

The starting point for any consideration of changes in property rights therefore includes both the existing set of property rights of workers, the employment position of workers, and the rights and obligations of members of the community to receive government services and benefits and to pay the taxes necessary to finance those services and benefits.

Any change in property rights involves an opportunity cost, as does a decision to leave property rights unchanged. Since market outcomes are determined by property rights, One Lesson economics is of no use here. We need to make choices as a society and understand the opportunity costs of these choices. These issues will be discussed further in chapter 12.

7.4. Property Rights and Natural Law

There have been many attempts to ground property rights, particularly rights in land, in so-called natural law, independent of government. The most famous is that of the English philosopher John Locke, who took the view that ownership of land was originally acquired by "mixing one's labour with the land," that is, by cultivation.

Locke's doctrine was self-serving, to put it mildly. Locke's personal wealth derived largely from investments in England's American colonies, including the slave trade. The viability of these investments depended, in the end, on the capacity of the colonists to dispossess the indigenous inhabitants who were mostly hunters and gatherers rather than farmers.[5] By making agricultural labor the crucial factor in the original acquisition, Locke could justify the expropriation that made colonization

---

[5] Those who were farmers, such as the Cherokee, were ignored by Locke and, ultimately, dispossessed anyway.

feasible, while still presenting a case for natural rights in property, independent of the state.[6]

More fundamentally even disregarding the native inhabitants, the idea of natural rights depended on the assumption that there was so much land beyond the frontier of existing settlement that anyone who wanted to could acquire enough to support themselves, while leaving "enough and as good" for those who followed. Thomas Jefferson expressed this belief when he said that his Louisiana Purchase would provide "room enough for our descendants to the thousandth and thousandth generation."

In reality, within a couple of generations, all the usable agricultural land in North America had been occupied and had become the scene of "range wars" between farmers and ranchers. Similar conflicts emerged in Australia, South America, and wherever Europeans settled in the New World.

Locke's idea that one person can acquire rights in land without making things worse for anyone else is an obvious example of a spurious "free lunch." The idea at the core of the Two Lessons is that we need to look at the opportunity costs of any benefit even when they are not directly obvious. Once we do this, it is clear that the use of land by one person always has an opportunity cost, namely the best alternative use.

Locke's whole theory is based on ignoring opportunity costs, which are central to both our lessons. It is striking, then, that it is the main justification used by One Lesson economists for ignoring the distribution of property rights. The idea of founding a defense of capitalism on Locke's doctrine of just acquisition of property is inherently contradictory. Such a defense pits the role

---

[6] Of course, neither Locke nor his aristocratic friends were going to do any labor themselves to acquire their "natural" rights. Rather, in Locke's model, work is done by "servants" and the benefits accrue to their masters. In the American context, servants were either black slaves or white indentured laborers. Indentures were effectively a form of slavery, though for a limited period of 7 to 14 years.

of prices in signaling opportunity costs against an origin story in which opportunity costs are assumed out of existence.

Today, wealth is no longer derived from the ownership of agricultural land, however that land might have been originally acquired. This opens another possibility: even if the natural rights theory was false when it was first put forward, the development of the modern capitalist economy—where property is acquired through competition and innovation—posthumously validates it.

But this claim fails for a number of reasons. First, though most large fortunes don't depend on agriculture, control of natural resources remains important. Some of the world's largest companies (most notably ExxonMobil) and richest families (like the Kochs and the Gettys) were built on oil profits. And, as the long history of struggle over the control of oil resources has shown, everyone who depends on natural resources is acutely aware of opportunity costs.

Even more important is the central role played by intellectual property (IP) in the modern economy. IP is the core of the value of information technology companies like Apple and Google, and of major pharmaceutical companies. As we will see in chapter 15, the creation of property rights in ideas has opportunity costs that often outweigh the benefits.

More fundamentally still, a natural rights theory of property only makes sense if we believe that unaided individual effort can generate wealth. This was at least superficially plausible for small farmers, who worked a small plot of land with only the aid of animals and some simple tools and supplied most of their own needs, including food and clothing.[7]

In a modern economy, however, interdependence reveals itself immediately. No one can acquire any kind of income or

---

[7] In reality, their agricultural technology was the product of millennia of human development and their self-sufficiency was ultimately underpinned by access to a market economy.

property without countless other people's assistance. Believers in One Lesson economics are outraged when this is pointed out to them as evidence against ideas of natural rights to property. A striking example was the furor that erupted when, against claims that business owners had built their own wealth and owed nothing to anyone else, former US president Barack Obama pointed to the roads and other infrastructure on which business depends and observed, "You didn't build that."

7.5. Pareto and Inequality

The situation where there is no way to make some people better off without making anyone worse off is often referred to as "Pareto-optimal," after the Italian economist and political theorist Vilfredo Pareto, who developed the underlying concept. "Pareto-optimal" is, arguably, the most misleading term in economics (and there are plenty of contenders). Before explaining this, it's important to understand Pareto's broader body of thought, one that led him in the end to support the fascist regime of Benito Mussolini.

Pareto sought to undermine the version of liberalism that dominated nineteenth-century economics, according to which the optimal (most desirable) economic outcome was the one that contributed most to human happiness, often (if somewhat loosely) summed up as "the greatest good for the greatest number." Particularly as developed by the great philosopher and economist John Stuart Mill, this is a naturally egalitarian doctrine.

The egalitarian implications of the classical framework reflect the fact that the needs of poor people are more urgent than the needs of those who are better off. The happiness of the community as a whole will be increased by policies that benefit the poorest members of the community, even if these benefits come at the expense of those who are better off. It follows that a substantial degree of income redistribution will be socially desirable and that large accumulations of individual wealth, which contribute only marginally to the happiness of a small number of people, are undesirable in themselves, though they may in some circumstances be a by-product of desirable policies.

Pareto's big achievement, further developed by a large number of twentieth-century economists, was to show that economic analysis could be undertaken without invoking the concept of utility. Hence, interpersonal comparisons of happiness, which invariably lead to the conclusion that redistributing wealth more equally is beneficial, could be dismissed as "unscientific."

Pareto didn't stop with an attack on the economic implications of Mill's approach. Mill's philosophical framework implied support for political democracy, including the enfranchisement of women. Since everyone's welfare counts equally in the classical calculus, the political process should, as far as possible, give everyone equal weight.

Pareto reversed this reasoning, arguing that a highly unequal distribution of income was both inevitable and desirable; he proposed what he called a power law, described by a statistical distribution which also bears his name. Pareto's "Law" may be summed up by the 80–20 proposition, that 20 percent of the population have 80 percent of the wealth.

The supposed constancy of income distribution implies that any attempt at redistribution must be essentially futile. Even if the aim is to benefit the poor at the expense of the rich, the effect will simply be to make some people newly rich at the expense of those who are currently rich. Pareto called this process "the circulation of elites."[8]

---

[8] In his dystopian classic *1984*, Orwell has the Trotsky-like character Emmanuel Goldstein present Pareto's idea as the starting point of *The Theory of Oligarchical Collectivism*. Orwell almost certainly derived the idea from James Burnham, an admirer of Pareto whose work Orwell saw as the embodiment of "power worship."

All of this led Pareto to become one of the first advocates of a political position that combined an extreme free-market position on economic issues with hostility to political liberalism and democracy. Pareto welcomed the rise of Mussolini's fascist regime and accepted a "royal" nomination to the Italian senate from Mussolini. However, he died in 1923, less than a year after Mussolini's rise to power.

Pareto was not really a fascist. Rather, he developed a version of liberalism similar to that of his more famous successors, Hayek and Mises, both of whom embraced and worked for murderous regimes that had come to power by suppressing democratic socialist parties. Like Pareto, neither Hayek nor Mises can properly be described as fascists—they weren't interested in nationalism or in the display of power for its own sake. Rather, their brand of liberalism was hostile to democracy and indifferent to political liberty, making them natural allies of any authoritarian regime that adheres to One Lesson orthodoxy in economics.[9]

7.5.1. Pareto Optimality

Now back to Pareto optimality, and why it is such a misleading term. Describing a situation as "optimal" implies that it is the unique best outcome. This is not the case. Pareto, and followers like Hazlitt, seek to claim unique social desirability for market outcomes by definition rather than demonstration.

In reality, there are infinitely many possible allocations of property rights, and infinitely many allocations of goods and

---

[9] Supporters of Hayek and Mises commonly describe themselves as "libertarians," but their alliance with brutal dictators makes a travesty of the term. They have been derisively described as "shmibertarian." A more precise description, used in this book, is "propertarian."

services, that meet the definition of Pareto optimality. A highly egalitarian allocation can be Pareto optimal. So can any allocation where one person has all the wealth and everyone else is reduced to a bare subsistence.

Recognizing the inappropriateness of describing radically unfair allocations as optimal, some economists have used the description "Pareto-efficient" instead, but this is not much better. It corresponds neither to the ordinary meaning of efficient nor to the meaning with which the term is commonly used in economics, which is also misleading, but in a different way.

The concept of opportunity cost gives us a better way to think about the possibility of making some people better off while no one is worse off. If such possibilities exist, then there are potential benefits that have no opportunity costs. Conversely, if there is a positive opportunity cost for any benefit, then we can't make anyone better off without making someone else worse off. A Pareto-optimal situation may be described more simply as one where all opportunity costs are positive, or, in the phrasing of section 2.4, as one in which there are no free lunches available.

7.6. Conclusion

The difference between One Lesson and Two Lesson economics is neatly reflected in the theory of welfare economics. One Lesson economists read the theory as far as the First Fundamental Theorem and then close the book, satisfied that they have discovered everything they need to know. They ignore the more important and interesting Second Theorem and fail to recognize that the allocation of property rights is the critical factor in determining which of the infinite range of possible market equilibrium outcomes is realized.

As Samuelson observed in the quotation that opens this book,

When someone preaches "Economics in One Lesson," I advise: Go back for the second lesson.

Further Reading

Blaug (2007) provides some valuable historical background on the Fundamental Theorems. Little (1950) and Graaff (1968) give critical accounts of the theoretical foundations of welfare economics.

Orwell's *1984* is available in many editions, as is Mill's *On Liberty*. I've referenced some easily accessible editions. Burnham (1941) is still influential on the right of US politics, despite Orwell's (1946, republished as Orwell 1968) acute diagnosis of "power worship" and demolition of Burnham's theoretical ideas.

Nye (1977) discusses the anti-democratic elite theory put forward by Pareto and others in the late nineteenth century.

My critique of Locke is developed in more detail in three articles in *Jacobin* (Quiggin 2015a, 2015b, 2016). A more scholarly and less polemical account of Locke's role as a defender of colonialist exploitation is given by Arneil (1996).

For the Hayek-Pinochet connection, see Farrant, McPhail, and Berger (2012). One side of an exchange of letters between Hayek and Thatcher is discussed by Corey Robin (2013).

CHAPTER 8

■

Unemployment

No country can afford to lose a generation to unemployment.
—Sharan Burrow, General Secretary of the
International Trade Union Confederation[1]

In this chapter, we will look at the business cycle, that is, the tendency of market economies to fall into periods of recession, characterized by high unemployment, idle capital, and declining or stagnant output. According to One Lesson economics, recessions ought to be impossible; markets should ensure that all resources are used up to the point where their opportunity cost matches their marginal product. Since recessions obviously do happen, most One Lesson economists don't state this explicitly. Instead, they tell a story in which recessions may arise due to momentary disruptions of business, but the economy will recover rapidly as long as governments do nothing to harm business confidence.

As we will see, the economy is in recession almost as often as it is operating at full capacity. The fact that recessions are part of the ordinary workings of a market economy, and not temporary aberrations, has important implications for the way we think about opportunity cost.

---

[1] https://www.huffingtonpost.com/sharan-burrow/its-not-the-economy
-stupi_1_b_1523115.html.

Although the term "recession" refers to the reduction in output that characterizes a recession, the critical feature of a recession is large-scale unemployment and the suffering and dislocation it causes. Whenever workers who could usefully contribute to production, and want to do so, are unemployed, we need to consider Lesson Two. Prices (remember that wages are the price of labor) are not properly reflecting the opportunity cost of resources, in this case unemployed productive resources. In this chapter, we will consider in detail how Lesson Two applies to unemployment.

Pulling all this together, we'll see that the microeconomic analysis of Lesson One only makes sense if full employment can be sustained. This doesn't happen automatically in market economies. It requires government action, through monetary and fiscal policy, to smooth out the business cycle.

With this in mind, we will reconsider Hazlitt's discussion of Bastiat's "glazier's fallacy." We will show that the story told by Bastiat only makes sense in an environment of high unemployment. In this context, the apparent fallacy needs more careful consideration.

8.1. Macroeconomics and Microeconomics

Economists commonly distinguish "macroeconomic" issues like unemployment, which affect the economy as a whole, from "microeconomic" issues arising in particular markets. Microeconomics leads us, with some important qualifications, to Lesson One. Microeconomic analysis shows us how prices signal, and respond to, opportunity costs. By contrast, the core concern of macroeconomics is the periodic failure of markets to function properly, resulting in recessions and depressions. Macroeconomic analysis is, therefore, part of Lesson Two.

The macro-micro distinction goes back to John Maynard Keynes, the great British economist who produced the first serious analysis of why market economies can experience prolonged periods of depression, including high unemployment and widespread business failure.[2] The core idea in Keynes's analysis is that of a failure of coordination, in which people may be willing to trade at the prices prevailing in the market but are unable to do so.

In standard economics courses, analysis of opportunity cost and market failure is typically confined to courses on microeconomics. This is a mistake. Lesson Two tells us that market prices don't reflect all the opportunity costs we face as a society. There can be no clearer case of this than that of an unemployed worker, willing to work for the prevailing market wage, but unable to find a job. Workers trade their labor for the goods and services that they buy with their wages.

Under conditions of high unemployment, workers would like to make this trade at current wages and prices but are unable to do so. Yet when the economy recovers, the same workers regain employment and are sufficiently productive that employers can pay their wages and earn a profit margin. This is possible because of the additional demand for goods and services that arises when the labor force is fully employed.

Mass unemployment, then, is a clear illustration of Lesson Two. The market wage does not reflect the opportunity cost faced by unemployed workers, who would willingly work at this wage and could, under full employment conditions, produce enough to justify their employment.

Wages represent most, or at least a large part of, the cost of every one of the goods and services produced in the economy.

---

[2] The terms are due to Keynes's Norwegian contemporary, Ragnar Frisch, but without Keynes, macroeconomics as we know it would not exist.

For the majority of households, wages are the primary source of income. When wages do not properly reflect the social opportunity cost of labor, no price in the economy reflects the true social opportunity cost of the goods and services concerned.

A simple application of Lesson One suggests that unemployment could be resolved if only wages were reduced until they matched opportunity costs. This does not work for a number of reasons. First, workers, quite sensibly, resist cuts in wages, even when employers claim they are necessary; such claims can always be made whether or not they are justified. Second, and more subtly, declining wages and prices reduce the profitability of long-term investment since the price level at which final goods are sold is lower than that prevailing when inputs to production are increased. Equivalently, the real rate of interest is higher when prices are falling, as can be seen from the discussion in chapter 3.

To put it simply, Lesson One, important as it is, holds true only in an economy that is working at full employment. Wages properly represent opportunity costs only when all workers can obtain jobs at the market wage determined by their skills and occupation. In recessions, this does not happen.

The standard results of microeconomics are valid only when the macroeconomy is working properly. This fact is why Keynes saw his macroeconomic theory as a means of saving market capitalism, not from its socialist critics, but from its own potentially fatal flaws.

8.2. The Business Cycle

In the United States, recessions are officially measured by the Business Cycle Dating Committee of the National Bureau of Economic Research (NBER). When the NBER was founded in 1920, its primary task was to document and analyze business cycles, of which recessions and depressions are the most distinctive features. To this day, it is the announcement and definition of recessions for which the NBER is best known to the general public.

To understand recessions, and the way they are measured, therefore, it is useful to take a brief look at the idea of the business cycle. NBER defines a recession as "a significant decline in economic activity spread across the economy, lasting more than a few months, normally visible in real GDP, real income, employment, industrial production, and wholesale-retail sales."

Almost as soon as global capitalism emerged around the beginning of the nineteenth century, it became evident that capitalist economies were subject to fluctuations arising, not from external causes like wars and crop failures, but from the operation of markets themselves. More or less regularly, the economy would fall into recession, frequently as the result of a panic in financial or commodity markets. At other times, the gloom of recession was replaced by the feverish optimism of booms. The argument that these crises were not aberrations but an inherent feature of a capitalist economy was a central theme of the work of Karl Marx.[3]

The idea that these alternating periods of boom, recession, and "normal" economic expansion reflected an underlying cyclical pattern was immediately appealing. A variety of cyclical theories were proposed in the nineteenth century of which the most influential have been those of Clement Juglar and Nikolai Kondratiev. Kondratiev proposed the idea of "long waves" of expansion

---

[3] Marx's expectation that crises would grow steadily more severe, leading to a final collapse and the revolutionary overthrow of the system, has not been fulfilled. Neither, however, have numerous predictions that the economy has entered a new, crisis-free era. For that reason, Marx's ideas attract renewed attention whenever there is a particularly severe global crisis, like that of 2008.

and contraction, with each phase lasting up to 30 years. Juglar proposed a cycle of 7 to 11 years encompassing phases of expansion, crisis, recession, and recovery. This roughly corresponds to the business cycle concepts in use today by the NBER.

The NBER approach is based on identifying "peaks" and "troughs" in economic activity. A recession is then defined as the period between a peak and a trough, while an expansion is the period between a trough and a peak. The typical view of the US business cycle is one in which recessions are relatively short and involve a steep decline in economic activity, followed by a similarly rapid recovery, which gives rise to the notion of a "V-shaped" recession. The recovery phase is followed by a more durable period of steady expansion, which is ended either by an economic crisis or by a sharp tightening of monetary policy designed to reduce the risk of inflation. The phases of a cycle including a V-shaped recession correspond fairly closely to the classic Juglar cycle.

However, the biggest macroeconomic events, namely, major depressions such as the Great Depression of the 1930s and the Lesser Depression that began in 2008, do not fit into this pattern. These episodes will be examined in the next section.

8.3. The Experience of the Great and Lesser Depressions

Most of the time, booms and recessions fit the "typical" business cycle pattern first described by Juglar. Recessions are relatively short, occur in different countries at different times, and are followed by a fairly rapid return to the long-term trend path of economic growth.

In the past 100 years, however, the developed world has experienced two prolonged periods of depression that do not fit the typical pattern: the Great Depression of the 1930s and the Lesser Depression that began with the Global Financial Crisis of 2008, the effects of which are still being felt.[4]

The experience of depressions is very different from that of the standard cyclical downturn. Depressions typically follow a period of sustained growth and financial excess, culminating in a crisis and financial panic. The immediate contraction is rapid and deep. Worse still, in most cases, any recovery is choked off by mistaken policy decisions, commonly labeled as "austerity."

The Great Depression followed this pattern, beginning with a crash in the US stock market in October 1929. The US stock market lost 25 percent of its value in two days and continued falling for three years. At its lowest point, in July 1932, the market had lost 89 percent of its pre-crisis value.

Consumer spending fell sharply as a result of stock market losses and a general decline in confidence. Companies responded to the lack of demand by cutting investment and laying off workers. The result was a downward spiral that cut US industrial production in half between 1929 and 1932.

The decline in the US economy had a direct impact on European exporters. But the biggest impact was financial. A series of banking crises in the wake of the US crash led to the collapse, in 1931, of the Austrian Credit-Anstalt bank, which had been forced to rescue weaker competitors. This turned the general European slowdown into a full-blown crisis.

The US economy did not begin to recover until the presidential inauguration of Franklin D. Roosevelt in 1933. Roosevelt did not have a coherent policy program, but he was willing to

---

[4] The terms Great Depression and Lesser Depression are appropriate when the focus is on US unemployment. But, as Olivier Blanchard and Lawrence Summers have shown, the loss in output since 2008 has actually been worse than in the Great Depression. Many European countries have fared still worse on both unemployment and output.

take action to bring about an economic recovery, regardless of the constraints of market orthodoxy.

Over time, Roosevelt's New Deal program became broadly Keynesian in its orientation and provided a substantial stimulus. Similar responses emerged in Sweden. Elsewhere, however, the general response to the Depression was the adoption of a set of contractionary policies commonly described as "austerity," with consequences that ranged from bad to disastrous.

The biggest disasters occurred in Germany and Japan. In his book, *Austerity: The History of a Dangerous Idea*, Mark Blyth describes the way in which the austerity policies of the conservative Brüning administration in Germany paved the way for the rise of Adolf Hitler. Similar policies in Japan led to the replacement of limited democracy by an expansionist military dictatorship.

The Global Financial Crisis that began in September 2008 led to a broadly similar set of economic outcomes and threatens to generate similar social and political consequences, including the rise of authoritarian governments. Although the immediate response to the crisis was to adopt Keynesian stimulus measures, there was a sharp swing back to austerity following the emergence of debt crises in European countries such as Greece and the rise of the Tea Party in the United States.

Keynesian policies prevented the complete economic collapse that seemed imminent when the crisis broke. However, the shift to austerity meant that there was no real recovery. Rather, the United States and other developed countries experienced a long period of economic weakness sometimes described as the Lesser Depression.

The Lesser Depression is reflected in economic data. After a sharp drop in both employment and production, the US economy returned to slow economic growth in 2010. However, the lost output and jobs were never regained.

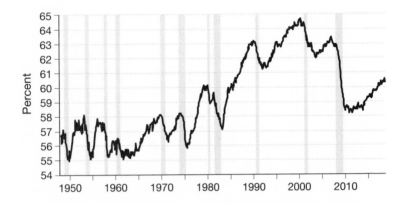

Figure 8.1. Civilian employment-population ratio, 1948–2018. *Note*: Shaded areas indicate US recessions. *Source*: Data from US Bureau of Labor Statistics. Graph from Federal Reserve Bank of St. Louis Economic Database.

Even though official unemployment rates have fallen to low levels, this outcome has arisen largely because people have given up looking for work. The employment-population ratio (the proportion of the adult population in employment) fell sharply in 2009, to levels not seen since the large-scale entry of women into the workforce in the 1970s and 1980s. A decade later, the ratio remains far below its pre-crisis level, as shown in figure 8.1.

This experience is common to other long-lasting recessions and depressions, particularly those that have followed financial crises. Potentially productive workers can remain unemployed for years at a time.

In these circumstances, Lesson One does not apply, even approximately. Attempts to pretend that it does, through misguided austerity policies, will only make matters worse.

After a decade of stagnation, the social and political effects of failed austerity policies have emerged in a form reminiscent of the 1930s, with the rise of right-wing extremist parties and factions. The most consequential outcome has been the election of Donald Trump to the US presidency, with the support of a variety of racist groups (the so-called alt-right) and the collaboration or acquiescence of mainstream Republicans. The United States is not alone in this respect. Similar extreme groups have emerged in many countries. Historical studies suggest that, perversely, failures of capitalism benefit the political right more than the left, at least in the short run.

8.4. Are Recessions Abnormal?

As was mentioned above, much economic discussion is based on the implicit assumption that the "normal" state of the economic or business cycle is one of full employment, and that mass unemployment is a rare exception to this state. On this view of the world, recessions are temporary interruptions to a pattern of stable growth.

The pattern of economic activity associated with a "typical" recession is V-shaped, with two or three quarters of sharp contraction followed by an equally rapid expansion, which restores the economy to something close to full employment. The widely used informal definition of a recession as "two quarters of negative growth" reflects this view.

There have, however, been lengthy periods when the economy has behaved quite differently. In deep depressions such as those following the Wall Street Crash of 1929 and the Global Financial Crisis of 2008, the contraction is sharper and the recovery, when it comes, is slow and fragile. Even after years of "recovery," employment remains far below normal levels.

During the Great Depression, the ratio of employment to population in the United States fell from 55 percent in 1929 to 42 percent at the depths of the slump in 1933. Despite the expansionary effects of the New Deal, employment remained weak throughout the 1930s, with the ratio only reaching 47 percent in 1940.

The same is true of the Lesser Depression, which began with the Global Financial Crisis at the end of 2008 and continued for most of the next decade. The ratio of employment to population in the United States fell from 63 percent to 58.5 percent at the onset of the crisis. Despite years of "recovery," the ratio has remained at or near that level ever since.

There have also been lengthy periods when recessions were consistently mild, so mild that many observers believed the business cycle had ceased to operate. The longest such period began with the outbreak of World War II in 1939 and came to an end in the 1970s. This "long boom" began when wartime economic planning mobilized all available economic resources.

Most economists expected the economy to decline when the war ended, as had happened after World War I. However, under the influence of Keynesian economics, governments in the decades after World War II were committed to maintaining full employment and did so with substantial success. Internationally, this commitment was embodied in the Bretton Woods system of fixed exchange rates, and the associated institutions, the International Monetary Fund and the World Bank. The Keynesian system of economic policies ran into difficulties at the end of the 1960s, leading to the breakdown of the Bretton Woods system in 1971. The 1970s was a chaotic period of high inflation and periodic high unemployment.

In the mid-1980s, the US economy began to recover, as the Federal Reserve developed new tools for economic management. Recessions continued to occur, as in 1990 and 2000, but they were relatively brief and mild. By the early 2000s, economists discerned a period of relative stability, which was quickly christened the "Great Moderation."

However, the Great Moderation turned out to be an illusion. Whereas the Keynesian long boom had lasted for decades, the Great Moderation was already over by the time it was discovered." The bursting of the Internet bubble in 2000 marked the end of strong employment growth in much of the developed world. The Global Financial Crisis turned slow growth into sharp decline, followed by stagnation.

Taking these disparate periods into account, can we regard full employment as the normal state of the economy, subject to temporary interruptions associated with downturns in the business cycle? The evidence suggests that we cannot.

Before looking at the business cycle, it's important to observe that, even under the conditions normally described as representing full employment, around 5 percent of the labor force is unemployed and actively looking for work at any given time. In addition, substantial numbers of workers would like to work longer hours, while others would enter the labor force and seek work if they thought such a search would be successful. In treating such a state as one of full employment, the underlying assumption is that, under these conditions, unemployment arises from difficulties in matching workers with jobs, rather than from a shortage of jobs in aggregate.

Turning to the cyclical data, the NBER estimates that, over the one-hundred-year period since 1914, around 25 years have been spent in recession, that is, in the contraction phase of the economic cycle. However, this classification is, in critical respects, an underestimate. In deep depressions, economic weakness persists long after the end of the contraction phase. At least from the perspective of labor markets it would make more sense to treat the recession as continuing until the economy returns to its pre-crisis growth path. In particular, as long as the employment-population ratio is far below its pre-crisis level, implying the existence of large numbers of unemployed or discouraged workers, wages do not properly represent opportunity costs.

To see the implications of this, consider the NBER data separately for the periods before and after 1929. Before 1929, contractions and expansions were about equally long, so that the economy was in recession a little under half the time.

Now, in addition to the NBER data, treat the whole of the Great Depression 1929–1939 and the years since the Global Financial Crisis as recessions. On that basis, the US economy has been in recession for about a third of the period since 1929, only a modest improvement on the period 1854–1929.

But this is still an underestimate. The post-1929 average was pulled up by World War II when the government actively worked to ensure that everyone capable of working toward the war effort did so, and by the period of Keynesian macroeconomic management from 1945 to 1970. If these periods are excluded, the proportion of time spent in recession is around 40 percent.

To sum up, except when governments are actively working to maintain full employment, the economy is in recession almost as often as not. The idea of full employment as the natural state of a market economy is an illusion.

8.5. Unemployment and Opportunity Cost

In the immediate aftermath of an economic crisis, such as the Global Financial Crisis of 2008, markets of all kinds are paralyzed. Unsold goods pile up in warehouses and on wharfs, crops rot in fields because it is not worthwhile to harvest them, and half-built houses are abandoned. As a slump continues, firms reduce their production, laying off workers and idling factories. The visible surpluses of unsold goods are gradually wound down, but the surplus of unused productive capacity continues to grow.

The most obvious feature of a recession is mass unemployment, sustained for a long period. Workers find it impossible to get jobs, even though they would be willing to work at prevailing wages. When jobs are advertised, the number of applicants greatly exceeds the number of vacancies.

Mass unemployment is an example, and arguably the most important example, of Lesson Two. The prevailing wage does not reflect the opportunity cost faced by unemployed workers, who would willingly work at this wage and could, under full employment conditions, produce enough to justify their employment.

If an increase in production is achieved by hiring previously unemployed workers, then the true opportunity cost is not the wages they receive but the value of whatever they were doing while unemployed. This value is usually low, for example, doing odd jobs for cash or around the home. It may even be negative, if idle workers sit at home while their skills become obsolete and their work habits are eroded.

Workers are not the only ones affected by recessions. A less obvious but nevertheless important feature of recessions is that capital, as well as labor, is unemployed or underemployed.[5]

If a recession persists long enough, market pressures force wages and prices down to a level where consumers are willing to spend rather than save, and where domestically produced goods and services are more affordable than imports. The process is slow and painful, especially because the immediate impact of

---

[5] At this point, it's worth mentioning the theory of the business cycle put forward by members of the Austrian School, most notably Hayek. According to this theory, business cycle slumps are the result of excessive and unsound investment during a boom phase. The slump continues until the excess capital stock is liquidated through depreciation and scrappage. While this theory represented an advance on the classical view, in which recessions were impossible, it fails to explain why recessions and depressions lead to unemployment among workers. Given an excess capital stock, the demand for workers should be greater than usual, not less.

lower wages is to reduce the purchasing power of wages and therefore the demand for the "wage goods" typically consumed by workers.[6] Only when prices also fall to a level where they reflect opportunity costs does Lesson One become applicable again. In the long run, with lower wages and prices, the recession ends and full employment is restored.

But, as Keynes observed in a much-misquoted statement, this is no reason not to worry about unemployment.[7]

> The long run is a misleading guide to current affairs. In the long run we are all dead. Economists set themselves too easy, too useless a task if in tempestuous seasons they can only tell us that when the storm is past the ocean is flat again.

The fact that mass unemployment is a regular occurrence in market economies rather than an occasional aberration means that full employment, taken for granted in One Lesson economics, is better considered a special case. It is for this reason that Keynes named his classic work *The **General** Theory of Employment, Interest and Money* (emphasis added).

To sum up in terms of Lesson Two,

> Under recession conditions, market prices do not work as accurate signals of opportunity costs for the economy as a whole.

---

[6] The pain is greatest where the value of the currency is tied to a gold standard or fixed to the currency of other countries, as in the eurozone. Henry Farrell and I have compared austerity in the eurozone to the failure of the gold standard in the Great Depression.

[7] Keynes is not saying that we should ignore the long run. Rather, his point is that we can't afford to ignore the "short run," which may involve years of recession and depression, on the basis that the economy will eventually return to long-run equilibrium.

8.6. The Macro Foundations of Micro

In the heyday of Keynesian economics, the majority of attention was focused on macroeconomic issues: unemployment, inflation, economic growth, and the balance of international payments. These were the big issues that determined whether the economy was performing well or badly. Microeconomic issues like the determination of prices in individual markets received plenty of attention but were definitely seen as a less pressing concern.

As Keynes himself observed, markets can work properly only if governments maintain full employment and economic growth. In the Keynesian period, the typical economics course began with a description of the economy as a whole, and the basic macroeconomics of the business cycle. Only after presenting this background did the course move on to supply and demand, under implicitly assumed conditions of full employment. In the terms of this book, Lesson Two was taught before Lesson One.

When Keynesian economics fell from favor in the 1970s, the crucial objection was that it lacked foundations in microeconomics. The hope was that a single consistent body of economic analysis could be developed to overcome the inconsistencies between macroeconomics and microeconomics. This project has proved to be a disastrous failure. Micro-based macroeconomics proved unable to predict the Global Financial Crisis or to provide any useful guidance on how to respond to the Crisis. Logically, this failure should have cast doubt on the microeconomic foundations of the model as well as the macroeconomic implications derived from it.

However, the majority response among One Lesson microeconomists has been to treat this as "somebody else's problem."[8]

---

[8] In the radio series *Hitchhiker's Guide to the Galaxy* first broadcast in the late 1970s, the character Ford Prefect describes an invisibility device based on the

Even if macroeconomic problems appear insoluble, microeconomists assume that the validity of their own analysis is unaffected. The implication is that, even if macro is totally wrong, only a minority of economists do it, and microeconomists are in the clear. This defense doesn't work, at least not in general.

The problem is that One Lesson microeconomics is itself a macroeconomic theory in the sense that it's derived from a general equilibrium model of the economy as a whole. The general equilibrium model takes full employment as given and derives a whole series of fundamental results from this. Conversely, if the economy can exhibit sustained high unemployment, there must be something seriously wrong with One Lesson microeconomics.

As we saw in chapter 2, Lesson One applies in a competitive general equilibrium with full information, no externalities, and so on. Under these circumstances, prices of goods reflect the social opportunity cost of producing them. This means, that, other than redistributing the initial endowments of property rights, governments can't do anything to improve on the competitive market allocation of resources.

Once you have involuntary unemployment, all of this fails. Keynes's famous thought experiment of burying pound notes in coal mines made the point that an intervention that would be totally absurd in terms of standard microeconomic reasoning might nonetheless help to alleviate a recession and therefore make society better off.

The point can be made in more detail with respect to labor economics, finance theory, public economics, and industrial organization. None of the standard conclusions of these fields of microeconomics can be assumed to be valid under conditions of sustained high unemployment.

"Somebody Else's Problem Field" as follows: "An SEP is something we can't see, or don't see, or our brain doesn't let us see, because we think that it's somebody else's problem," https://en.wikipedia.org/wiki/Somebody_else's_problem.

8.7. Hazlitt and the Glazier's Fallacy

With Lesson Two in mind, let's look at the "glazier's fallacy," due to Bastiat and recycled by Hazlitt as a critique of Keynesian economics. In the passage quoted in section 6.1, Hazlitt criticizes the idea that a smashed window might be beneficial because it generates work for glaziers. He points out that the opportunity cost of the money spent on the window repair might be, for example, a new suit that the shopkeeper had planned to buy.

The argument is compelling at first, but there's a subtle problem. Implicit in the crowd's reaction is the assumption that glaziers are short of work. If (as sometimes happens) glaziers have more jobs than they can handle, then there is no extra window—at best, the shopkeeper's order simply displaces some other, less urgent, repair. Similarly, for Hazlitt's riposte about the tailor to work, there must exist unemployed resources in the tailoring industry, so that the shopkeeper's suit represents an addition to output. If not, the additional demand from the shopkeeper will raise the price of suits marginally, just enough to lead some other customer to buy one less suit. That is, the story implies that the economy is in recession, with unemployment across a wide range of industries.

With these facts in mind, we can tell a different story. Suppose that the glazier, having been out of work for some time, has worn out his clothes. Having fixed the window and been paid, he may take his $50 and buy a new suit from a tailor, who was also previously unemployed. The tailor might spend $25 of his earnings on, say, a new pair of shoes from the cobbler.[9]

In this version of the story, the glazier, the tailor, and the cobbler are all paid. The social product is increased by a new suit

---

[9] In general, the cobbler's expenditure would also increase, but we won't trace the story any further here. A more complex and realistic version of this analysis, using the Keynesian concept of the "multiplier," is given in chapter 14.

and a pair of shoes (plus any additional value associated with the replacement of an old window by a new one).

What if the window had not been broken? Under the assumptions made so far, the shopkeeper would buy a new suit for $50, the tailor would hoard the money, and the glazier would remain unemployed. The shopkeeper is better off, since (before the window was broken) he preferred a new suit to a new window. On the other hand, the glazier is worse off, since he gets no work and no suit. For society as a whole, employment has increased: if the new window is better than the old one, output has also increased.

The argument is illustrated using tables 8.1 and 8.2. Table 8.1 gives the story as told by Bastiat and Hazlitt, with the simplifying assumption that the window and the suit each require one day of work.

As we can see, the only thing that changes is that the glazier replaces the broken window instead of making a new one. The tailor produces a suit, as before, but someone other than the shopkeeper buys it. The total amount of work done is unchanged, by the (implicit) assumption of full employment. The final outcome, that there is no additional work or output, is built into the story by this assumption.

Now let's look at the case when the glazier, the tailor, and the cobbler are initially unemployed, with the assumption that making a pair of shoes takes half a day of work.

In table 8.2, the initial stimulus to activity provided by the broken window sets off a virtuous circle, which leads to the production of a new suit, a new pair of shoes, and additional work for everyone in the story.

Hazlitt's seeming refutation of the glazier's fallacy falls apart on closer examination. On the one hand, Hazlitt uses language that implies the existence of unemployment. On the other hand, he is implicitly assuming that private and social opportunity

Table 8.1. Output and Employment in the Glazier's Story under Full Employment

	No broken window	Broken window
New windows	1	0
New suits	1	1
Days of work	2	2

Table 8.2. Output and Employment in the Glazier's Story in Recession

	No broken window	Broken window
New windows	0	0
New suits	0	1
New pairs of shoes	0	1
Days of work	0	2.5

costs are the same. The Second Lesson tells us that this won't be true in general if the economy is in recession.

That's not to say that breaking windows is a good thing, even in a recession. As we saw in chapter 6, destruction is rarely beneficial. There are always more productive activities available. As will be discussed in chapter 14, the crucial role of macroeconomic policy is to ensure that available resources, the most important being the skills and effort of workers, are used productively, regardless of the ups and downs of the business cycle.

Further Reading

Kondratiev (2014) is a translation of his major work on long waves. Van Duijn (2006) surveys the various "long-wave" theories. There are a great many stock market advisers who will, for a fee, explain how to make money by exploiting cyclical patterns, but I do not suggest consulting them.

Keynes's (1936) *General Theory of Employment, Interest and Money* is probably the most important work in economics other than Smith's *Wealth of Nations*. Some, but not all, of his insights have been incorporated into mainstream Keynesian macroeconomics. Hayek (1966) is rather less rewarding, but I'm including it for completeness.

Bernanke's (2004) *Essays on the Great Depression* give an insight into how contemporary New Keynesian economists viewed the Great Depression and help to explain the policy reaction to the Global Financial Crisis. I've written a couple of essays with Henry Farrell looking at Keynesian and anti-Keynesian reactions to the Global Financial Crisis and Lesser Depression (Farrell and Quiggin 2011, 2017), as well as my previous book, *Zombie Economics: How Dead Ideas Still Walk Among Us*. The paperback edition (Quiggin 2011) has a chapter on austerity. Another useful book on this topic is Mark Blyth's *Austerity: The History of a Dangerous Idea* (2012).

Figure 8.1 is from the Federal Reserve Economic Database (FRED) maintained by the Federal Reserve Bank of St. Louis. The data are originally derived from the Bureau of Labor Statistics and may be accessed at https://fred.stlouisfed.org/series /EMRATIO. The National Bureau of Economic Research (NBER) Business Cycle Dating Committee maintains a chronology of the US business cycle dating back to 1854 (http:// www.nber.org/cycles.html). Unemployment statistics for the Great Depression are from http://www.u-s-history.com/pages /h1528.html.

CHAPTER 9

■

Monopoly and Market Failure

> People of the same trade seldom meet together, even for merriment and diversion, but the conversation ends in a conspiracy against the public, or in some contrivance to raise prices.
> —Adam Smith, *The Wealth of Nations*

Two hundred years after the birth of Karl Marx, and 50 years after the last upsurge of revolutionary ferment in 1968, the term "monopoly capitalism" sounds antiquated, a relic of past enthusiasms and obsolete ideas. In reality, however, the problems of monopoly and associated market failures have never been more significant.

In the twentieth century, the market power of large firms was offset, to a large extent, by the "countervailing power" of trade unions and governments. As unions have declined, and governments have increasingly followed the dictates of financial markets, that countervailing power has dissipated. As a result, market failure has become ever more important.

9.1. The Idea of Market Failure

The idea of market failure comes directly from the theory of general equilibrium described in Lesson One. Under the ideal conditions of competitive general equilibrium, market prices for all goods and services would reflect their opportunity cost for society as a whole. But not all markets are competitive. In many sectors of the economy, individual firms have substantial power over the prices they charge and the wages they pay.

We have already seen that, for macroeconomic reasons, market processes may fail to reach the general equilibrium outcome. During periods of crisis and recession, goods go unsold, workers are unemployed, and financial assets become unsaleable. Moreover, the desirability of any particular market equilibrium depends on the allocation of property rights from which it is generated. The choice of property rights systems and allocations determines opportunity costs in markets, but this choice is itself subject to the logic of social opportunity cost.

But even in a full employment general equilibrium, and taking the allocation of property rights as given, markets may fail to generate prices that reflect social opportunity cost. This can happen in many different ways, a fact that has resulted in the development of various typologies of market failure, that is, attempts to classify the main possible problems with market outcomes.[1] There have also been attempts to reduce all the many kinds of market failure to a single underlying cause, such as the absence of a market, or an inadequate definition of property rights. While elegant at first sight, the attempt to fit a range of disparate phenomena into a single analytical box usually ends up reminiscent of a Procrustean bed.[2]

---

[1] One of the first such typologies, and one of the most useful, was developed by Francis Bator in the 1950s. Bator distinguished between ownership externalities, technical externalities, and public good externalities.

[2] Procrustes was a character in Greek mythology who forced overnight guests to sleep in an iron bed. If they were too short for the bed, he stretched them to fit; if too long, he amputated the excess length. The myth was recently used by Nassim Taleb as the title of a collection of critical aphorisms about mistaken ways of thinking.

The framing of the problem in terms of market prices and social opportunity costs suggests two broad classes of market failure. First, market prices may not reflect the opportunity costs facing buyers and sellers. Second, the opportunity costs of a given transaction may be borne, wholly or in part, by people other than the buyer and seller who are directly involved.

Most obviously, market failures arise when markets are not perfectly competitive. The classic example is monopoly, where a single firm is the sole supplier of a good. Such a firm can set prices higher than opportunity costs and thereby reap additional profits. Monopoly is the extreme case of a large class of what are commonly called "market imperfections."

Like many other terms in economics, the concept of market imperfections is subtly misleading, implying that markets are, if not perfect, at least close enough that the perfect market case is the appropriate benchmark. In reality, the competitive markets assumed in One Lesson economics are responsible for only a small part of economic activity.[3] In this chapter, we will look at the implications of various kinds of monopoly as well as the case of bargaining between two parties.

9.2. Economies of Size

The idea that the opportunity cost of production declines as the volume of production increases goes back to the starting point of modern economics, Adam Smith's *Wealth of Nations*. Smith focused on the idea that, by dividing production processes into small parts, the amount produced by given groups of workers, each specializing in one operation, could be greatly increased. His classic example was that of a pin factory, in which the

---

[3] See section 15.6 on *I, Pencil.*

relatively simple process of making a pin was divided into 18 distinct operations. Using this division of labor, ten workers could produce 48,000 pins a day among them. Working separately, Smith estimated, the same ten workers could produce no more than 200 pins.

Other economies of large-scale operation arise from the physical characteristics of technology. For example, the cost of a boiler, the central element of steam technology, depends on its surface area, while the capacity depends on its volume. Roughly speaking, doubling the volume of a sphere requires a 60 percent increase in surface area. This physical fact (the square-cube law) forms the basis of a rule of thumb that engineers have found applicable to estimating scale economies in many different contexts. The "point six power rule" states that changing the size of a piece of equipment will change the capital cost by the 0.6 power of the capacity ratio.

The 0.6 rule for scale economies is illustrated in table 9.1, which is derived from data on cane-sugar processing plants. As the capacity of the plant increases by a factor of 8, from 1,350 tons/day to 10,000 tons/day, the total cost increases by a factor of only 3.5. As a result, the average cost per ton crushed falls by more than half.

Cost savings associated with increasing the volume of output are called "economies of scale." Another way large firms can reduce their unit costs of production is by spreading fixed costs across a wide range of products. The savings realized in this way are called "economies of scope." The combined benefits of economies of scale and scope are called "economies of size."

A classic example of economies of scope is that of airlines. It is possible to operate an airline offering only a single product, that is, flights connecting a single pair of cities. Operating the service requires airplanes and crews, and the opportunity cost of flying the route is that these planes and crews cannot be

Table 9.1. *Illustrative Example of Scale Economies*

Capacity*	Total cost**	Average cost***
1,250	1.0	800
2,500	1.4	540
5,000	2.0	400
7,500	2.7	360
10,000	3.5	350

* Tons crushed per day; ** $million; *** $ per ton crushed.

used anywhere else. If these were the only costs, and the planes and crews were fully employed on the route, there would be no economies of scope.

However, an airline also requires a ticketing and reservation system which, once established, may be used to support multiple routes, serving many city pairs. For fixed costs like this, most of the opportunity cost is borne when the system is established. The additional cost of supporting multiple routes is small.

Similarly, an airline must establish baggage handling facilities at each airport where it operates. Economies of scale in baggage handling give rise to economies of scope when flights to many destinations depart from the same airport. This logic leads to the development of "hub and spoke" networks such as those of Delta, based in Atlanta, and FedEx, based in Memphis. Again, the opportunity cost of flying additional routes is less than the opportunity cost of establishing the service in the first place.

As a result of these interactions, the airline industry provides examples of a variety of market structures. Low traffic routes are often served by only a single carrier, whose prices are constrained mainly by the threat that some other airline might decide to enter the market. Many more markets are served by two or three carriers, which tend to charge prices in excess of opportunity costs. Travelers between major cities have a wide choice of carriers and get better deals, with prices close to opportunity costs.

There are other benefits that arise when a number of firms in a given industry are located in close proximity. These firms can share technical knowledge, either by agreement, or as skilled workers move between firms. The more firms are concentrated in a given location, the more suppliers and skilled workers seek out opportunities in that location, thereby benefiting the whole industry. Transport networks and supply chains similarly benefit all firms in an industry. These benefits are sometimes called "external economies of scale" as opposed to the "internal economies of scale" realized when an individual firm increases its output.[4]

In many cases, co-location is so significant that a physical location serves as a figure of speech for the industry that is located there.[5] "Hollywood" refers to the movie industry, "Wall Street," to financial markets, and "Silicon Valley," to the information technology sector.

It might seem that, since all the firms in an industry both contribute to and benefit from these economies of co-location, the effects cancel out, leaving prices equal to opportunity costs. This is not the case. Each firm treats the benefits generated by others as part of its technology of production but treats its own contribution to the industry as an opportunity cost for which no benefit is received. Because firms take no account of the external scale economies they generate, industries where such economies are important are likely, in a competitive equilibrium, to be smaller than would be required if prices were equal to social opportunity cost.

---

[4] As discussed in section 10.5, this distinction gave rise to the term "externality."

[5] More precisely, a "synecdoche," or "container for the thing contained."

Moreover, even if the co-location of firms is motivated by the desire to take advantage of economies of size, it also provides enhanced opportunities for collusion, as Adam Smith observed in the quotation at the chapter opening.

Whatever their source, economies of size create a problem for One Lesson economics. When economies of size are present, the opportunity cost of additional output is less than the average cost of the total quantity produced. If prices are set high enough to cover the average cost of production, they will be higher than the opportunity cost of producing more.

In most cases, firms in markets with significant economies of size will have enough market power to set prices above average cost, earning additional profits and increasing the gap between prices and opportunity cost. The extreme case is that of monopoly, to which we now turn.

9.3. Monopoly

The term "monopoly" means "one seller" (from Greek). A monopoly arises when there is only a single seller of a given good or service.[6] Monopoly prices are an instance of the Second Lesson. Monopolists have the power to set whatever price they choose and will always choose a price higher than the opportunity cost of the goods and services they sell, thereby reaping extra profits.

Despite the market power, monopolists are, like all producers, subject to the logic of opportunity cost. Since the price they receive is greater than the opportunity cost of production, they would like to produce and sell more.

---

[6] The term is often used more broadly to cover situations where there are only a few providers (oligopoly, discussed in section 9.4) or only a single buyer (monopsony, discussed in section 9.5).

However, to sell the additional output, the monopolist must set a lower price. This involves an opportunity cost additional to the cost of production, namely, the opportunity of charging the original, higher price to those consumers willing to pay it. A monopolist will produce and sell extra output only if the price received exceeds the sum of the two components of opportunity cost: the marginal cost of production and the profits forgone by lowering prices for everyone. As a result, the monopolist will set a price higher than that of a firm in a market where prices are set by competition.

Since the monopolist could always choose to charge the competitive market price, it's clear that profits are higher under monopoly. But consumers are worse off, both those who pay the higher price and those who would buy the good or service at the opportunity cost price but are not willing to pay the higher price demanded by the monopolist.

The first kind of loss is a transfer of wealth from consumers to the monopoly supplier, but the second kind of loss benefits no one. In aggregate, therefore, the losses to consumers are larger than the benefit to the monopolist.

The loss of profits on existing sales when prices are lowered is an opportunity cost to monopolists when they increase production. However, since this loss is matched by a gain to consumers, it is not an opportunity cost for society as a whole. Monopoly is, then, an instance of Lesson Two: even when market prices represent opportunity costs for producers and consumers, they may not reflect opportunity costs for society as a whole.

9.3.1. Natural Monopoly

If production is characterized by economies of scale, large firms will have lower costs than their smaller competitors and will tend to drive them out of business. If the process goes far enough, a single firm will come to dominate the industry, leading to what is called a "natural monopoly." More formally, a market is a natural monopoly if the opportunity cost of supplying the market demand is lower when the entire market is served by a single firm than when multiple firms compete.

The fact that a monopoly arises naturally from market competition does not mean that it is socially beneficial. Most important, the prices set by a monopoly will not correspond to the (marginal) opportunity cost of production. Just to cover the opportunity costs of serving the market, the monopolist must set a price at least equal to the average cost of production. In a natural monopoly, this average cost must be higher than the marginal cost of additional production, which is the opportunity cost of serving an additional customer.

In the absence of external regulation, a monopolist won't be content with covering the opportunity costs of serving the market but will seek to maximize profits. Lowering prices to reach additional customers involves reducing revenue from existing customers. Unless the monopolist can successfully discriminate between customers, it will be more profitable to keep prices high.

Most economic analysis of monopoly focuses on the case where a monopoly has already been established and looks at the way in which the monopoly firm sets prices to maximize a profit. However, precisely because monopolies are so profitable, it is worth expending effort and money to secure monopoly control of a market. In the case of natural monopoly, the best way to achieve this goal is to grow faster than your competitors, thereby securing economies of size. This can be a profitable strategy for the winning firm, even if it incurs losses in the short run.

The strategy of making losses to secure market dominance proved highly successful for Amazon, the first big online retailer. Firms like Google, Twitter, and Facebook took this strategy further, giving their services away free of charge, and largely free of advertising, in the hope of securing enough users to sell advertising later.[7] Against these successes must be set the many startup firms, particularly during the dot-com boom of the 1990s, for whom initial losses turned into bigger losses and then into bankruptcy and liquidation.

The easiest way to achieve rapid growth is to set prices below the opportunity cost of production. This phase of the struggle for market share is good for consumers in the short run, though the firm that is successful in securing the natural monopoly will recoup its losses and more. From a social point of view, however, prices that are below the opportunity cost of production are just as much an instance of Lesson Two as are prices that are too high. Either way, the resources available to society are not being used to yield the greatest possible benefits. Other methods of increasing market share, such as unnecessary duplication of infrastructure, are even more wasteful.

Natural monopoly provides a powerful example of Lesson Two. Under the conditions of natural monopoly, the prices that arise from leaving markets to themselves will not reflect the opportunity costs facing society. Some policy responses to this problem will be discussed in chapter 15.

9.3.2. Unnatural Monopoly

"Unnatural" monopolies may arise because one firm acquires or squeezes out all its competitors, perhaps by gaining control of an essential and unique input to the production process. The classic example of monopoly by acquisition was the Standard Oil Trust, dominated by John D. Rockefeller. Starting in Cleveland, Standard Oil acquired its rivals or drove them out of business. By the time the Supreme Court ordered it broken up in 1911, under the

---

[7] The bundling of "free" services with advertising was discussed in section 4.5.

terms of 1890's Sherman Antitrust Act, Standard Oil controlled between 85 and 90 percent of the US oil markets.

Monopolies can also arise because the first firm to enter a market creates barriers that keep out rivals. For example, monopolies can sign exclusive long-term contracts with customers and suppliers. Standard Oil used this technique with pipelines and railroads, demanding and securing terms much more favorable than those available to potential competitors.

Alternatively, they can threaten entrants with a price war that would cause the entrants to lose their investment, a practice referred to as "predatory pricing." The development of game theory has provided tools for the analysis of predatory pricing.

Accusations of predatory pricing played a major role in the Standard Oil case. In the second half of the century, One Lesson economists associated with the Chicago School mounted a vigorous and largely successful counterattack, arguing that there was no clear evidence of predatory pricing in the Standard Oil case.[8] More recent scholarship has examined the historical record more closely, finding further evidence of predatory pricing. However, the influence of the Chicago School, combined with the increased political power of big business, has contributed to a rolling back of antitrust policy.

Last, but not least, governments create legal monopoly rights for a variety of good or bad reasons. For example, inventors are granted patents which give them, for a limited period, monopoly rights to sell any product that uses their invention. Similarly, authors receive copyright for their work. If the copyright is valuable, it usually ends up as the property of a corporation.

Over the course of the late twentieth century, the scope and duration of these intellectual property rights were greatly expanded.

---

[8] The Chicago School was so called because its leading figures were economists at the University of Chicago, notably including Gary Becker, Milton Friedman, and George Stigler.

The term of copyright, for example, which was once just seven years, now extends 70 years past the end of the author's life.

Even if they are not explicitly time-limited, unnatural monopolies don't last forever. If governments don't act to break them up, changes in market conditions will usually do so, in the long run. But Keynes's aphorism that "we are all dead in the long run" is just as applicable here as in macroeconomics.

The computer market provides an example. A series of firms have risen to market dominance, eventually failing. IBM dominated the market for many decades, successfully making the transition from large mainframe computers to PCs. IBM lost its dominance, not to a rival manufacturer, but because the source of monopoly power shifted to the operating system MS-DOS, controlled by Microsoft. Clever reverse engineering allowed rival companies to make IBM-compatible "clones" that would run MS-DOS programs exactly like IBM's PCs, but copyright law prevented anyone from duplicating MS-DOS.

The rise of mobile computing shifted the dominant model again. Apple, which supplied both the physical device and the operating system in a more elegant package, emerged as the dominant supplier. Meanwhile the Internet, originally created by the not-for-profit university sector with public funding from the Defense Advanced Research Projects Agency (DARPA), became the basis of a new dominant firm, Google. It turned out that the crucial key to control of this market was the search function, and this market was quickly dominated by Google.[9]

None of these firms has remained dominant forever. In the long run, then, the power of any given monopoly is likely to dissipate. But, with brief interruptions, the history of information technology has been one in which markets are dominated by a

---

[9] Google has leveraged its dominant role in search functions into other areas, such as mapping. In many of these markets, there were already well-established services, but Google drove them out of business.

single firm, with a great deal of power over pricing. There is only a tenuous relationship between prices and opportunity costs.

In particular, the profits of these enterprises depend at least as much on their ability to gain and retain monopoly profits as on the social value of their products. In these circumstances, it is unlikely that capital markets, by increasing the precision with which the profits are valued, are adding anything at all of value to society. As of 2016, according to *Business Insider* magazine, the six most valuable companies in the world were Apple, Exxon, Alphabet (Google), Microsoft, Amazon, and Facebook, all firms depending, to a greater or lesser extent, on monopoly power. The market value of these firms depends more on the question of whether they can maintain that monopoly position than on whether the total return on their investments is greater than the social opportunity cost.

9.3.3. One Lesson Defenses of Monopoly

Because of the divergence between prices and opportunity costs, One Lesson economists are uncomfortable with the existence of monopoly and look for ways to dodge the issue. Some avoid the topic altogether, while others downplay its importance.

Hazlitt's *Economics in One Lesson* doesn't even mention monopoly. In an essay on prices, published in 1967, Hazlitt asserts that

> The fears of most economists concerning the evils of "monopoly" have been unwarranted and certainly excessive.

Hazlitt then runs through some of the standard defenses of monopoly. First, he argues that monopoly is hard to define, since it depends on defining the scope of the market for a particular good or service. Since all goods have substitutes, defining markets are problematic. Second, he argues that monopolists can't know for sure how much pricing power they have, since, if the price is too high, competitors may enter.

Neither of these claims stands up to scrutiny. The first is just a quibble. The second point is more substantive, but it merely shows that monopolists can't make arbitrarily large profits or raise prices without limit.

Other defenses of monopoly used by One Lesson economists are based on the idea that any potential cure based on government action is worse than the disease. As discussed above, no monopoly lasts forever, and some monopolies only exist because of government intervention. A more fundamental claim is that even if monopoly is bad, government intervention will only make matters worse.[10]

Because this set of defenses of monopoly was largely developed at the University of Chicago, the bastion of One Lesson economics in the mid-twentieth century, it is often referred to as the "Chicago critique" of antitrust policy.

The Chicago critique does contain a grain of truth. The fact that markets differ from the ideal of One Lesson economics doesn't necessarily mean that there is an easy policy solution available to governments, or that governments will choose the best possible solution that is available. The central point of Two Lesson economics is to examine both sides of problems like this, rather than presuming that the market solution is the best one.

9.4. Oligopoly

A related set of problems arise when the market is dominated by a few firms, typically offering branded products that are similar in essentials but differ in important details. Such firms will compete

---

[10] This claim can be, and is, made about any market failure, and has been generalized to a theory of "government failure."

both on price and in terms of the quality of their offerings. However, their choices will be determined by the desire to strengthen their own market position and undermine that of their rivals. Economists call a market with few sellers an "oligopoly."

Firms in an oligopoly will seek to secure parts of the market in which they can obtain an effective monopoly. This may involve tacit agreements with rival firms, backed up by the threat of aggressive price competition, setting prices below opportunity cost. Consumers benefit from occasional price wars, but this will be offset by higher prices at other times.

In ordinary language, markets in which a small number of firms struggle for dominance are often seen as highly competitive. But this kind of competition is quite different from what economists refer to as "perfect competition." In perfect competition, firms respond to prices set by the market as a whole, not by any individual competitor or small group.

Oligopoly prices will not, in general, reflect opportunity costs. Firms will produce too little of some goods and too much of others, at different times and places, depending on their strategic imperatives.

9.5. Monopsony and Labor Markets

Economists have always been concerned about monopolies. By contrast, until recently, much less attention was paid to the other side of the coin, monopsony (markets with only one buyer). Obviously, markets for consumer goods are almost never monopsonies; even for specialized goods and services, there are more than the handful of buyers needed to ensure effective competition on the consumer side.

Problems of monopsony mostly arise in markets for labor and other inputs to production, and often in conjunction with monopoly in consumer markets. If one or a few firms dominate the market for some class of goods, they will also dominate the market for suppliers of components and for workers with specialized skills in producing those goods.

For most of the twentieth century, economists tended to ignore monopsony in labor markets. Except in the case of specialized skills, it was assumed that labor markets were more or less competitive. Any market power held by employers was assumed to be offset by the bargaining power of unionized workers (see chapter 12 for more on this). An important implication was that minimum wages, which impose a wage higher than that in a competitive market, must generate reductions in employment. By the late twentieth century, with unions in retreat and the real value of minimum wages in decline, the foundation for this view was obsolete.

The first big shift came with a series of studies of the fast food industry by Card and Krueger showing that higher minimum wages did not appear to reduce employment and might actually lead to an increase in employment. Card and Krueger argued that this outcome might be explained if employers had monopsony power.

As usual in economics, the work of Card and Krueger set off a lengthy controversy, full of rebuttals and counter-rebuttals. Over time, however, the view that many, perhaps most, labor markets are monopsonistic has gained ground, at least among those economists open to empirical evidence.[11]

Monopsonistic labor markets are a crucial instance of Lesson Two. Wages in these markets do not represent the opportunity cost of the production forgone when employers hire fewer workers. The gap between the wage and the marginal product of

---

[11] As on other issues, One Lesson economists have preferred the simplicity of their model to the complex reality of the world.

additional workers benefits employers with market power and offsets the opportunity cost of lower production.

9.6. Bargaining

Many of the most important prices in the economy do not emerge from competitive markets, or even from the decisions of monopolists, but from bargaining between two parties. The most important single example is the wage bargain made between an employer and a worker, or between employers and unions representing workers as a group. Bargaining is also the appropriate model for bargaining between large corporations, for example, between manufacturers and their suppliers.

There need not be anything fair about this bargaining process. A bargain involves benefits for both parties. For example, when an employer hires a suitably qualified employee, the outcome should be better for both parties than the alternative when the worker remains unemployed and the employer's job opening remains unfilled. Ideally, the bargained outcome will maximize the combined benefits. But that leaves open the question of how the benefits will be divided.

Recall, for a moment, the example of Robinson Crusoe and his barter exchanges with Friday, discussed in section 1.1. This example is very helpful in understanding opportunity cost, but it does not involve markets or prices. Rather, the two parties bargain to reach an alternative that is better for both of them than the alternative of not trading.

In the typical One Lesson textbook version of the story, Crusoe and Friday bargain on equal terms and share the gains from trade more or less equally. In Defoe's novel, however, Crusoe rescues Friday from a rival tribe who intend to kill him, and then makes Friday his servant. Crusoe has much more power in the relationship than Friday, and he exploits it to secure most of the benefits from the bargain.

Understanding opportunity costs, and their relationship to bargaining power, can help to explain outcomes like this. The great mathematician John Nash, most famous for his work on game theory, also developed a theory to explain the outcome of bargaining. The crucial idea in Nash's theory is to compare the outcome of the bargain with the "disagreement point," that is, the outcome that would be achieved if the bargain is not made.

In the simplest kinds of bargaining problems, the two parties get equal shares of the benefits of the bargained outcome, relative to the disagreement outcome. The model may take account of the bargaining skill of the parties and of issues such as attitudes to risk. Nevertheless, the disagreement point is crucial.

In the case of Crusoe and Friday, the disagreement point would see Crusoe return to his previous solitary life, forgoing a lot of benefits. For Friday, who would be left to the mercy of his enemies, the disagreement point is, literally, death. Any agreement is much better than this. So, the Nash bargaining solution gives Crusoe most of the additional goods and services generated by the bargain, while Friday gets his life and not much else.

The idea of the disagreement point may naturally be expressed in terms of opportunity cost. For each of these parties, the difference between the disagreement point and a potential bargained agreement is the opportunity cost of failing to agree.

The case of wage bargaining illustrates the critical importance of the disagreement point. First, let's look at the case where an employer is bargaining with a currently unemployed worker. The disagreement point is the outcome when the worker remains unemployed and the employer's job opening remains unfilled. The worker must go on looking for a job, and the employer must go on seeking to fill the vacancy.

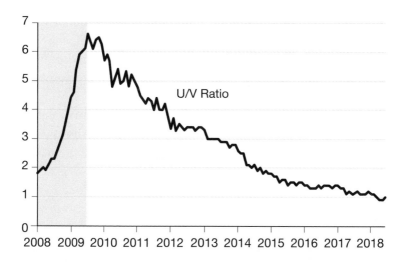

Figure 9.1. Number of unemployed persons per job opening (seasonally adjusted). The ratio of unemployed persons (U) per job vacancy (V) varies with the business cycle. When the most recent recession began (December 2007), the ratio of unemployed persons per job opening was 1.9. The ratio peaked at 6.6 unemployed persons per job opening in July 2009. The ratio of unemployed persons per job opening was 1.0 in June 2018. *Note:* Shaded area represents recession as determined by the National Bureau of Economic Research (NBER). *Source:* Bureau of Labor Statistics (2018b).

Under conditions of full employment, with as many jobs available as there are workers to fill them, the balance of bargaining power is roughly equal. But such conditions are not the norm. As we've already seen, in the absence of a Keynesian macroeconomic policy, with full employment as a policy objective, the economy is in recession around half the time. And even under "normal" conditions, as defined by the NBER, there are typically more unemployed workers than unfilled vacancies. Boom conditions, with more vacancies than workers, are exceptional and almost always short-lived.

As evidenced in figure 9.1, the ratio of unemployed job seekers per opening rose rapidly during the Global Financial Crisis but declined only very slowly. The ratio reached 1.0 in June 2018. This was the first time since 2000 that the number of vacancies was equal to the number of job seekers. Moreover, this balance was achieved, in large measure, because large numbers of people withdrew from the labor force altogether.

In general, therefore, a worker who rejects an offer will find it harder to get another offer than the employer will find it to get an alternative candidate. So, the disagreement point will be worse for the worker. This allows employers to make "take-it-or-leave-it" offers in which the employer gains the larger share of benefits.

Employers have other advantages in a typical bargaining situation. Employers have efficiencies of scale and specialization in hiring and bargaining that employees lack. They may also impose noncompete agreements that prevent workers from moving to another employer in the same field if they quit. The result is that, in subsequent negotiations, the disagreement point is less favorable to the worker.

The bargaining power of employers is reduced somewhat if they have difficulty in monitoring employees' performance on the job. Under such circumstances, employers may seek to encourage higher work effort by paying a wage higher than the worker's "outside option" in order to increase the cost of being fired for inadequate performance. Such a wage premium is referred to as an "efficiency wage."

The bargaining situation is very different when workers are represented by a union. In this case, the disagreement point is an industrial dispute, of which the archetypal examples are strikes and lockouts. In such a dispute, the workers go without wages (though they may receive strike pay from union funds) while the employers must shut down their plants, unless they can rely on strikebreakers to do the necessary work. The costs of a dispute are the same, or perhaps lower, for workers as in the case of individual bargaining, but are much higher for employers. Unions can also resist management practices that reduce workers' autonomy and bargaining power.

One Lesson economists like Hazlitt typically assume a very different pattern of bargaining power: one in which unions act as a monopoly supplier of labor to a market that is implicitly assumed to consist of a large number of small firms, none of which has any individual bargaining power. If this were true, even approximately, we would expect to see unions doing best, and therefore gaining the highest levels of membership, in industries dominated by small businesses. In reality, the opposite is true: unionism is strongest in industries dominated by large employers, both private and public.

9.7. Monopoly and Inequality

The increased inequality of income and wealth since the 1980s in the United States, reversing a seemingly inevitable trend toward greater equality, has been one of the most striking developments in recent economic history. Research has pointed to a number of factors, including regressive changes in tax and welfare policy, the globalization of markets, and the rise of the financial sector. Increasingly, however, attention has been focused on the growth of monopoly and monopsony as a cause of greater inequality.

The main patterns are clear. Returns to capital exceed the rate of growth of the economy in the long term. As Thomas Piketty argued in *Capital*, this implies that inequality will increase in the absence of equalizing forces. Under current circumstances, however, a number of factors are working to accelerate the growth of inequality.

Markets are increasingly concentrated, and the leading firms are taking an increasing share of total profits. A study by the Obama administration's Council of Economic Advisers (2016)

Table 9.2. Change in Market Concentration by Sector, 1997–2012

Industry	Revenue share earned by 50 largest firms, 2012 (%)	Percentage point change in revenue share earned by 50 largest firms, 1997–2012
Transportation and warehousing	42.1	11.4
Retail trade	36.9	11.2
Finance and insurance	48.5	9.9
Wholesale trade	27.6	7.3
Real estate	24.9	5.4
Utilities	69.1	4.6
Educational services	22.7	3.1
Professional and technical	18.8	2.6
Administrative / support	23.7	1.6
Accommodation and food	21.2	0.1

Source: Economic Census (1997 and 2012), US Census Bureau.

showed that the share of revenue going to the 50 largest firms increased in nearly all sectors of the economy between 1997 and 2012. The results are shown in table 9.2.

This outcome is unsurprising, given that public policy has increasingly favored monopoly over competition. *The Great Leveler: Capitalism and Competition in the Court of Law* by Brett Christophers looks at the balance between competition and monopoly in capitalist economies and makes the case that it has shifted heavily toward monopoly. Moreover, profits increasingly rely on intellectual property such as patents and copyrights. As we discussed in section 9.3.2, intellectual property rights are monopolies created and enforced by law. Monopoly in product markets is associated with monopsony in labor markets and with lower wages.

The causal links between increasing monopoly power and increasing inequality have yet to be fully clarified. But the very complexity of the problems shows the need for Two Lesson economics, taking account of all the ways in which Lesson One fails to capture the reality of the economy. As we've seen, monopoly pricing is an important instance of Lesson Two in itself. Monopolies also change the distribution of property rights over time, creating new effective property rights associated with monopoly power in employment and contract relationships. This, again, is an instance of Lesson Two, as we discussed in chapter 7.

Further Reading

The cost conditions under which natural monopoly arises are discussed in more detail by Baumol (1977) and Sharkey (1982). Gold (1981) summarizes much of the economic literature on this topic. Morrison and Schwartz (1994) provide a useful discussion of the distinction between internal and external scale economies, with an application to public infrastructure. Bilotkach (2017) is a useful reference on the economics of the airline industry. An accessible and informative discussion of the rise of large corporations is Chandler (1990).

Keynes (1923), in which he coined the aphorism "we are all dead in the long run," was primarily a critique of the gold standard, a topic that remains controversial.

Howe (2016) gives a brief and accessible history of the Internet, showing that all the major development until the mid-1990s took place in the education and research sectors. For the broader history of the personal computer, Wikipedia is probably the best source. The *Business Insider* article is Leswing (2016).

Hazlitt's defense of monopoly is contained in Hazlitt (1967).

The term "government failure" as contrasted with "market failure" appears to be due to Coase (1964). The argument was developed in more detail by McKean (1965). The general point is referred to by Demsetz (1969) as the "grass is always greener fallacy." Demsetz fails to note that this fallacy is just as relevant for proposals that reduce government intervention as for those that increase it.

Nash (1950) characterized the bargaining problem and characterized his solution. A range of other solutions have been proposed, all of which depend, in differing ways, on the disagreement point.

Card and Krueger (1995a, 1995b) summarize a large body of work challenging the then-conventional view that minimum wages cause higher unemployment. Leonard (2000) gives an excellent history of the minimum wage debate. Leonard concludes that those economists who have rejected Card and Krueger have mostly done so because of a theoretical commitment to One Lesson economics, rather than on the basis of an unprejudiced reading of the empirical evidence.

The impact of monopsony on the labor share has been discussed by Azar, Marinescu, and Steinbaum (2017) and Barkai (2016). Yellen (1984) provides an introduction to the literature on efficiency wages.

The growth of monopoly power was documented by the Obama administration's Council of Economic Advisers (2016), which is the source for table 9.1 and figure 9.1, and by Christophers (2016). The growth of monopoly power as a source of profits and its role in increased inequality of income has been emphasized by a number of recent papers (Barkai 2016; Taylor 2016; Autor et al. 2017; De Loecker and Eeckhout 2017; Ingraham 2017; Eggertsson, Robbins, and Wold 2018).

Piketty (2014) is important, and very readable, drawing not only on economic data but also on the great literature of the nineteenth century to show the working of a patrimonial society (that is, one based on inherited wealth). Piketty argues that wealth will become increasingly concentrated whenever the rate of return on capital consistently exceeds the rate of growth of output. The work of Jorda et al. (2017) shows that this has been true, particularly for large concentrations of capital.

Other works cited include Taleb (2010).

CHAPTER 10

∎

Market Failure:
Externalities and Pollution

We pay for power plant pollution through higher health costs.
—Senator Sheldon Whitehouse[1]

The idea of market failures is most commonly associated with the term "externalities." Historically, this term referred to "external" economies of scale arising as industries expanded. The resulting problems of natural monopoly were discussed in chapter 9.

By the early twentieth century, the term "externality" had been broadened to encompass production and consumption activities that affect people other than the producers and consumers concerned. The most prominent examples of such effects are pollution problems. These include air pollution generated by factories that harm nearby residents or, in cases like acid rain and CO_2 emissions, people far removed from the point at which pollution is generated.

As a result, the term externalities is most commonly associated with the negative externalities that arise from pollution. However, positive externalities, such as the amenity that neighbors gain from well-kept gardens, are also important.

---

[1] https://www.whitehouse.senate.gov/news/op-eds/lets-have-the-presidents-back-on-climate-change.

Extending the idea of externalities leads to the idea of public goods. These are goods such as broadcast television where the technology of production and distribution means that the good must be supplied equally to the entire population.[2]

Market failures due to externalities and public goods are closely related to each other and to the failures of competition discussed in chapter 9. For example, monopolies arise most frequently where the technology displays economies of scale. Similarly, the public good of air quality is affected by pollution externalities. Applying Lesson Two, we can see how all market failures arise from a divergence between prices and opportunity costs.

Market failures such as externalities are sometimes described as "imperfections," a term that might be applied to superficial blemishes on an otherwise perfect piece of fruit. But externalities are pervasive. Almost everything we do in markets, as consumers, workers, and business owners, affects people other than those with whom we are directly engaged in transactions. In particular, every use of energy has an impact on the consumption of fossil fuels and therefore on the amount of carbon dioxide in the atmosphere. In the absence of active public policy, we would be overwhelmed by air and water pollution, along with many other externalities.

10.1. Externalities

The key feature of an externality is that the person who is affected has no say in the matter, and therefore cannot demand a price to offset the negative effects of the actions of others. As a result, the costs of these negative effects are not reflected in

---

[2] Pollution externalities affecting everyone in a given area are sometimes referred to as "public bads."

the opportunity costs of the firm or consumer generating the externality.

The first economist to examine this issue seriously was A. C. Pigou. Pigou extended the idea of "external economies of scale" to the more general concept of "externalities." External economies of scale involve externalities between firms within a given industry. More generally, externalities may arise between production and consumption activities, or between producers, consumers, and households who may be affected by problems like pollution.

Externalities may be classified in various ways. The simplest cases are unilateral externalities, where the actions of one party affect another; for example, air pollution from a factory. There are also bilateral externalities, where each of the parties affects the other, for example, noisy neighbors, each of whom annoys the other.

More complex cases arise with congestion and network externalities, where many people are involved, both contributing to the externality and being affected by it. Examples include traffic jams and crowds at open access facilities like beaches.

Some externalities are beneficial. A common example is that of a flower garden, which improves the amenity, and therefore the land value, of neighboring properties. Similarly, if shops of the same kind are located in close proximity, they may attract more customers than they would if located separately, since buyers will benefit from a wider range of choice without the need to travel between shops. Positive network externalities arise when many people use the same software or take part in a social media network such as Facebook.

There are, however, good reasons for expecting negative externalities, such as pollution, to predominate. As Pigou observed, firms have no particular incentive to organize themselves in ways that produce positive externalities. By contrast, a negative externality involves shifting some of the costs of production onto others. In the absence of a policy response, this will increase profit. Since negative externalities are profitable and positive externalities are not, we expect to see more production of goods that generate negative externalities, and less of goods that generate positive externalities, than we would if market prices fully reflected social opportunity costs.

10.1.1. Externalities and Property Rights

Pigou's analysis of the externality problem was challenged by Ronald Coase in a classic paper entitled "The Problem of Social Cost." Coase argued that, given well-defined property rights, market transactions could bring opportunity costs into line with prices, even in the presence of what would otherwise be considered externalities. For example, suppose that a company's ownership of a factory was associated with an explicit right to dump waste into a river, and that downstream water users were harmed by this pollution.

Then, Coase argued, the downstream users could pay the company not to pollute, effectively purchasing the property right. Conversely, if the downstream users had a right to stop the company dumping waste, but could obtain clean water elsewhere, the company could pay them not to exercise their rights.

Obviously, this doesn't happen in practice. That's in part because "rights to pollute" and "rights not to be polluted" are typically not assigned to particular individuals or groups, but are general rights governing access to unowned resources. Coase did not analyze this problem very satisfactorily but observed that unspecified "transaction costs" might prevent the parties from reaching an agreement.

In these cases, Coase suggested that the best outcomes would be realized if the property rights were allocated to the party for whom they were most valuable. Coase thought that the common law judicial system performed this function. However, the court system is just one part of the state machinery that creates and enforces property rights. States can create (and restrict or abolish) property rights through legislation or through executive actions such as regulatory determinations.

As was stressed in chapter 7, the creation of property rights invariably involves an opportunity cost. Although many One Lesson economists, following Coase, have stressed the importance of property rights, they have mostly avoided this point.

Coase's discussion of transaction costs has also given rise to a large literature. A transaction cost may be regarded as a difference between the (higher) price paid by a buyer and the (lower) price received by a seller. The existence of such differences violates a crucial assumption in the theory of competitive equilibrium, namely that both buyers and sellers face the same market-determined prices; this is part of assumption (A) in section 2.4. If there are two different prices, one for buyers and one for sellers, they cannot both be equal to social opportunity cost. The appearance of social cost in the title of Coase's paper refers directly to this point.

Where transaction costs are large, market outcomes will not be satisfactory. Whether there is a better alternative, however, depends on the nature of the costs involved. Unfortunately, despite extensive research on the topic, transaction costs generally end up being treated as something of a "black box," the contents of which remain inaccessible. For this reason, analysis in the "market failure" tradition that began with Pigou continues to be a more useful tool.

10.2. Pollution

The characteristic product of industrial society is not cotton, cars, or computers, but smoke. Cities have always been smoky places: as early as 1272, King Edward I banned the burning of coal in London. But it was only after the Industrial Revolution that human activity became a major influence on the atmosphere and the climate, first locally and then globally.

As factories and mills sprang up in the nineteenth century, the city became "the Big Smoke." London, the great metropolis of the Industrial Revolution, was the birthplace of "smog," the meeting of smoke and fog in the infamous "pea-souper," a characteristic feature of nineteenth-century novels set in the metropolis. The smogs only got worse as time went on. The Great London smog of 1952, which killed more than 10,000 people, was the point at which the problem became too big to ignore.

Smoke pouring out of a factory chimney is a perfect symbol of one of the most important parts of Lesson Two. Factory production requires the disposal and management of the associated waste products. In the absence of special measures, the resulting pollution harms people living nearby and business activities such as tourist ventures that depend on clean air.

Water was also badly polluted, with everything ranging from human waste to heavy metals and industrial chemicals. The Great Stink of 1858, arising from human and industrial waste in the River Thames, forced the British House of Commons to abandon its meetings, and led to a large-scale project to improve sanitation. But even 100 years later the Thames was little better than an open sewer. The same was true of other great rivers like the Rhine and the Hudson. The Cuyahoga river flowing into Lake Erie was so polluted that it regularly caught fire, most famously in 1969 when it made the pages of *Time* magazine (though the picture was of an earlier, and larger, fire in 1952).

Pollution is part of the social opportunity cost of production. But, under the rules that prevailed until the mid-twentieth century, this component of opportunity cost was not borne by factory owners. Rather, it was shifted to the public as a whole, through the adverse health effects of pollution and the cost of cleaning it up. So, the market prices for inputs to production do not represent the full opportunity costs.

The rise of the automobile provided a new, less tractable, and more pervasive source of pollution externalities. The most notable example of automobile-driven pollution was in Los Angeles, where a massively car-dependent transport system combined with temperature inversions to trap large quantities of emissions, most notably carbon monoxide and hydrocarbons. By the 1950s, the air in Los Angeles was dangerous to breathe more days than not.

Fresh air was sold in the streets as a novelty item, an idea that has been reinvented recently and exported to heavily polluted cities in Asia and elsewhere.

Less obvious, but more pernicious, was the effect of tetraethyl lead, added to gasoline to improve performance and prevent engine "knocking." Lead in the atmosphere affects child development and can cause serious brain damage.[3] It has even been claimed that the increase of youth crime in the late twentieth century and its subsequent decline reflected the rise and fall of exposure to atmospheric lead. The correlation behind this claim is illustrated in figure 10.1.

Not only do cars contribute to a choking atmosphere, they also choke each other through traffic jams. With old-style pollution externalities, the generator of the externality and the bearer of the cost were separate. By contrast, with congestion externalities like those associated with motor vehicles, the people who generate the externality also bear the costs.

This might seem to solve the problem. But a careful analysis of opportunity costs shows that the opportunity cost of using the road, for any individual motorist, does not include the

---

[3] This is also true of paint, where lead was used until the 1970s.

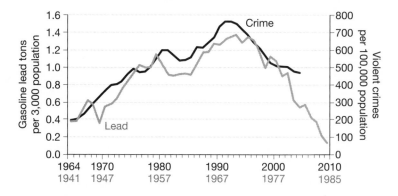

Figure 10.1. Lead exposure and violent crime. *Source*: Nevin (2000).

congestion they themselves create.[4] As a result, social opportunity costs are not equal to private costs.

10.3. Climate Change

As our technological capacities have grown, so has the scope of our ability to damage our environment. Problems like air pollution, which once affected individual cities, have expanded to become national and then transnational problems changing the climate of the entire planet.

One of the first examples of a transnational pollution problem was that of "acid rain," formed when emissions of sulfur dioxide from the burning of coal combined with water vapor to produce a dilute form of sulfuric acid in the atmosphere. The resulting acidic clouds could be transported over large distances

---

[4] A further complication arises from the fact that, most of the time, motorists aren't charged for using a road (the exception being toll roads). Rather, they pay indirectly through gasoline taxes, vehicle registration fees, and general taxation.

and across national boundaries by wind, before falling as rain, resulting in large-scale damage to forests and lakes, particularly those that were naturally adapted to neutral or slightly alkaline conditions.[5] As we'll discuss in chapter 16, policy responses to acid rain foreshadowed some of those later used or advocated in response to global warming.

The second major example of a global pollution problem was that of the damage to the ozone layer caused by chlorofluorocarbons (CFCs), gases used in refrigeration and cooling. In the 1970s, a group of chemists determined that CFCs could combine with ozone (a molecule with three oxygen atoms) at such a rate that they would destroy the thin layer of ozone that protects Earth from the Sun's ultraviolet rays.[6] A decade later, their theory was confirmed by the discovery of a "hole" in the ozone layer over Antarctica. An international agreement called the Montreal Protocol phased out the use of the most damaging CFCs, but these gases will take many decades to dissipate. The ozone hole has only recently begun to shrink.

By far the most serious form of climate change is the enhanced "greenhouse effect" caused by emissions of carbon dioxide, methane, and other gases. The term "greenhouse effect" refers to the fact that gases in Earth's atmosphere trap some of the heat from sunlight, thereby maintaining Earth's temperature at a higher level than, for example, that of Mars, which has little or no atmosphere. Our other planetary neighbor, Venus, has undergone a runaway version of the greenhouse effect, with the result that surface temperatures exceed 450 degrees Celsius (850 degrees Fahrenheit). The more limited greenhouse effect on Earth

---

[5] Acidity is measured by the pH value scale. The neutral value is 7 and values below 7 are acidic.

[6] Molina and Rowlands, who led the team, were later awarded the Nobel Prize for their work.

keeps the planet at an average temperature sufficiently warm to support human life and the ecosystems that sustain us.[7]

The mechanism of the greenhouse effect was first identified in the nineteenth century. The first known study of the warming effects of carbon dioxide was presented in 1856 by Eunice Foote, the second female member of the American Association for the Advancement of Science.[8] Foote's work was neglected, but the effect was independently discovered a few years later by Irish physicist John Tyndall.

The link between carbon dioxide and global warming was quantified toward the end of the nineteenth century by the Swedish chemist, Svante Arrhenius, who estimated that a doubling of atmospheric CO_2 concentrations would increase global mean temperatures by 5 to 6 degrees Celsius. A century of subsequent work has refined this estimate (referred to as climate sensitivity) to 3.5 degrees, plus or minus 1.5 degrees.

Human activity over the past century or so has led to greatly increased emissions of the main greenhouse gases. Carbon dioxide emissions arise from burning "fossil fuels," such as coal, oil, and natural gas, and from clearing of forests that would otherwise act as "sinks" absorbing CO_2 from the atmosphere. Methane emissions are generated from irrigated agriculture (particularly rice paddies), from the belches of ruminant animals (cows and sheep), and from leakage during the extraction of natural gas (which consists primarily of methane). As well as damaging the ozone layer, CFCs are powerful greenhouse gases and their phaseout will help to alleviate the problem. Unfortunately,

---

[7] Sometimes called the "Goldilocks" zone. It is often argued that the fact that Earth is so ideally suited to human life suggests some kind of intelligent design or inherent capacity of the planet to maintain itself in a state suitable for life (the Gaia hypothesis). This is an example of the "anthropic fallacy." If Earth were like Mars or Venus, there would be no humans to observe the fact and speculate on its causes.

[8] The first was astronomer Maria Mitchell.

many of the gases (hydrofluorocarbons or HFCs) initially used to replace CFCs, while less damaging to the ozone layer, also contribute to the greenhouse effect. These HFCs are now also being phased out.

The science of climate change is complex, and much remains to be learned. The best estimates are that, if the concentration of CO_2 and other greenhouse gases can be held below 450 parts per million (ppm), the mean global temperature will ultimately rise by 2 degrees Celsius or less.[9] With the more ambitious goal of 350 ppm, which would require the removal of some greenhouse gases that are already in the atmosphere, warming could be held below 1.5 degrees Celsius.

Climate change has been described by Nicholas Stern as "the greatest market failure in history." The magnitude of the problem is hard to estimate precisely, but it certainly justifies Stern's description. Even if carbon dioxide emissions stopped tomorrow, global temperatures would continue to rise, resulting in more extreme weather events, species extinction, and substantial adjustment costs. On the other hand, the investment required to replace fossil fuels with non-polluting energy sources will amount to many trillions of dollars.[10]

---

[9] Considerable attention has been paid to the minority of scientists who argued that the likely impact of greenhouse gas emissions has been overestimated. We should be much more concerned about the opposite view, that potential warming has been greatly underestimated. If the low estimates turn out to be correct, and there is little or no warming, the world community will have made unnecessary investments equal to perhaps 2 percent of total income. On the other hand, warming of 4 degrees would be catastrophic and warming of 6 degrees would amount to the end of life as we know it. As I've shown in some recent work, any calculation of the costs and benefits of climate policy must take these high estimates seriously, even if they are "extremely unlikely" (less than 5 percent probability) to be realized.

[10] That is, an amount comparable to the cost of the Iraq and Afghanistan wars, equal to about 1 percent of world income for the next 10–20 years. This amount is

Markets, as they currently exist, do not reflect the opportunity costs of CO_2 emissions. Most of the costs will be borne by people who either are not yet born or are too young to have much influence.[11]

Economists have lots of ideas about how to mitigate and adapt to climate change (see chapter 16). In one way or another, they all reflect Lesson Two: market prices do not reflect the opportunity costs faced by society as a whole.

10.3.1. One Lesson Economists and Climate Change

The problems of pollution, particularly global pollution such as acid rain, ozone depletion, and global warming, pose major theoretical difficulties for One Lesson economists. In an interview with *Reason* magazine, Hazlitt admitted finding the issue of pollution "very tough" and said he chose not to write about it, having not made up his mind on the topic.

The most common One Lesson response, beginning with the work of Ronald Coase, has begun with the observation that pollution problems can, in principle, be resolved by negotiation between the parties. For example, if an upstream factory pollutes the water that is used by a downstream community, the community could pay the factory to install filtering equipment or could even buy the factory and shut it down.

The last refuge, and increasingly the standard response, of One Lesson economists has been to abandon the debate over

---

huge in absolute terms, but small compared to the potential cost of uncontrolled climate change.

[11] The phrase "future generations" is often used in this context, but it is inexact and misleading. A large proportion of the people who will bear the brunt of climate change, in the middle and later decades of this century, are already alive. They are the children and grandchildren of the people most likely to be reading this book.

the proper economic response to pollution problems and instead dispute the scientific evidence about those problems.

This response first emerged in the 1990s, when the tobacco industry sought to dispute evidence about the health dangers of second-hand smoke. As well as funding scientists willing to bend the results of their research in support of the industry agenda, the tobacco lobby supported a network of think tanks and commentators willing to push their case.[12] Many of them later moved on to climate science denial.

The result of this effort has been to delay action on climate change, but also to undermine the credibility of economics and economists. In this context, it's encouraging to note that the vast majority of economists who have actually worked on the issue are convinced of the need for action. One survey showed that 95 percent of economists with climate expertise favored cuts in CO_2, a figure comparable to the 97 percent of climate scientists who support the mainstream view that human-caused climate change is a serious problem.

10.4. Public Goods

The term "public good" is used in various ways, most commonly to refer to goods and services that, for one reason or another, are provided free of charge by governments and public agencies, rather than by private firms charging market prices. Economists use the term differently, to describe certain characteristics of a good that may make it suitable for public provision.

---

[12] Notable think tanks that have promoted both tobacco and climate science denial include the American Enterprise Institute, the Cato Institute, the Competitive Enterprise Institute, and the Heartland Institute.

The economist's ideal concept of public goods takes the concepts of scale economies and externalities to a logical extreme. A pure public good is one that:

(a) once provided to one consumer can be provided to everyone at no additional cost (non-rivalry); and

(b) if made available to one consumer, cannot be withheld from others (non-excludability).

Non-rivalry means that, once the service has been provided for some users, there is no additional cost in providing it to everyone. The standard example is broadcast TV. Producing the programming for TV and constructing the system for broadcasting are costly. But once the signal has been sent out, anyone with an appropriate TV set can receive it. The cost is the same whether one viewer or one thousand tune in. Here, the opportunity cost for any individual consumer tuning in is zero, but the opportunity cost for the TV station to produce and broadcast the program is substantial. There is no price that is equal to opportunity cost for both producers and consumers.

Non-excludability means that, if the good is provided at all, it is not possible to restrict access to those who are willing to pay for it. In these circumstances, users do not pay the opportunity cost of the goods they consume. If the value of the good to the consumer is less than the opportunity cost to society, then there is a net loss of social welfare.

For example, if a city council creates a new public park, it may not be practical to construct gates and fences around the park so that those using it can be charged for access. As a result, the park may be overcrowded. Park users with a high value for the amenities of the park will have a less pleasant experience as a result of entry by other users with a low value. In the worst case, it may be that the total value of the park is lower than the cost of provision, so that, if the council anticipates the outcome correctly, the park will not be provided at all.

Public goods are, in some ways, the opposite of negative externalities like pollution.[13] This is most obvious in the case of public health measures that remove hazards (whether natural or human-caused) from the environment. For example, sanitation measures make water supplies safe to drink, removing hazards that may arise naturally, or be caused by industrial pollution, agricultural runoff, or human waste.

Public goods illustrate Lesson Two in two ways. First, non-rivalry means that when one person produces some of the public good for his or her own benefit, everyone else benefits. If the price is equal to the benefit received by the producer, it will be below the benefit for society as a whole. Moreover, non-excludability means that no one can be made to pay a price for access to the good, assuming that it is provided at all. Even though the total benefit of providing the good might exceed the cost, no single person has an incentive to pay that cost. In summary, Lesson One does not apply to non-excludable public goods.

10.5. The Origins of Externality

The term "externality" is one of those bits of technical jargon that most economists would be at a loss to explain. Certainly, until I looked into it for this book, I had only the vaguest idea of its original meaning. The term originates with the analysis of economies of scale, discussed in section 9.2.

---

[13] A key distinction is that externalities (positive or negative) arise as a by-product of some production or consumption activity. Public goods are produced for their own sake.

The great English economist Alfred Marshall, who systematized the subject in the late nineteenth century, examined the issue of economies of scale in detail. He observed that the economies described above, available to a single firm as it increased the scale of its operations, were not the only, or even the most important, sources of lower production costs. Rather, as discussed in section 9.2, there are benefits that arise when a number of firms in a given industry are located in close proximity.

Based on this observation, Marshall drew a distinction between internal economies of scale (those arising when a given firm expands its output) and external economies of scale (those arising from the growth of an industry). Over time, the second class came to be referred to as "externalities."

Marshall's greatest successor, A. C. Pigou, realized that the issues arising from externalities arose in many contexts other than those of industry-level scale economies. As Pigou observed, any situation where the actions of one firm affect the costs of another (for example, upstream water pollution affecting downstream farmers) is a kind of externality; more specifically a technological externality. Pigou then generalized to cover cases such as air pollution, where the effects are felt by households rather than firms.

Importantly, whereas the external economies of scale observed by Marshall were beneficial, these externalities are negative. As we saw in section 10.1, market incentives encourage the generation of negative externalities and fail to reward the generation of positive externalities.

As a result of these developments, the term externality now typically refers to negative effects such as pollution and congestion. The external economies of scale discussed by Marshall are now more commonly referred to as sources of "endogenous growth."

Further Reading

Pigou's (1920) *Economics of Welfare* is the classic work that introduced the modern concept of externalities but is now mainly of historical interest. The modern approach begins with Francis Bator's classic article "The Anatomy of Market Failure" (Bator 1958). The classic paper on the theory of public goods is Samuelson (1954), but this is hard going. Tietenberg and Lewis (2013) is a good modern text.

American Amnesia by Hacker and Pierson (2017) puts the issues in a political context.

Latson (2013) tells the story of how *Time*'s picture of a burning river in 1969 contributed to the passing of the Clean Water Act. Rae (2012) and Klekociuk and Krummel (2017) give useful background on CFCs and the Montreal Protocol.

The interview with Hazlitt is Zupan (1984). Oreskes and Conway (2011), *Merchants of Doubt*, showed how the denial industry operates, beginning with tobacco and moving on to CFCs and then to climate change denial. Her earlier work (Oreskes 2004) established the strength of the agreement within mainstream science on the role of greenhouse gas emissions in climate change. Howard and Sylvan (2015) report a similarly strong consensus among economists who study climate change on the need for urgent reductions in emissions. The Skeptical Science website, https://www.skepticalscience .com/, provides a summary of mainstream climate science along with rebuttals of the talking points commonly put forward to challenge science.

The literature on the economics of climate change is vast. A good starting point, though somewhat out of date now, is the *Stern Review of Climate Change* (Stern 2007). The survey of economists is reported by Nuccitelli (2016). My most important contributions are Quiggin (2008) and Quiggin (2018).

Rosenberg (2012) discusses how Los Angeles began to put its smoggy days behind it and provides the photos. Moshakis (2018) describes the contemporary market for cans of fresh air. The relationship between crime and atmospheric lead was analyzed by Reyes (2007). Casciani (2014) provides an accessible summary.

Cornes and Sandler (1996) give a good summary of the theory of public goods, drawing on the classic text of Richard and Peggy Musgrave (1973), which established the definition in terms of non-rivalry and non-excludability. The formal definition of public goods is due to Samuelson (1954), who drew on the work of Richard Musgrave.

The large literature on endogenous growth is beyond the scope of this book. The central ideas, including the link to Marshall, are discussed by Romer (1994).

CHAPTER 11

■

Market Failure: Information,
Uncertainty, and Financial Markets

Information wants to be free.
—Stewart Brand, *Whole Earth Review* (May 1985, p. 49)

As we saw in chapter 3, it's a commonplace to say that we live in an information economy, but in reality this has always been true. Humans are different from other animals precisely because we can make better and more flexible use of information through reasoning and share complex information through language. Such information is embodied either in the technology we employ or in the knowledge of how to use it, held in human brains.

As was discussed in Part I (Lesson One), market prices give us information about the opportunity costs we face and are therefore central to our decisions about buying and selling goods and services of all kinds. But what about information itself? Is it a private good that can be bought and sold, and if so what is its price? If it is a pure public good, who will supply it? And what is the opportunity cost of information? We will examine some of these questions in this chapter.

Information is what we know. The other side of the coin, what we don't know, may be described as ignorance, ambiguity, or unawareness, among other terms. The profusion of names for what we don't know reflects the difficulty of coming to grips with this problem. The most commonly used general term in economics is "uncertainty."

To a greater or lesser extent, all economic choices involve uncertainty. We don't know for sure what we will get when we make a choice, or what we are forgoing as a result. That's obviously a problem in working out opportunity cost. In this chapter, we'll look at information and uncertainty, and at how markets sometimes help us in managing uncertainty, but sometimes make matters worse.

In particular, our two Lessons provide a useful way to look at the large body of evidence about the performance of financial markets. To the extent that Lesson One is applicable, financial markets will provide information about the likelihood of different possible outcomes for the economy as a whole and for particular businesses and industries. Lesson Two is more relevant where financial markets fail, generating inappropriate investment signals and leading to speculative bubbles and busts.

11.1. Market Prices, Information, and Public Goods

The price mechanism is a marvelous social device for collecting and combining information about the value and cost of goods and services. In an open market, everyone can see the price at which suppliers are willing to sell goods and services, which ensures that all suppliers will charge much the same price at any given time. Suppliers will only be willing to accept the market price if it is at least as great as the opportunity cost of the good or service concerned. If buyers are willing to pay that price, they are showing that the value of the good to them is more than the opportunity cost.

As we saw in section 3.2, Hayek makes this point very effectively in his classic article, "The Use of Knowledge in Society" (quoted again for convenience):

> Assume that somewhere in the world a new opportunity for the use of some raw material, say tin, has arisen, or that one of the sources of supply of tin has been eliminated. It does not matter for our purpose and it is very significant that it does not matter which of these two causes has made tin more scarce. All that the users of tin need to know is that some of the tin they used to consume is now more profitably employed elsewhere, and that in consequence they must economize tin. There is no need for the great majority of them even to know where the more urgent need has arisen, or in favor of what other uses they ought to husband the supply. (Hayek 1945, p. 526)

But there is a paradox here. In an open market setting, the information conveyed by the price system is a pure public good. The use of price information by one buyer or seller does not reduce its availability to everyone else. Information, once someone knows it, has no opportunity cost. Sharing the information with someone else does not mean that it is no longer available. That is, market information, like all information, is non-rival.

Moreover, unlike many other kinds of information, which can be kept secret, market information is non-excludable. In open markets, everyone can observe the prevailing prices. Everyone who buys or sells in the market automatically contributes information about their willingness to buy or sell, whether or not they wish to reveal this information. Aggregated over all participants, this information is reflected in the price.

Market information is a pure public good. But as we have already seen, pure public goods are generally undersupplied, relative to the socially desirable level. Does this conclusion apply to the information contained in market prices? There's no easy answer to this question.

In this context, economists commonly distinguish between "thick" and "thin" markets. Thick markets are characterized by homogenous products, large numbers of buyers and sellers who regularly engage in repeat transactions, transparent pricing, and, ideally, forward markets for purchase or delivery at future dates. Thin markets are missing one or more of these characteristics. Broadly speaking, prices emerging from thick markets are regarded as capturing all the information of market participants that is relevant to opportunity costs. By contrast, prices in thin markets are relatively uninformative.

One way of telling whether the public good of market price information is undersupplied is to look at the characteristics of the market in question, to see whether it is thick or thin. Another is to look at the volatility of market prices. In a market where available information is widely shared, prices will move only if there is an unanticipated change in the technology of production, such as an unexpected invention, or in consumer preferences, for example because of the emergence of a competing product. In the absence of such major changes, price volatility suggests an inadequate supply of information.

A third approach is to look at the willingness of market participants to spend money and resources on information about the demand for and supply of particular goods and services. Getting such information early can yield significant benefits to producers making investment plans, to large-scale consumers, and, as we will see in the following section, to speculators. Unlike market price information, which anyone can observe, this kind of information is not, in general, a public good. As long as it can be kept secret, it is, in the technical terminology of public goods theory, an excludable good. But it is difficult to make use of information without revealing it to others, and thereby losing the ability to gain additional private benefits.

So, we have a further paradox, best summed up by Stewart Brand, who was quoted at the beginning of this chapter. The full quotation is:

> On the one hand information wants to be expensive, because it's so valuable. The right information in the right place just changes your life. On the other hand, information wants to be free, because the cost of getting it out is getting lower and lower all the time. So you have these two fighting against each other.

Returning to the paradox with which we started, the amazing ability of market prices to combine information about opportunity costs from diverse and disparate groups of buyers and sellers is the best illustration imaginable of Lesson One. But, the fact that market information, like all publicly available information, is a pure public good means that Lesson Two is applicable even here. Economics needs two lessons, not one.

11.2. The Efficient Markets Hypothesis

The discussion in section 11.1 showed how prices collect and combine information about the value and cost of goods and services, but also how markets may fail to use information properly. These points are particularly applicable to financial markets where assets are bought and sold on the basis of estimates of the returns they will generate in the future.

History has shown that prices in financial markets fluctuate widely, with no obvious link to any underlying reality. Yet One Lesson economists claim that financial markets make the best possible use of all available information, public and private. This claim, referred to in the jargon of economics as the efficient markets hypothesis (EMH), represents One Lesson economics in its purest form.[1]

Casual observation suggests that both the private and public sectors have difficulty in managing investments. Public sector investments, from the time of the Pharaohs onward, have included plenty of boondoggles, white elephants, and outright failures. But the private sector has not obviously done better. Waves of extreme optimism, leading to massive investment in particular sectors, have been followed by slumps in which the assets built at great expense in the boom lie unfinished or idle for years on end.

The EMH supports the first of these observations. Since public investments are not subject to the disciplines of financial markets, there is no reason to expect their allocation to be efficient. By contrast, the second observation tends to refute the EMH. According to the EMH, private investment decisions are the product of an information system that is automatically self-correcting. The value assigned by the stock market to any given asset, such as a corporation, is the best possible estimate of the economic value of its future earnings. If the owners and managers of a given corporation make bad investment decisions, the value of shares will decline to the point where the corporation is subject to takeover by new owners, who will hire better managers.

The EMH, which enshrines the market price of assets as the summary of all relevant information, is inconsistent with any idea that managers should pursue the long-term interests of corporations, disregarding short-term fluctuations in share prices.

---

[1] As I discuss in my book *Zombie Economics*, a more complete and accurate description of the efficient markets hypothesis would be the *strong* efficient *financial* markets hypothesis.

On the EMH view, the short-term share price is the best possible estimate of the long-term share price and therefore of the long-term interests of the corporation.

If the EMH is accepted, public investment decisions may be improved through the use of formal evaluation procedures like benefit-cost analysis, but the only really satisfactory solution is to turn the business over to the private sector. In the 1980s and 1990s this reasoning fit neatly with the global push for privatization.[2]

The EMH implies that governments can never outperform well-informed financial markets, except in cases where mistaken government policies, or a failure to define property rights adequately, leads to distorted market outcomes. If governments are better informed than private market participants, they should make this information public rather than using superior government information as a substitute for public policy.

To sum up, the EMH implies that private enterprises will always outperform governments, and that governments should confine their activities to the correction of market failures, and to whatever income redistribution is needed to offset the inequality of market outcomes.[3]

This is why the EMH is so central to One Lesson economics. Conversely, evidence of the failure of the EMH makes a powerful case for Two Lesson economics. The most striking evidence of this kind is found in the repeated occurrence of financial bubbles and busts. The most notable recent example is that of the Global Financial Crisis, but there have been many others.

Finally, and perhaps most significantly, the share of profits going to the financial sector has grown dramatically. This understates the problem since the finance sector employs few

---

[2] Discussed in *Zombie Economics*, chapter 5.
[3] In the view of most One Lesson economists, not very much.

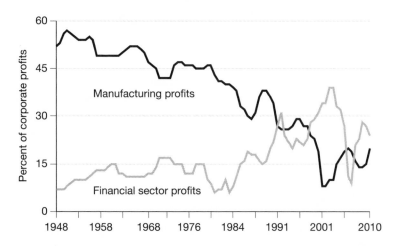

Figure 11.1. Profit shares for finance and manufacturing. *Source*: BEA, NIPA table 6.16, annual data. 2012 is based on annualized Q3 data. "Finance" totals are based on "other financial," which excludes Federal Reserve banks.

workers relative to its size. Much of its revenue goes to pay a relatively small group of highly paid professionals, whose incomes are, in effect, profits rather than wages. As shown in figure 11.1, the share of profits going to the financial sector is now around 30 percent, having fallen from a peak of 40 percent before the Global Financial Crisis. As the restrictions imposed after the crisis are unwound, it seems likely that financial sector profits will continue to rise both absolutely and relative to the economy as a whole.

11.3. Financial Markets, Bubbles, and Busts

Financial markets are essential to the functioning of a capitalist economy. Yet they are also a source of disastrous disruption. Both the Great Depression of the 1930s and the Lesser

CHAPTER 11

Depression of the recent past had their origin in financial market failures. The same is true of a string of panics and slumps going back to the bursting of the South Sea Bubble in 1720.

Even disregarding spectacular crashes like those of 1929, 2000, and 2008, financial markets are many times more volatile than the economy as a whole. Even in a deep recession, the aggregate output of the economy rarely falls more than 10 percent below its long-run trend values. By contrast, exchange rates and stock market indexes frequently double (or halve) their value over the course of a few years.

The extreme volatility of financial markets is associated with a phenomenon that has perplexed economists for decades: the "equity premium puzzle." Equities (shares traded on stock markets) commonly generate high returns at times when the economy is strong (booms) and low returns or losses when the economy is weak (recessions and depressions). By contrast, high-quality bonds, such as those issued by the US government, provide a return, in the form of interest, that does not vary with the state of the economy.

Because equities are riskier than bonds, equity investors expect a premium rate of return to compensate them. Historically, the equity premium has been large: around six percentage points in addition to the long-term rate of interest on bonds, which has averaged about 2 percent, adjusted for inflation. Because equity investments pay off in booms, but not in recessions, they represent one way of increasing income in boom periods with the opportunity cost of reducing income in recessions.

The magnitude of the equity premium is a puzzle because it seems to imply that the opportunity cost of additional income or consumption in periods of booms is very low. An additional dollar of income in a boom period is given the same value, by stock markets, as an additional 50 cents of income in a recession. Yet even in a deep recession, total income rarely falls more than 10 percent below its trend value. Reasoning in terms of opportunity cost suggests that the premium is higher than it should be, if Lesson One were applicable.

What this means is that the equity premium puzzle is an illustration of Lesson Two. The prices generated in financial markets do not, in general, give us an accurate measure of the opportunity costs facing society as a whole.

11.4. Financial Markets and Speculation

Financial markets provide incentives to gather information about the value of all kinds of assets. The central, and false, claim of the EMH is that financial markets provide the best possible way of generating and aggregating such information.

Information is socially valuable because it allows investors, producers, and consumers to make decisions that align the benefits of production and consumption with the opportunity costs. The more information that is publicly available, the closer the economy is to satisfying the conditions for Lesson One to apply, as set out in chapter 2.

Information is also privately valuable. The importance of obtaining more information than is contained in current market prices is most obvious in the case of speculators. Speculators make their living by predicting market price movements in advance, buying if they expect the price to rise and selling if they expect it to fall.[4]

For an ordinary buyer or seller of tin, the price conveys information about opportunity costs. Additional information

---

[4] In some markets, speculators can "sell short," promising to deliver goods or securities they do not own, in the expectation that they will be able to buy later at a lower price.

about, for example, the likely movement of prices can further refine these decisions. For example, buyers who think the price of tin is likely to fall might rearrange their plans so that they can hold off buying. Sellers who think the price is going to rise might stockpile their production rather than sell at the current low price. These judgments reflect the role of prices in signaling current and future opportunity costs.

But what about a participant in the market for tin futures? This market allows anyone who can correctly predict movements in the price of tin to make large profits, irrespective of whether they have any need for, or ability to supply, the commodity. That in turn means that information is highly valuable, as long as it can be obtained and exploited before it is learned by other market players. Players in the futures market will be willing to pay a substantial amount for being the first to gain information. In modern markets, with automated high-frequency trading systems, even microseconds can matter.

In speculative markets, private information about prices will itself have a price. But there is no obvious way that this price corresponds to the social value of information. There is no reason to think that there is much social value in obtaining information about tin prices a day earlier, let alone a microsecond earlier, than we would otherwise. The amount of tin produced and consumed will not change noticeably as a result of such short-term improvements in information. There is no necessary match between the private value of information and the social value.

On the other hand, markets such as commodity futures markets provide useful services to producers and users, allowing them to reduce the risk associated with future price movements. And, in many cases, an active group of speculators is needed to provide a "thick" market, in which prices are truly informative.

There is no general answer to the question of whether speculation is beneficial or harmful. As with many other questions in economics, it is necessary to weigh whether Lesson One or Lesson Two is more relevant in any particular case.

Looking at the explosive growth of speculation over recent decades, however, it seems clear that the opportunity cost of the resources allocated to speculation exceeds any conceivable benefit. The volume of financial transactions is startling. To take just one example, the total value of world trade (exports and imports of physical goods) is around $15 trillion a year. International investment flows account for another $1.5 trillion a year. By contrast, the value of transactions in foreign exchange markets is $5 trillion *a day*.

That is, only about 1 percent of activity in foreign exchange markets reflects the exchange that takes place when goods are exported from one country to another, or in international investment flows. The rest is devoted to speculative financial "engineering," largely designed to minimize taxation and exploit inconsistencies in regulation.

These gigantic numbers appear in ledgers but don't reflect actual opportunity cost. The opportunity cost of speculation lies in the resources devoted to the financial sector and its supporting inputs such as legal and accounting services.

The growth of the financial sector since the 1970s has been staggering. Great world cities like London and New York are now dominated almost entirely by finance. The financial sector accounts directly for around a third of the economic activity in London, and indirectly for much of the rest.

This growth is striking when we consider that advances in information and communications technology have drastically reduced the cost of routine financial transactions. Even as the financial sector has grown, banks have been closing branches and laying off the people who work in them.

In principle, as we have discussed, the growth of the financial sector could be justified by bringing the price of financial assets closer to their opportunity cost and making capital markets more like the model of Lesson One. There is no evidence that this is happening. On the contrary, over the past few decades, as the financial sector has grown, the frequency and severity of bubbles, and the subsequent busts, have grown.

11.5. Risk and Insurance

Unlike speculative financial markets, insurance markets provide an unambiguously useful service. One of the most important kinds of uncertainty is that relating to large and small disasters, from minor car crashes, to losing a job, to life-threatening illnesses. For some of these disasters, such as car crashes, it is possible to obtain insurance that largely offsets the risk of loss. As we saw in chapter 3, insurance against such disasters provides an illustration of Lesson One. Nevertheless, they are subject to market failures that illustrate Lesson Two.

A striking feature of market societies is that for some risks, including job loss, crop failure, and health costs, market insurance is typically unavailable. In these cases, insurance is commonly provided by governments, either directly or through a combination of mandate and subsidy policies.

Why is insurance available for some risks and not for others? Insurance companies operate by offering insurance to many clients on the assumption that only a small proportion will need to make a claim in any given year. The premiums of all the clients, including those who don't claim, can be used to pay out claims, as well as covering the insurers' operating costs and providing a profit margin.

One problem with insurance arises if the insured event affects a large proportion of the insured group at once, as in a natural disaster. The smaller and less diversified the insurance company, the bigger the problem. This is, in essence, a problem of economies of scale, so the analysis of section 9.2 is relevant.

The bigger problem is the need for insurers to estimate, with reasonable accuracy, the probability that any particular client will make a claim. This depends on the risk faced by the client in the absence of insurance, as well as on whether they respond to insurance by taking more risks. In most cases, the client knows more about this than does the insurance company. This problem is referred to in the economic literature as "asymmetric information."[5]

Insurers can deal with the problem of asymmetric information in various ways. In some cases, public information about potential clients is sufficient to estimate the probability of a claim with reasonable accuracy. For example, a driver aged twenty-five with a poor driving record is more likely to be involved in a crash and will therefore face higher premiums than a forty-five-year-old with a clean sheet. Another is to design contracts with features that appeal more to low-risk clients. For example, a contract with low premiums and high deductibles will be more attractive to someone who does not expect to make many claims.

For many important risks in life, however, the problem of asymmetric information cannot be overcome, and markets do not provide insurance. Perhaps the most important is unemployment insurance. Market insurance against job loss is typically unavailable. That's because workers often have much better information about the likelihood of losing their job than an outside insurer can hope to obtain. A private firm offering unemployment insurance would sell lots of insurance to people

---

[5] In the technical jargon of insurance, this form of asymmetric information is referred to as "adverse selection" and distinguished from "moral hazard," where the client fails to take appropriate action to reduce the risk of an adverse outcome. For rather abstruse theoretical reasons, I don't find this distinction particularly useful.

who expected to lose their jobs, and not much to those confident of retaining them. In the technical jargon of the field, this problem is called "adverse selection."

Public unemployment insurance programs work because all employers are required to pay contributions on behalf of all their employees. The premium varies depending on past experience. Firms with a history of stable employment pay less, while those who regularly lay off workers pay more. Because participation is compulsory, adverse selection is not a problem.

Lesson One explains the potential benefits of insurance. Lesson Two is relevant whenever problems of asymmetric information prevent the emergence of properly functioning insurance markets.

11.6. Bounded Rationality

Human beings are incredibly clever at processing and responding to information. We have a general capacity for reasoning that far exceeds that of other animals. In addition, genetic and cultural evolution has equipped us with a variety of cognitive "modules" that enable us to perform specific tasks rapidly and efficiently. For example, we can naturally throw objects much better than any other animal and we are also good at catching objects (though birds of prey are even better).

We can improve our ability to catch thrown objects in a couple of ways. One, based on general reasoning, involves estimating the speed and trajectory of the object, and running to the point where we expect it to fall within our reach. Going further, we can use mathematics and physics to make incredibly accurate predictions, enabling humanity to send spaceships to the edge of the solar system and beyond with exact knowledge of the course they will follow.

Such rational optimization takes a lot of time and mental effort, however. Beginning with the work of Herbert Simon in the 1950s, psychologists and some economists have investigated the implications of "bounded rationality," that is, the fact that we have only a limited capacity to reason about the choices we face.

To catch a ball flung in the air, a much simpler solution is the "gaze heuristic." A fielder using the gaze heuristic observes the initial angle of the ball and runs toward it in such a way as to keep this angle constant. Baseball fielders learn the gaze heuristic through trial and error, or through "cultural transmission" (that is, advice from coaches or fellow players). But it can also be arrived at as the solution to an optimization problem.

The gaze heuristic appears to work well in practice.[6] It is therefore described as "ecologically rational" for the environment in question. Heuristics are examples of cognitive modules.

Heuristics work well in the environments in which they evolve. However, they may fail in other environments. Some, researchers, most notably Daniel Kahneman and Amos Tversky, have examined ways in which heuristics may lead to good decisions in some contexts and bad ones in others. Others, such as Goldstein and Gigerenzer, have focused more on the cases where, given our cognitive limitations, decision-making requires a combination of heuristics and rational calculation.

One Lesson economics ignores this. In the standard One Lesson model of decision-making, human beings are replaced by "rational agents" who are assumed to be members of the species *Homo economicus*. Rational agents have an infinite capacity

---

[6] There is a large and contentious literature in cognitive science and psychology on whether human catchers actually use the gaze heuristic and on whether terms like "heuristic" are even useful for the purposes of psychology. This need not concern us here. The term is certainly helpful as an alternative to the standard One Lesson assumption of unboundedly rational choice.

to calculate the consequences of their actions under every possible contingency.[7] Not only that, but they can use their reasoning capacity to model the actions of other agents, taking into account the fact that the other agents are modeling them, and so on, ad infinitum. In economics jargon, this assumption is referred to as "common knowledge of rationality."

The problem of making decisions under uncertainty is an important case where bounded rationality plays a crucial role. The efficient markets hypothesis rests on the assumption that market participants are rational agents making decisions to maximize their "expected utility."

It has long been known, however, that real-life choices aren't consistent with the theory of expected utility and that more general and flexible models are needed. Much of my career as an academic economist has been devoted to this task.

One aspect of the problem is that people tend to place more weight than they should (at least according to the EMH) on low-probability extreme events, like winning the lottery or dying in a plane crash. It's possible to develop models of this behavior involving weighted probabilities, but these aren't necessarily consistent with the rationality required for the EMH.

Another, more fundamental, difficulty is that we can't possibly be aware of all contingencies relevant to a decision. Contingencies of which we suddenly (and often painfully) become aware have been described as "unknown unknowns" and "Black Swans." When participants in financial markets, unaware of their own unawareness, attempt to apply rational optimization to an incomplete model of the world, the results

---

[7] The sole exception to this model of unbounded rationality is in the case of economic policymakers and, in particular, central planners. One Lesson economists are more than happy to point out the cognitive limitations of their opponents.

can be disastrous. Financial crises typically involve a rapid spread of awareness about a possibility (such as a simultaneous default by a number of borrowers) that had previously been disregarded.

In the face of our incapacity to take account of all possibilities, it is often better to rely on heuristics rather than attempting to achieve a solution that is optimal for our mental model of the world but may fail in reality. The simplest such heuristic, as stated by Gerd Gigerenzer, is "Never buy financial products you do not understand." Another is the "1/N rule." Rather than attempting the complex calculations needed to optimize the trade-off between risk and return, simply identify N assets and divide your investments equally among them.

Bounded rationality is most significant in financial choices involving time and uncertainty, but it can arise in spot markets where these factors are not important. Dominant firms in a market (for example the market for phone and Internet service) sometimes offer a vast and confusing range of options. The idea is that consumers with the time and ability to pick out the best offer will do so, rather than defecting to a competitor, while more loyal customers will stick with bad deals, on the mistaken assumption that there is nothing better on offer.

The exploitation of loyalty is one of many ways in which firms may exploit bounded rationality to trick consumers into choices that are profitable for the firms but harmful to consumers. Nobel Prize winners George Akerlof and Robert Shiller develop this theme in their amusingly titled book, *Phishing for Phools*.

Moreover, given our bounded rationality, it is possible to have too many choices, most of which differ from one another only marginally. This point has been stressed by psychologists such as Barry Schwartz, who argues that too much choice can lead to depression, as people feel overwhelmed and anxious about making the right choices.

Taking all these points together, the complex relationship between markets and information is even more fraught once we take bounded rationality into account. Markets create incentives to produce information, but also to conceal it, or to overwhelm useful information in meaningless noise.[8]

The fact that our reasoning capacity is bounded is another instance of Lesson Two. Prices give us information about opportunity costs, but only if we have the capacity to process that information.

11.7. What Bitcoin Reveals about Financial Markets

The Bitcoin bubble, in which the price of a valueless "cryptocurrency" rose from virtually zero to $20,000 in December 2017, before beginning a gradual decline, should finally destroy our faith in the EMH.

The EMH survived the absurdities of the dot-com bubble in the late 1990s and early 2000s, as well as the meltdown in derivative markets that led to the Global Financial Crisis in 2007 and 2008. Although the hypothesis should have been refuted by those disasters, it lived on, if only in zombie form.

But at least each of those earlier bubbles began with a plausible premise. The ascent of the Internet has transformed our lives and given rise to some very profitable companies, such as Amazon and Google. Even though it was obvious that most 1990s dot-coms would fail, it was easy to make a case for any of them individually.

---

[8] This problem is not unique to markets, as the phenomenon of "fake news" has shown.

As for the derivative assets that gave us the Global Financial Crisis, they were viewed favorably in light of a widely held theory known as the "Great Moderation," which suggested that major economic crises were a thing of the past, thanks to certain systemic changes in the way developed nations ran their economies.[9] The theory was backed by leading economists, politicians, and central bankers.[10] Asset-backed derivatives were, ultimately, a bet on the great moderation.

The contrast with Bitcoin is stark. The Bitcoin bubble rests on no plausible premise. When Bitcoin was created about a decade ago, the underlying idea was that it would displace existing currencies for transactions of all kinds. But by the time the Bitcoin bubble took off last year, it was obvious that this would not happen. Only a handful of legitimate merchants ever accepted Bitcoin. And as the Bitcoin bubble drove up transactions charges and waiting times, even this handful walked away.

For a while, Bitcoin was used for transactions that people wanted to keep secret from government authorities, like drug deals and money laundering. It soon became apparent, however, that if authorities wanted to track these transactions, they could. For instance, Silk Road, the first major online drug market, which made use of Bitcoin, was shut down by the FBI in 2013.

Hardly anyone now suggests that Bitcoin has value as a currency. Rather, the new claim is that Bitcoin is a "store of value" and that its price reflects its inherent scarcity. (By design, no more than 21 million Bitcoins can be created.)

---

[9] Discussed in my book, *Zombie Economics*.

[10] This endorsement was, perhaps, unsurprising, since the theory reflected well on all three groups: the central bankers who managed the economy, the politicians who appointed them, and the economists who advised them.

Most economists, including me, dismiss this claim. And if the claim is false, Bitcoin's value is obviously another deadly strike against the efficient market hypothesis.

But even if the claim is true, the idea that Bitcoin is valuable simply because people value it and because it is scarce should shake any remaining faith in the efficient market hypothesis.

Consider: If Bitcoin is a "store of value," then asset prices are entirely arbitrary. As the proliferation of cryptocurrencies has shown, nothing is easier than creating a scarce asset. The same argument would apply to any existing financial assets. Any stock in the S&P 500 could be priced, not in terms of future earnings prospects, but on the basis that people choose to value it highly.

Suppose, more plausibly, that Bitcoin has no underlying value and will eventually become worthless. According to the efficient market hypothesis, financial markets will correctly estimate the true value of Bitcoin and will drive the price to zero immediately.

But that hasn't happened either. Until recently, it wasn't even possible because the Bitcoin markets were themselves as opaque as the currency.

Now it is possible: Futures trading for Bitcoin on the Chicago Mercantile Exchange has been going on since December 2017. But Bitcoin prices rose after the creation of futures trading and began their gradual decline only when governments took measures to limit speculation.

Whatever happens to Bitcoin, we must not lose sight of a more fundamental, and more worrisome, development. A financial product with a purely arbitrary value has been successfully introduced in the world's most sophisticated financial markets.

Bitcoin probably won't bring financial markets crashing down. But it shows that regulators need to cut those markets down to size.

Further Reading

Hayek (1945) has been discussed already. Brand (1987) is interesting, and still relevant, as a representative of the techno-utopianism that prevailed in the early days of the Internet.

Greenwood and Scharfstein (2013) document the growth of the financial sector. For anyone interested in the rise and fall of the efficient markets hypothesis, Justin Fox's (2009) *The Myth of the Rational Market: A History of Risk, Reward, and Delusion on Wall Street* is essential reading. The "Adam Smith"/George Goodman classic, *The Money Game* (1968), is still full of insights after 40 years. John Kay (2004) provides an excellent, and sympathetic, view of the strengths and weaknesses of markets, and the way in which markets can only work if they are embedded in social and cultural institutions. The discussion in this chapter draws on my 2010 book *Zombie Economics: How Dead Ideas Still Walk Among Us*.

Important articles in support of the efficient markets hypothesis are Manne (1965) on the market for corporate control and Fama (1970) on the efficiency of financial markets.

The classic reference on early bubbles is Charles Mackay's (1841) *Extraordinary Popular Delusions and the Madness of Crowds*. I've written a lot on the equity premium puzzle and its implications. Links in the speculation section are World Trade Organization (2017), UN Conference on Trade and Development (2017), Bank for International Settlements (2016), and Wadwha (2016).

Classic works on bounded rationality include Simon (1957), Tversky and Kahneman (1974), and Thaler (1990). More recent contributions include Gigerenzer and Selten (2002); Kahneman (2013) *Thinking Fast and Slow*; Gigerenzer et al. (2015) *Heuristics: The Foundations of Adaptive Behavior*; Ortmann and Spiliopoulos (2017); and Schwartz (2005). Taleb's (2007)

The Black Swan is also of interest, though the author's claims to unique insights, not shared by any mainstream economist, should be taken with a large grain of salt. The Wikipedia article on ecological rationality is also useful.

Anyone interested in my analysis of moral hazard and adverse selection, mentioned briefly in footnote 5, will find the argument set out in my book with Bob Chambers, *Uncertainty, Production, Choice, and Agency: The State-Contingent Approach* (Chambers and Quiggin 2000). Warning: there's lots of math.

LESSON TWO

■

PART II

Public Policy

The philosophers have only interpreted the world, in various ways. The point, however, is to change it.
——Karl Marx, *Eleven Theses on Feuerbach*

In this, the final part of the book, we will examine the implications of Two Lesson economics for public policy. First, we will consider how public policy can respond to inequities in the distribution of income and wealth. In chapter 12, we will consider "predistribution," that is, the idea that it is better to fix the inequitable allocation of property rights in the first place than to fix the resulting market outcome. Examples of predistribution include the rights of employers and workers, the setting of minimum wages, the creation of intellectual property, and institutions for managing business risk, such as bankruptcy and limited liability.

In chapter 13, we will examine income redistribution through the tax and welfare systems. We will show how tax and social welfare systems combine to create an effective marginal tax rate. Finally, we will consider some principles for weighing the opportunity costs involved in predistribution and redistribution.

In chapter 14, we will consider policies for full employment. We will begin with the traditional tools of fiscal and monetary policy, then consider direct intervention in labor markets, through programs including training and wage subsidies. The most direct form of intervention is a Job Guarantee, aimed at ensuring paid work for anyone who is willing to undertake it. We will discuss the Job Guarantee and its relationship to opportunity cost. Finally, we will discuss the way in which One Lesson economists, from Bastiat to Hazlitt and beyond, have tried, and increasingly failed, to address the problem of unemployment.

In chapter 15, we will examine responses to the growing power of monopolies and monopsonies. After considering the option of a revival in antitrust policy, we will argue that the best solution is a "mixed economy" in which governments, as well as private firms, play a major role in producing and delivering crucial services, including health, education, and infrastructure services.

Finally, in chapter 16 we will discuss environmental policy with a focus on climate change. An understanding of the Two Lessons allows an assessment of the strengths and weaknesses of responses including direct regulation, pollution taxes, and emission permits. By contrast, the inability of One Lesson economists to address these problems has led many of them to embrace climate science denial.[1]

---

[1] Surprisingly, this pattern of denial stretches right back to Bastiat in the nineteenth century (see section 16.5).

CHAPTER 12

∎

Income Distribution:
Predistribution

The Golden Rule: Whoever Has the Gold Makes the Rules.
—"The Wizard of Id" comic strip, May 3, 1965,
created by Johnny Hart and Brant Parker

In chapter 7, we saw that the logic of opportunity cost does not begin, as Hazlitt and others in the propertarian tradition assume, with a preordained distribution of property rights. Rather, the allocation of property rights, including entitlements such as Social Security and labor rights, is itself a social choice. Every such choice involves both benefits and opportunity costs.

One way to think about the way society determines the allocation of income and consumption is based on a distinction between "predistribution" and "redistribution." Here predistribution, a term coined by Jacob Hacker, refers to the setting of the property rights and other rules that determine the distribution of wages, profits, and other incomes arising from markets. Redistribution refers to taxation and expenditure policies that change the final distribution of income and consumption relative to the market outcome.

In this chapter, we will begin with some examples of predistribution and redistribution, before considering the issue of predistribution in more detail.

12.1. Income Distribution and Opportunity Cost

There are many policy changes that will improve the economic position of some members of the community. Examples include

(A) Making it easier for workers to form unions and negotiate for higher wages

(B) Increasing the legal minimum wage

(C) Making Social Security payments and unemployment insurance more accessible, which will benefit those who are unable to work because of age or inability to find a job

(D) Increasing the number of publicly funded places in colleges and universities, which will benefit the young people who are entitled to apply for those places

(E) Increasing the duration of intellectual property rights such as copyrights and patents, which will benefit the owners of those rights

(F) Making it easier for corporations to wipe out their debts through bankruptcy

(G) Reducing marginal rates of income tax above some income level, which will benefit those with taxable incomes above that level

Over the past 40 years, we have seen substantial changes of types (E), (F), and (G) in the United States and elsewhere around the world. These changes benefit high-income earners and the managers and stockholders of corporations.

The top marginal rate of income tax has been reduced from 70 percent to 39.6 percent. The maximum term of copyright protection has been extended from 56 years in 1975 to the duration of the author's life plus 70 years. Other measures, such as the use of Investor–State Dispute Settlement (ISDS) provisions in trade agreements, have created a variety of new and expanded property rights for corporations. The ease with which corporations can declare bankruptcy and re-emerge with their debts discharged has greatly increased.

By contrast, there have been few changes for types (A) and (B), which benefit workers, or types (C) and (D), which benefit the recipients of social welfare payments and public services. On the contrary, policy has been directed at reducing wages and at cutting public expenditure of all kinds.

These outcomes reflect the logic of opportunity cost, in a context where political power has shifted toward corporations and the wealthy. To finance increased expenditure on some goal or to reduce the taxes paid by one group, the government must find offsetting cuts in expenditure or increased taxes elsewhere, or else accept a larger deficit, incurring a debt that will have to be serviced in the future. The least unattractive of these options, as evidenced by the choices of policymakers, will constitute the opportunity cost of providing the benefit.

Policy changes like (E), (F), and (G) generally benefit those who are already relatively well-off. The opportunity cost, as we have seen, is that fewer resources are available to improve the position of those with less initial wealth through policies such (A), (B), (C), and (D).

In the list above, policies like (A), (B), (E), and (F) involve predistribution, and particularly the distribution of market income between workers and employers. Policies like (C), (D), and (G) involve redistribution. The distinction is not hard and fast. The provision of education can be regarded as fitting into both categories. To the extent that education is seen as a universal right, its provision is a kind of predistribution. On the other hand, if education is seen as a discretionary purchase or investment, public support for education is better viewed as redistribution. We will consider the provision of education and other public services, financed by taxation, as a form of redistribution.

In this chapter, we'll look at the four examples of predistribution given above. Section 12.2 will deal with unions, section 12.3 with minimum wages, section 12.4 with intellectual property, and section 12.5 with corporate bankruptcy and limited liability.

12.2. Predistribution: Unions

The biggest single factor in determining the distribution of market income is the relative shares going to wages on the one hand and to capital incomes (rent, interest, dividends, and capital gains) on the other.[1] This division is often treated as the outcome of a competitive market process, beginning with an allocation of property rights in which workers own their labor, while everything else belongs to property owners. This is, however, a drastic oversimplification.

The wages that emerge from labor markets are the products of a complex process of implicit and explicit bargaining between workers, employers, and (where they exist) unions. The outcomes of those bargains depend on the relative power of the parties and that in turn depends on the rules set out by society.

The historical starting point for the relationship between workers and employers is the master-servant relationship that formed the basis of English and American common law. In the common law framework, servants were legally bound to their masters. A competing employer offering higher wages could

---

[1] The division is even sharper if the incomes of top executives and financial sector professionals are regarded as reflecting control over capital, rather than as wages for labor.

be sued for "enticement," and workers who left their employers could be prosecuted criminally.[2] As late as 1864, more than 10,000 workers were imprisoned for such crimes in England (Jones 1867).

In this context, workers joining together to bargain for better wages constituted a criminal conspiracy. The United States took over the English common law position, as was established in the case of *Commonwealth v. Pullis* (1806). Under these circumstances, the jibe of Southern slave-owners that Northern workers were nothing more than "wage slaves" had an uncomfortable grain of truth. Bargaining between masters and servants was so lopsided as to ensure that all the benefits went to the master and none to the servant.[3]

Over the course of the nineteenth century and through the first half of the twentieth century, the political and economic environment became increasingly favorable to unions and workers. *Commonwealth v. Pullis* was overturned in 1846. The establishment of the American Federation of Labor in 1886 marked the beginning of an era in which unions were considered a normal part of modern society, rather than a conspiracy against the market. Nevertheless, the normal stance of government remained one of backing employers against workers, and actively assisting in the breaking of strikes.

The great gains of the labor movement were made under the New Deal. The Wagner Act of 1935 guaranteed the right to join trade unions and to take strike action. In addition, it created

---

[2] The same action could be brought against someone who induced a wife to leave her lawful master, namely her husband.

[3] The gradual erosion of this imbalance, to the point where workers in general and domestic workers in particular could demand better wages and conditions and leave if dissatisfied, was the core of the "servant problem." The servant problem was continually discussed in upper-middle-class households from the mid-nineteenth century until the near-disappearance of live-in domestic servants after 1945.

the National Labor Relations Board, which conducts ballots to allow workers in a given workplace to organize as a union. The Wagner Act specifically set out to redress the inequality of bargaining power between workers and employers and required employers to engage in collective bargaining with unions.

Of equal or greater importance in enhancing the bargaining power of workers was the unprecedented era of full employment that began with the outbreak of World War II in 1939 and continued until the early 1970s. In conditions of full employment, employers found it difficult or impossible to break strikes by hiring non-union workers, and threats to fire workers who supported union votes were less daunting.

As a result, union membership boomed, reaching its peak in the 1950s. The result, along with other elements of the New Deal, was a massive reduction in economic inequality in the United States (and other developed countries), to the lowest levels in history. Combined with strong economic growth, this produced an era of middle-class prosperity which, even as it fades into history, dominates our expectations of the way an economy ought to work. For most of the 1950s and 1960s, the position of unions remained strong. More important, the idea of unions as a central part of a modern society was completely normalized.

As part of this process, unions broadened their coverage. The craft unions of the mid-nineteenth century, from which the American Federation of Labor (AFL) emerged, were restricted to skilled manual workers, predominantly white males. The shift toward industrial unions, associated with the rise of the Congress of Industrial Organizations (CIO), expanded membership to cover unskilled workers and provided a model for white-collar workers to unionize, particularly in the public sector.

The expansion of unionism inevitably raised the issues of racism and sexism. As with the rest of society, racist and sexist attitudes were prevalent in the early union movement. However, the CIO challenged the entrenched racism of many of the old AFL unions. The merged AFL-CIO, created in 1955, banned racial discrimination in member unions and strongly supported the civil rights movement. Equally important, the struggles of women in the garment industry led to the rapid growth of the International Ladies' Garment Workers' Union (now UNITE) and the union movement was one of the major forces behind the Equal Pay Act of 1963.

Throughout the 1950s and 1960s, it seemed that the United States was leading the world on an upward trajectory, toward a society in which inequalities based on class, race, and sex would become less and less acceptable. Unions played a central role in that development.

The US experience was replicated, with variations, in other developed countries with market economies. By the mid-twentieth century, governments generally presented themselves as neutral arbiters between workers and employers, seeking to promote fair and harmonious outcomes consistent with widely shared prosperity. There was a general acceptance of the legitimacy of trade unions, as reflected in international conventions such as those of the International Labor Organization.

Since the 1950s, however, unions have been steadily weakened both by changes in the law and by increasingly aggressive and effective anti-union strategies. The process began in the United States with the Taft-Hartley Act of 1947, which outlawed closed shops and greatly restricted the right to strike. However, Taft-Hartley was an isolated defeat that did not, initially, harm unions very much.

The global inflationary upsurge of the 1960s was a disaster for the union movement, and for workers. In retrospect, it is clear that the acceleration of inflation was primarily the result of mistakes in macroeconomic policy. At the time, however, it seemed more plausible to place the blame on a wage–price spiral caused by the greed of unions and big corporations, acting in concert.

Because the process of keeping wages ahead of inflation required virtually continuous strike action, unions came to be seen (and to some extent to see themselves) as being in conflict with society as a whole. By contrast, attempts to control increases in prices, most notably during the Nixon wage-price freezes from 1971 to 1973, ended in ignominious failure.

The attack on unions accelerated markedly throughout the developed world in the 1970s, following the explosive growth of the financial sector and the resurgence of One Lesson economics. Anti-union legislation was reinforced by discretionary policy.

From the 1980s onward, the stance of government was one of overt or covert hostility, depending on whether the party in office was nominally of the right or the center-left. The iconic leaders of the right, such as then-president Ronald Reagan and then-prime minister Margaret Thatcher, established themselves by breaking strikes and crushing the unions involved. The anti-union position was enshrined in UK legislation such as the Employment Acts of 1980 and 1982 and the Trade Union legislation. The Reagan administration, lacking a majority in Congress, relied primarily on appointing anti-union officials to bodies such as the National Labor Relations Board. The rulings of these officials greatly restricted the scope of strike action and enhanced the power of employers to dismiss striking workers.

Notionally center-left leaders such as former president Bill Clinton and former prime minister Tony Blair retained, and in some cases, extended, the anti-union legislation and regulation of their predecessors. These advocates of the "Third Way" were particularly hostile to unionism among public sector workers, most notably teachers' unions. This is still evident, for example, in the policies of Rahm Emanuel, an adviser to Bill Clinton, and chief of staff under the Obama administration. As mayor of Chicago, Emanuel has consistently pursued an anti-union campaign. The result of all of these developments has been a dramatic decline in union membership, particularly in English-speaking countries.

The decline in unionism has gone in parallel with a decline in the labor share of national income and stagnant or declining wages for large groups of workers, particularly in the United States. A large number of economic studies have demonstrated that declining unionism is a major factor in the worsening position of workers. Even such a defender of the market as the International Monetary Fund (IMF) recently published a summary concluding that

> On average, the decline in unionization explains about half of the 5 percentage point rise in the top 10 percent income share. Similarly, about half of the increase in the Gini of net income is driven by deunionization.

This decline has been accompanied by an increase in inequality among workers. Highly educated professionals have done better than manual workers, though both have lost ground relative to managers and owners of capital. A study of the United States by Bruce Western and Jake Rosenfeld attributed about 33 percent of the rise in within-group wage inequality among men to deunionization. The effect was lower for women because their initial rate of unionization was lower.

It is often assumed that the decline of unionism is irreversible and that unions are simply irrelevant under modern conditions. There is no good reason to believe this. On the contrary, survey evidence shows that a great many workers would like to join unions, but are unable, or too worried about the prospect of reprisal, to do so. This reinforces the point that the decline of unionism is the product of decades of anti-union law and policy.

What has been legislated can be repealed. The more fundamental change that is needed is a revision of assumptions that are taken for granted, throughout the political process, that corporations are a natural feature of market economies, while unions are an alien intrusion. This attitude, shared across the spectrum of mainstream political opinion, is only now under challenge.

As we will see in the next section, corporations, like unions, are social constructions, which could not exist except as a result of conscious policy decisions to change the rules of a market economy. A policy that begins with implicit assumptions in favor of corporations, and against unions, is one in which inequality is guaranteed to increase.

There is not enough space in a book of this kind to discuss the many changes that would be needed to restore balance in bargaining between workers and employers. But in the US context, the obvious political demand is to begin at the beginning, by repealing the Taft-Hartley Act and restoring the pro-labor framework of the New Deal's Wagner Act.

As unions have declined, many groups of workers have sought to protect their position through occupational licensing, which restricts entry to a variety of jobs and professions. Workers in jobs requiring a license generally receive higher wages. However, unlike unionization, licensing tends to promote wage inequality, both within licensed occupations and between licensed and unlicensed occupations.[4]

Finally, it is necessary to consider the other side of the bargaining table. While there is some room for mutually beneficial agreements, an imbalance of bargaining power means gains for one side and losses for the other. In addition to strengthening

---

[4] There is an interesting parallel with generous bankruptcy laws, which act as a political substitute for redistributive taxation, but tend to increase inequality, as discussed in section 12.5.

the position of workers, it is important to look at the way the bargaining power of employers, particularly large corporations, has increased, and how that power can be reduced. This issue will be discussed further in chapter 14.

12.3. Predistribution: Minimum Wages

The most direct way for government to influence the distribution of market income is to set minimum wage rates. The benefits to workers who receive the higher wage are obvious. But what are the opportunity costs, and who bears them?

The effects of minimum wages on the distribution of income have been the subject of a vast economic literature. Much of this literature starts from a simple (or simplistic) version of Lesson One. The starting point is the assumption that the price of labor (that is, the wage) is the product of a competitive market of the kind we discussed in chapter 2.

If this is correct, then a minimum wage involves setting a price above the opportunity cost of labor. This means that some workers who would be willing to work at a wage below the minimum will remain unemployed, while potential jobs that yield less production than is needed to cover the cost of a minimum-wage worker will remain unfilled or will not be created at all.

Even within this framework, workers may benefit from an increased minimum wage. Suppose for example that the minimum wage is increased by 10 percent, and that employers respond by reducing the hours of work, for all minimum wage workers, by 5 percent. In this case, workers would get 5 percent more total pay, and work 5 percent fewer hours, gaining both more income and more leisure.

Economists working in this framework point to a number of reasons to doubt this favorable projection. First, the gain to the workers here is associated with a larger increase in cost to the employer. This is because some potential jobs, which would yield a positive return to both parties, are not created.

Second, typical estimates of the change in hours of work associated with a given change in wages (referred to as the elasticity of demand for labor) are derived for small changes in the wage. Larger proportional effects might arise with a large and rapid increase in the wage.

Third, the idea of a uniform reduction in hours of work for all minimum-wage employees is clearly unrealistic. More likely, many workers will experience no change in their hours (getting the full benefit of the increase), while others will lose their jobs or fail to find jobs when they try to enter the market.

The third of these points is the most important. However, far from strengthening the case for an analysis based on Lesson One, it undermines it. Hours of work are not a commodity that can be supplied and demanded in order to match prices and opportunity costs. Rather, each worker is typically matched with one job which largely determines their living standards.[5]

With the allocation of property rights to employers that normally prevails in the United States, referred to as "employment at will," the job is the property of the employer who can withdraw it at any time, for any reason, or none. Donald Trump's catchphrase, "You're Fired," is the simple and brutal expression of this reality.

Because of this imbalance of power, Lesson Two is just as relevant to the determination of wages as Lesson One. In the absence of offsetting institutions like unions and minimum wages, the imbalance of bargaining power will ensure that most of the benefits of the bargain go to the employer.

---

[5] Except where they have to patch two or three jobs together, almost invariably ending up with worse wages and conditions than similar workers with a single job.

Approaches based solely on Lesson One dominated the economics literature until the early 1990s. The central concern of this literature was to estimate the elasticity of demand for minimum-wage workers. The elasticity of demand is the ratio of the percentage change in hours worked resulting from a given percentage change in the minimum wage. In the example above, where the minimum wage is increased by 10 percent, and employers respond by reducing the hours of work, for all minimum-wage workers, by 5 percent, the elasticity would be 0.5 (that is, 5/10).

Economists using this approach expected to find a moderately elastic demand for labor, and they did so. Econometric analysis undertaken in the 1970s and 1980s typically yielded estimated elasticities above 0 (no response) but below 0.5. However, over the course of the 1980s, the estimates tended to decline. Moreover, with the re-emergence of chronic high unemployment after the economic crises of the 1970s, the idea that wages could be regarded as prices emerging from a competitive equilibrium (for which full employment is a prerequisite) became less and less plausible.

The debate changed radically in the 1990s. The biggest single event was the publication of research by two young economists, David Card and Alan Krueger, discussed in chapter 9. Card and Krueger examined differential changes in minimum wages in neighboring states and found that they had no discernible effect on employment in the fast food industry. These estimates were subject to lots of reanalysis, the majority of which tended to confirm the original Card and Krueger analysis.

More important perhaps, Card and Krueger shifted the terms of the debate to include the key point of Lesson Two, that market prices do not always reflect social opportunity costs. In particular, they stressed the imbalance of bargaining power between employers and potential workers. This is reflected in what is called, in the jargon of economics, "monopsony power." Monopsony is the other side of monopoly: literally interpreted, it means that there is only a single buyer for the good or service in question, in this case labor hours. But more generally, monopoly and monopsony are relevant whenever one of the parties to a transaction has sufficient bargaining power to influence the price (in this case, the wage).

The central implication of the Card-Krueger analysis is that the primary effect of higher minimum wages will be to redistribute the benefits of the wage bargain from employers to workers, rather than to raise the opportunity cost of hiring to a level exceeding the private and social benefit.

Minimum wages are not a panacea. There must exist some level of minimum wage at which the wage is greater than both the opportunity cost of working and the social value of the output produced. At this point Lesson One would be more relevant than Lesson Two.

There is, however, no reason to believe that the current (as of 2018) US national minimum wage of $7.25 an hour (far lower in real terms than the level prevailing 50 years ago) is high enough to produce such effects.

12.3.1. A Data Point on Minimum Wages

A comparison with Australia, a country very similar in many respects to the United States, suggests that an adult minimum wage of $15 per hour could be achieved over time with few, if any, adverse effects on employment. Australia's minimum wage, evaluated at current exchange rates, is about US$13.50 an hour. Other benefits available to all full-time workers, such as four weeks' annual vacation, mean that the effective minimum wage for Australian workers is close to US$15. Yet Australia's labor market has generally performed better than that in the United States.

A trickier question is whether a big increase in the US minimum wage would result in outcomes similar to those observed in Australia. Labor market institutions develop over time, and under specific historical conditions, which determine the expectations and plans of workers and employers.

The minimum wage in Australia has always been high, relative to the average wage, reflecting an institutional history in which the "basic wage" was, for most of the twentieth century, the starting point for setting all wages. Labor market institutions and expectations were formed on this basis. For example, a high minimum wage means that it is not profitable to organize workplaces in ways that require minimal skill from workers. So, it is in the interest of employers to invest in capital that enhances labor productivity, and in the interest of both employers and workers to invest in training.

The policy question is: what impact have these high minimum wages had on employment and unemployment? That's too big a question to answer comprehensively, but we can look at the obvious data points: the official unemployment rates (averaging 5 percent in both countries over recent years) and the 15–64 employment population ratios (72 percent for Australia, 67 percent for the United States). It doesn't look as if the Australian labor market has been crippled by minimum wages.

By contrast, in the US context, the minimum wage has never been particularly high, and fell in real terms from the late 1960s until 2007, when it was restored to the value that had prevailed in 1973. Work by Lawrence Mishel of the Economic Policy Institute identifies the declining value of the federal minimum wage as a major factor driving inequality.

In these circumstances, and with high unemployment for most of the period, many businesses have organized their workplaces on the basis of an effectively unlimited supply of cheap labor. Such workplaces would require substantial reorganization, or else go out of business, if faced with a sudden large increase in minimum wages.

The implication is not that the minimum wage should be held down to maintain this economic structure. Rather, the necessity is to combine increases in minimum wages with other measures to encourage the emergence of high-wage businesses. Most obviously, these include the pro-union measures discussion in section 12.2. In the longer term, improvements in vocational education and training will also be important.

12.4. Predistribution: Intellectual Property

The system of property rights in market societies is based primarily on private property rights, that is, the exclusive allocation of control over some asset to a single person (or, in modern forms of capitalism, to a corporate entity). The concept of "private goods" in economics refers to goods that are rival and excludable in consumption. There are obvious similarities between these concepts, which often leads to the assumption that the two are identical.

In reality, there are crucial differences. The economic concept of private goods relates to the technological properties of the good in question. Private property is a right created and ultimately enforced by law, which may be applied, or not, to almost anything, whether or not it corresponds to the economic idea of a private good.[6]

In particular, public goods (in the economic sense) may be the subject of private property rights. The most important example is that of "intellectual property" (IP), that is, rights to control the use of information, such as copyrights, patents, and

---

[6] In nineteenth-century Britain, for example, army officers could buy and sell their commissions, a practice that continued until 1871.

trademarks. Enforcement of such rights typically involves the imposition, after the fact, of penalties for reproducing information without the consent of the owner of the rights.

More than any other kind of property, intellectual property rights such as patents are obviously creations of the states that define and enforce them. Patents were originally monopolies over common goods such as playing cards, used by the Tudor and Stuart monarchs in England to reward favorites or sold off to raise money to fund wars and other expenditures.

Creating new property rights or extending old ones provides the owner with control over resources, including ideas, that were previously accessible to all. Users other than the owner are either excluded from the resource or required to negotiate terms with the owner; the associated costs represent the opportunity cost.

The creation of intellectual property rights provides an incentive to generate new ideas, or at least ideas that are sufficiently distinctive in their formulation to attract intellectual property protection. But the enforcement of these rights means that use of the ideas in question is restricted, even though, since ideas are non-rival, there is a social benefit to unrestricted use. Economists have examined the trade-off between the costs and benefits of intellectual property protection and have concluded, in general, that the costs of strong forms of intellectual property protection outweigh the benefits.

By the time the US Constitution was drawn up in the eighteenth century, patents and copyrights were recognized as a way to encourage innovation, as were the dangers of excessive restrictions on the flow of information. The powers of Congress included (emphasis added)

> To promote the Progress of Science and useful Arts, by securing **for limited Times** to Authors and Inventors the exclusive Right to their respective Writings and Discoveries.

The first Copyright Act, passed in 1790, granted authors the exclusive right to publish and vend "maps, charts and books" for a term of 14 years. This fourteen-year term was renewable for one additional fourteen-year term, if the author was alive at the end of the first term. Similarly, inventors could patent their ideas for 14 years.

The terms of copyrights and patents were extended moderately over the subsequent two centuries. Since the resurgence of market liberalism in the 1970s, however, both the duration and the scope of what now became known as intellectual property have expanded massively.

Just about anything, from colors to chromosomes, has now been made the subject of intellectual property. In 2010, Apple Inc. even attempted to claim a trademark for the lowercase letter "i," as in "iPhone," but an Australian court rejected the claim.

The duration of copyright was extended to the life of the author plus 50 years in 1976, and to life plus 70 years by the Sonny Bono Copyright Term Extension Act of 1998, with corporate owners of "work for hire" getting an additional 25 years. The passage of the Act was due in part to pressure from the European Union, which has generally supported strong versions of IP, and in part to the efforts of the Disney Corporation, whose copyrights on cartoon characters such as Mickey Mouse and Winnie the Pooh were in danger of expiry (leading to the derisive label of the Mickey Mouse Protection Act).[7]

The expansion of patents is equally problematic. The barriers to claiming a patent have been steadily lowered, and the scope of patents expanded. Among the most problematic results have

---

[7] Anecdotally, one of the forces pushing for protection was the Bavarian government, which held the copyright over Hitler's *Mein Kampf* and had prohibited publication. While we might sympathize with the desire to suppress this evil book, the case indicates the way in which copyright limits the flow of ideas of all kinds.

been the patenting of obvious and well-known ideas in computer programming and the development of "business method" patents. The two coincided during the dot-com boom of the 1990s, when just about any business transaction, from corporate procurement to selling dog food, could be patented with the simple addition of the words "on the Internet."[8]

Paradoxically, this expansion of intellectual property rights has happened at the same time as the explosive developments in information and communications technology. Ideas, in the form of text, audiovisual material, open source software, and the designs required to make physical products, can now be shared globally on a massive scale and at almost no cost.

The result is a mess. On the one hand, intellectual property rights are routinely violated, on a massive scale, by just about everybody. On the other hand, the combination of massive scope and haphazard enforcement creates a minefield for anyone in a position to be sued. A snippet of an old song playing in the background of a movie or a few lines of recycled computer code can open up scope for costly litigation, with the result that it is usually easier to pay up than to fight.

"Patent trolls" make a profitable living in this fashion. And despite the name, these trolls include major corporations. Warner Brothers made millions suing anyone who had the temerity to perform the song "Happy Birthday to You" in public, even though the song had been in the public domain for at least a century. (The tune, with different lyrics, dates back to 1893. The words we sing evolved over time, through what is sometimes called the "folk process.")

The claims of IP have also been used to suppress public debate and support secrecy about wrongdoing by governments and

---

[8] Something similar is now happening with respect to "blockchain," the distributed database technology underlying Bitcoin.

corporations. The Church of Scientology is particularly notorious for its use of copyright claims to silence critics. Less spectacular, but almost certainly more damaging, is the development of the doctrine of "commercial-in-confidence" intellectual property. This doctrine is used in particular to suppress information about dealings between corporations and governments, providing a convenient cloak for misrepresentation and corruption.

Economic studies of patents and copyright have reached the similar conclusion that the damage caused by IP enforcement exceeds the benefits in terms of innovation. In particular, the premium paid by US consumers for patented pharmaceuticals compared to generics far exceeds the total research and development expenditure of pharmaceutical companies.

The Copyright Term Extension Act of 1998 provoked an extraordinary response from the economics profession, spanning the gamut from free-market advocates like Milton Friedman to interventionists like George Akerlof. These and others (including a total of five winners of the Economics Nobel) joined an amicus brief to the US Supreme Court in a case challenging the constitutionality of the Act, a challenge that unfortunately failed.

The conversion of ideas into IP has had even more corrosive implications. Economists are increasingly realizing that the expansion of IP rights for corporations is one of the most important factors contributing to the growth of inequality and the decline of the labor share of national income.

As was observed in section 7.4, many of the most profitable firms in the modern economy, such as Google, Facebook, Apple, and Microsoft, depend critically on intellectual property rights for their profitability. The mechanisms by which these translate into growing inequality are still being explored, but one of the most notable is the role of IP as one of the key vehicles for global corporate tax avoidance.

The basic method is simple: ideas developed or bought by corporations based in the United States and other large countries are turned into the IP of a subsidiary located in a tax haven that specializes in concessional treatment of such property. Ireland, for example, charges only 6.25 percent on income from IP. Companies then pay themselves (or rather their Irish subsidiaries) large amounts for the right to use their own ideas. This payment reduces their profits at home, while the Irish subsidiary pays almost no tax.

Tax-dodging companies weren't willing to pay even this modest amount of tax. By using a second Irish company located in a Caribbean tax haven (the "double Irish") and then rerouting the profits through the Netherlands (the "Dutch sandwich"), some of them managed to eliminate tax liabilities altogether.

The problems of international tax avoidance and evasion are complex, and the effort to curb such avoidance will take many years to succeed, if indeed it does. But reversing the shift toward stronger and stronger IP would be an important step in the process, as well as being beneficial in itself.

12.4.1. Alternatives to Strong IP

What could take the place of strong IP? In many cases, no replacement is needed. No social purpose is served by restricting publication of the works of long-dead authors, who could not possibly have anticipated this outcome when they wrote. Even looking forward, it's absurd to suppose that I (or any author writing today) am writing in the hope of providing an income for my unborn great-grandchildren.

Similarly, most of the new categories of patents that have exploded in recent decades (business methods, adaptations of standard ideas to the Internet, and so on) are positively undesirable. If a new patent required a positive demonstration, rather than a mere assertion, that the alleged invention was in fact novel, non-obvious, and socially beneficial, most of these patents would disappear, along with the "patent trolls" who exploit them to blackmail genuine innovators. As things stand, it's often easier to pay the trolls than to demonstrate that they are simply claiming rights over well-known ideas ("prior art" in the terminology of patent law).

In some cases, such as pharmaceuticals, it is necessary to reward the private corporations that produce new medicines. Around 15 percent of the total revenue of pharmaceutical companies is allocated to research and development, a figure matched only by the information technology and communications sector.

But nearly all of the money these corporations receive from patent-protected medicines comes, directly or indirectly, from governments. In the United States, and other developed countries, governments contribute to the pharmaceutical industry through support for basic research. Much more important, however, are payments through Medicaid and Medicare, which have greatly expanded as a result of Medicare Part D, introduced under the (George W.) Bush administration. In addition, the US government subsidizes health insurance for most of the population through tax benefits for employer-provided health insurance and through the Affordable Care Act (Obamacare). A substantial part of this subsidy flows through to support the purchase of prescription drugs.

Unlike other governments, the US government does not bargain with pharmaceutical companies over the price of medications (Medicare is explicitly banned from doing so). Rather, companies set their own prices in bargains with private insurers. Unsurprisingly, US pharmaceutical prices are around 50 percent higher than those in other developed countries.[9]

---

[9] The absence of direct bargaining contributes substantially to this outcome, but it is not the only causal factor here. The quasi-private system prevailing in the United States produces higher costs in almost all areas of health care.

Advocates for the pharmaceutical industry claim that this system enables funding for research and development, and that other countries are effectively being subsidized by the United States. There is some truth in this claim, but the higher prices in the United States owe at least as much to marketing efforts and to the ability of pharmaceutical companies to secure monopoly profits thanks to the protection of intellectual property.

It would be far better for the United States to follow the example of other countries and negotiate directly with pharmaceutical companies through mechanisms like the Australian Pharmaceutical Benefits Scheme. Companies with a new medication (or even a prospective new medication) could negotiate for an agreed rate of payment and a period after which generic alternatives would be allowed. Ideally, the current exemptions for poor countries would be expanded to allow immediate access to lifesaving treatments at or near the cost of production.

There would certainly be difficulties in sharing the global costs of such an arrangement between the United States, European Union, and other governments, replacing the current effective US subsidy. But these would be minor compared to the amounts currently wasted through the IP system.

Finally, and most important, governments could do more to support contributions to the public domain. Historically, the most important form of government support has been the funding of (mainly university) research through bodies like the National Science Foundation. However, the public good motivation for funding research sits uneasily with continuing pressure to "commercialize" research through patents and other forms of intellectual property.

The emergence of the Internet has created a vast range of possibilities for expansion of the public domain. While much of this will take place spontaneously, governments could help in many ways. For example, "fair use" exemptions from copyright could be expanded to remove obstacles to creative mixing of material from many different sources (mashups) and, more generally, to take account of the fact that the idea of a "copy" as a discrete physical item is no longer relevant.

A more active form of support would be the provision of grants to assist creative projects, ranging from cultural work to open source software that make their outcomes available through the public domain or through variants like the Creative Commons licensing. While it would be undesirable for governments to seek to control the outcomes of such projects, this is an area where relatively modest financial support could yield substantial social benefits.

As far as intellectual property rights were concerned, the drafters of the US Constitution understood the Two Lessons better than their successors 200 years later.[10] Property rights are social constructions, with both benefits and opportunity costs. Markets cannot determine the appropriate balance between the two because they only permit trade in property rights that have already been created. The determination of property rights is a crucial aspect of predistribution.

12.5. Predistribution: Bankruptcy, Limited Liability, and Business Risk

As we've seen in previous sections, the social construction of property rights and institutions surrounding employment makes a big difference to the determination of wages and working conditions. These social constructions affect predistribution, that is, the distribution of income and wealth that

---

[10] Of course, in other respects, most importantly the implicit acceptance of slavery, the Constitution's treatment of property rights was appalling.

arises before the effects of taxes and public expenditure are taken into account.

Predistribution is equally relevant to the other big source of personal income: profit derived from private businesses and corporations. Without legal structures designed specifically to protect businesses from the risks of failure, profits would be far less secure, and the difficulty of establishing and running a business much greater. Corporate profits are not a natural outcome of a market society, but the product of specific structures of property rights introduced to promote corporate enterprise.

The risks of running a business in the eighteenth century, and well into the nineteenth, were substantial and personal. There was no such thing as bankruptcy: a business failure meant debtors' prison, where debtors could be held until they had worked off their debt through labor or had secured outside funds to pay the balance.

After a brief and disastrous experiment in the early years of the eighteenth century (the South Sea Bubble), joint stock companies were also viewed with grave suspicion. Exceptions were made only for specially authorized quasi-governmental ventures like the East India Company, which focused on foreign trade. In general, limited liability companies were not permitted in Britain or most other countries. The partners in a business were jointly liable for all its debts.

The prevailing view was summed up by the aphorism "Did you ever expect a corporation to have a conscience, when it has no soul to be damned, and no body to be kicked." Adam Smith was also critical of corporations, saying

> The directors of such [joint-stock] companies, however, being the managers rather of other people's money than of their own, it cannot well be expected, that they should watch over it with the same anxious vigilance with which

the partners in a private co-partnery frequently watch over their own. . . . Negligence and profusion, therefore, must always prevail, more or less, in the management of the affairs of such a company.

These same rules applied in Britain's American colonies and continued to prevail in the United States until the middle of the nineteenth century. The introduction of personal bankruptcy laws put an end to debtors' prison, greatly reducing the risks of running a business. The creation of the limited liability company was an even more radical change.

These changes faced vigorous resistance from advocates of the free market. David Moss, in *When All Else Fails*, his brilliant history of government as the ultimate risk manager, describes how the advocates of unlimited personal responsibility for debt were overwhelmed by the needs of business in an industrial economy. The introduction of bankruptcy and limited liability laws took much of the risk out of starting and operating a business.

By contrast, in *Economics in One Lesson*, Hazlitt doesn't mention limited liability or personal bankruptcy and seems to assume (like most propertarians) that these are a natural feature of market societies. More theoretically inclined propertarians have continued to debate the legitimacy of bankruptcy and limited liability laws, without reaching a conclusion.

This debate over whether bankruptcy and corporation laws are consistent with freedom of contract is really beside the point. The distribution of income and wealth is radically changed both by the existence of these institutions and by the details of their design. In particular, without limited liability the massive accumulations of personal wealth made possible by capital gains from share ownership would simply not exist. Perhaps there would be comparable accumulations of wealth derived in some other way, but the owners of that wealth would be different people.

A crucial policy question, therefore, is whether current laws and policies relating to corporate bankruptcy and limited liability have promoted the growth of inequality and contributed to the weak and crisis-ridden economy that has characterized the twentieth century. The combination of these factors has produced absolute stagnation or decline in living standards for much of the US population and relative decline for all but the top few percent.

There can be little doubt that this is the case. As recently as the 1970s, a corporate bankruptcy was the last resort for insolvent companies, typically leading to the liquidation of the company in question. As well as being a financial disaster, bankruptcy was a source of shame for all those involved. For this reason, nearly all major companies sought to maintain an investment-grade credit rating, indicating a judgment by ratings agencies that bankruptcy was, at most, a fairly remote possibility.

Since that time, bankruptcy has become a routine financial operation, used to avoid inconvenient liabilities like pension obligations to workers and the costs of cleaning up mine sites, among many others. The crucial innovation was "Chapter 11," introduced in the Bankruptcy Reform Act of 1978.

The intended effect of Chapter 11 was that companies could reorganize themselves while going through bankruptcy and re-emerge as going concerns. The (presumably) unintended effect was that corporate managers ceased to be scared of bankruptcy. This was reflected in the spectacular growth of the market for "junk bonds" (more politely called "high-yield bonds"), that is, securities with a high rate of interest reflecting a substantial probability of default. Once the preserve of fly-by-night operations, junk bonds became a standard source of finance even for companies in the S&P 500.

At the same time, legislative changes and the growth of global capital markets greatly enhanced the benefits of corporate structures, while eliminating many of the associated costs and limitations. At the bottom end of the scale, the "close corporation" with only a handful of shareholders became the standard method of organizing a small business. This process was aided by a long-series of pro-corporate legislative changes and court decisions.[11] At the top end, the rise of global financial markets from the 1970s onward allowed the creation of corporate structures of vast complexity, headquartered in tax havens and organized to resist scrutiny of any kind.

At the behest of these corporations, governments have negotiated agreements supposedly designed to ensure that corporate profits are not taxed twice in different jurisdictions. In reality, using a combination of complex corporate structures and governments (notably including those of Ireland and Luxembourg) eager to facilitate tax avoidance in return for a small slice of the proceeds, the effect has been to ensure that most global corporate profits are not taxed even once in the countries where they are earned.

What can be done to redress the balance that has been tipped so blatantly in favor of corporations? The obvious starting point is transparency. Havens of corporate secrecy, from Caribbean islands to US states like Delaware, must be made to reveal the true ownership of corporations, in the same way that tax havens like Switzerland, used mostly by wealthy individuals, have been forced to disclose the ownership of previously secret accounts.[12]

Another option, proposed by Gabriel Zucman, is to tax corporations on the basis of their sales in each country, rather than

---

[11] Notably in Delaware, which has long led the way in this process, and where vast numbers of US companies are incorporated.

[12] Most of the information we have at present comes from leaks such as those of the infamous "Panama Papers."

on their profits. The crucial point is that it is easy to shift profits through accounting manipulation but much harder to shift sales revenue. This proposal, commonly called a "Google tax" after one of the corporations that would be most affected, has been seriously discussed in Australia and the United Kingdom.

The use of complex corporate structures to avoid tax is a much more difficult problem to tackle. Some measures are being taken to attack what is called "Base Erosion and Profit Shifting," but past experience suggests that slow-moving processes of this kind will at best keep pace with the development of new forms of avoidance and evasion. It's necessary to re-examine the whole structure of global taxation agreements. Instead of focusing on the need to avoid taxing corporate profits twice, the central objective should be to ensure that they are taxed at least once, in the place where they are actually generated.

More generally, though, the idea that corporations are a natural part of the economic order, with all the human rights of human beings, and none of the obligations, needs to be challenged. Limited liability corporations are creations of public policy, useful to the extent that they promote the efficient use of capital but dangerous to the extent that they facilitate gross inequalities of income and opportunity.

Further Reading

Hacker (2011) introduces the idea of predistribution. *The Predistribution Agenda*, edited by Diamond and Chwalisz (2015), provides a range of useful perspectives.

Hattam (1993) gives a historical analysis of *Commonwealth v. Pullis* (1806) and its implications for the development of unionism in the United States. Swartz (2004) examines the case from the perspective of modern struggles over union rights.

The decline in unionism is discussed by Organization for Economic Co-operation and Development (2017). The IMF study on unionization is by Jaumotte and Buitron (2015a, 2015b). Evidence on the extent to which workers would like to join unions is from Freeman (2007).

The debate over minimum wages sparked by Card and Krueger (1994) has been extensive but unfortunately is difficult to summarize. Mishel (2012a, 2012b, 2013) discusses the relationship between minimum wages and inequality. Minimum wages in Australia are set by the Fair Work Commission, available online at https://www.fwc.gov.au/awards-and-agreements/minimum-wages-conditions/national-minimum-wage-orders/.

Nunn (2018) gives useful information on occupational licensing.

An early statement of the idea that "a social planner which cares about income distribution may in principle want to use a reduction in intellectual property rights" can be found in a paper (unfortunately very math-heavy) by Saint-Paul (2004). Stiglitz (2016) provides a more popular and accessible treatment.

Bebchuk and Fried (2004) present the most detailed study of what they call *Pay without Performance: The Unfulfilled Promise of Executive Compensation*.

The aphorism about corporations is an improvement on the original, quoted in Poynder (1841, p. 268):

> Corporations have neither bodies to be punished, nor souls to be condemned; they therefore do as they like.

The way in which aphorisms can be improved in circulation is a small illustration of Brand's point that "information wants to be free." In the world ultimately envisaged by advocates of strong IP, adapting a quotation like this would be illegal without the permission of the original writer, and impossible if the writer could not be found.

Biasi and Moser (2018) offer some striking evidence on the way copyright protections can harm scientific progress. A more detailed discussion of alternatives to strong IP is given by Baker, Jayadev, and Stiglitz (2017). Zucman (2018) discusses the "Google tax."

CHAPTER 13

∎

Income Distribution: Redistribution

> The money was all appropriated for the top in the hopes that it would trickle down to the needy. Mr. Hoover didn't know that money trickled up. Give it to the people at the bottom and the people at the top will have it before night, anyhow. But it will at least have passed through the poor fellow's hands.
> —Will Rogers

In chapter 12, we discussed "predistribution"; that is, the framework within which market interactions take place, and the rights and obligations with which people enter the market. That set of rights and obligations largely determines the incomes that people can obtain from the market.

Now we consider "redistribution"; that is, changing the distribution of income by levying taxes and charges on market incomes, and using the resulting revenue to provide public services such as health and education and transfer payments such as Social Security, unemployment insurance, and social welfare payments. As discussed in chapter 7, the relevant starting point is the existing system, including both the structure of property rights and the existing settings of tax rates, transfer payments, and public expenditure. Here we will focus on the existing system of taxes and transfers.

The US federal government relies mainly on taxes levied on income. There are three main taxes on income: personal income tax (nearly half of all revenue), payroll taxes to fund Social Security and other social insurance programs (about one-third of all revenues), and corporate income taxes (about 10 percent of all revenue). State and local governments rely on income taxes, sales taxes, and land taxes. Overall, around 27 percent of national income is paid to governments in the form of taxation, a proportion that has remained broadly constant for many decades.

Some tax revenues are paid out in the form of cash benefits, including Social Security, unemployment insurance, and welfare assistance to poor families (mainly food stamps and Temporary Assistance to Needy Families). The rest is used to fund publicly provided services, most importantly health, education, and national defense.

A final, and more subtle, aspect of public expenditure and tax policies arises when certain sources of income or items of spending are exempted from taxation, wholly or partially. The effect is the same as if these expenditures were subsidized using public funds.

Opportunity cost is critical in understanding the effects of taxation and public expenditure policies. Two aspects of opportunity cost are relevant.

First, reflecting Lesson One, when a transaction is subject to a tax, the buyer and seller face different opportunity costs. In particular, taxes on labor income, the main source of revenue for governments, imply a difference between opportunity costs facing workers and those facing employers.

Second, reflecting Lesson Two, any policy decision leading to a reduction in taxes or an increase in public expenditure must be assessed in terms of opportunity cost, namely the best alternative use that could have been made of the money needed to fund the decision.

The crucial concept here is that of the effective marginal tax rate, to which we now turn.

13.1. The Effective Marginal Tax Rate

Much of the time, discussion of the opportunity cost of redistribution focuses exclusively on taxes and their effects on incentives to work and save. This is a mistake.

To understand the full effects of redistributive policies, it is necessary to examine the interaction between the tax system, tax credits of various kinds, and transfer payments such as Social Security.

Most publicly funded benefits are subject to means testing. Over a certain range of income, the benefit is reduced as income is increased. This reduction is commonly called a "clawback." Out of each dollar of additional income, a taxpayer must not only pay the marginal rate of income tax (including payroll tax) but must also give up the clawback. Adding the clawback rate to the marginal rate of tax on income gives the *effective marginal tax rate*.

The Earned Income Tax Credit (EITC) is the most important example of a clawback. Although it is formally part of the tax system, the EITC is widely regarded as a welfare measure. The EITC provides working families with low to moderate income with a credit that partly or wholly offsets their obligation to pay federal income tax.

Families on moderate incomes typically pay 15 cents of each extra dollar they earn in federal income tax, along with 12.4 cents in Social Security payroll tax. In addition, as their income increases, EITC recipients have their credit reduced by 20 cents for each dollar of additional income. Adding these up, around 47 cents of each additional dollar is returned to the government. This is the effective marginal tax rate. For families in

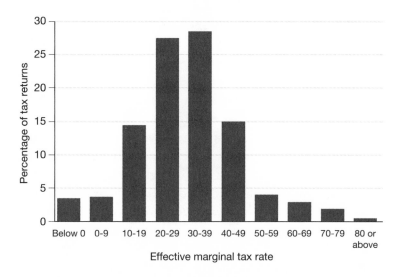

Figure 13.1. The distribution of effective marginal tax rates for low- and middle-income families. Combined effect of federal and state income taxes, payroll taxes, and SNAP benefits. *Source*: Congressional Budget Office (2012).

the Supplemental Nutrition Assistance Program (food stamps), additional clawbacks can push the effective marginal tax rate above 50 percent.

The Congressional Budget Office estimates that the average low- and moderate-income taxpayers in 2014 faced an effective marginal tax rate of 35 percent. However, this average conceals great variation. Single taxpayers without children face substantially lower rates, while families with children face higher rates. The range of variation is illustrated in figure 13.1.

By contrast, high-income earners are not subject to clawbacks and face no additional liability for Social Security taxes on income above $118,500. For these earners, the effective marginal tax rate is just the marginal rate of (federal) income tax, which reaches 37 percent for incomes above $500,000, along with any state income tax. This rate is only marginally different from the average rate for low- and moderate-income earners as a group, and well below the rate faced by low- and moderate-income families receiving means-tested benefits.

When the effective marginal tax rate, rather than the official rate of income tax, is considered, it is evident that the problems associated with high marginal tax rates are most serious for low-income working families, rather than for the high-income earners whose inadequate incentives attract so much concern in public commentary. In reality, most high-income earners have access to various legal devices to reduce income tax so that their effective marginal rate of tax is lower than the rate stated in the official schedule.[1]

The concept of the effective marginal tax rate is naturally expressed in terms of opportunity cost. The effective marginal tax rate represents the difference between the gross wage paid by an employer and the net amount received by a worker for doing a given job. For the employer, the wage represents the opportunity cost of employing the worker. For the employee, the opportunity cost of working must be compared to the net wage after paying the effective marginal tax rate.

There is a potential social gain from trade whenever the value to the employer of the work done by the employee is greater than the opportunity cost of working. However, this social gain may not be realized if the effective marginal tax rate is too high. In this case, there may be no wage lower than the employer's benefit from the job, but high enough, net of the effective marginal tax rate, to offset the worker's opportunity cost.

When the effective marginal tax rate is low (say, below 25 percent), the extent and value of the missed opportunities for

---

[1] A particularly egregious example is the "carried interest" loophole, which reduces the rate of tax paid by hedge fund managers and other financial executives to 20 percent.

beneficial trades is small enough to be disregarded. But as the rate rises, both the range of missed opportunities and the value of those opportunities increase. As a result, the value of the missed opportunities increases in line with the square of the rate. This means that the loss associated with a 50 percent effective marginal tax rate is around four times the loss associated a 25 percent rate.

It is, therefore, desirable to design the tax and transfer system in a way that does not result in very high effective marginal tax rates. This is particularly important for families on low and moderate incomes, who tend to face the highest effective marginal tax rates. Poorly designed tax and transfer systems, with high clawback rates, can generate effective marginal tax rates close to, or sometimes even higher than, 100 percent. Such high rates are often referred to as "poverty traps."

The situation is very different for high-income earners. For high-income earners in the United States, the effective marginal tax rate is the marginal rate of income tax, reduced by concessions and tax avoidance strategies. Moreover, in thinking about forgone opportunities for beneficial trades, the social benefits of additional consumption for high-income earners are small. So, the primary focus must be on the potential loss on the other side of the transaction.

13.2. Opportunity Cost of Redistribution: Example

Any change in the allocation of rights and obligations will create benefits for some people and costs for others. Consider a simple example: an increase of, say, $1 billion, in expenditure on the Supplemental Nutritional Assistance Program (SNAP, which replaced food stamps).

The opportunity cost of such a policy is the offsetting measure needed to finance it. Suppose that the policy is financed by an increase in the top marginal tax rate. How large must the increase be, and how should the opportunity cost be evaluated?

Both collecting taxes and operating unemployment insurance schemes involve administrative costs. Collecting taxes is costly, as is administering unemployment insurance. So, to transfer $1 billion to SNAP recipients, it is necessary to raise more than $1 billion in additional revenue. The resources spent in administration are necessary but yield no social benefit in themselves.

As advocates of One Lesson economics will be quick to point out, that's not all. Reducing tax rates on high-income earners will lead to changes in the opportunity costs that they face. In particular, the opportunity cost of taking additional leisure time, namely the additional expenditure that could be enjoyed with a higher post-tax income, falls as tax rates rise.

This change in opportunity costs, often referred to as an "incentive effect," means that high-income earners will tend to allocate less time to work, and more to leisure, when tax rates are increased. As a result, the additional revenue generated by an increase in tax will be less than might be expected from a simple calculation.

An extreme form of this effect arises with the so-called Laffer curve, which posits a marginal rate of taxation so high that an increase in tax rates will actually reduce tax revenue. As a matter of logic, such a rate must exist; at a tax rate of 100 percent, no one, except workaholics and extreme altruists, would do any paid work. This point has been well understood for centuries. What made Laffer politically important was the "Laffer hypothesis," that currently prevailing tax rates are at or near this level. As we shall see, this is far off the mark. The marginal rate of taxation at which no additional revenue can be realized has been estimated at 70–80 percent (see section 13.4).

Faced with higher rates of income tax, and therefore lower effective returns to earning additional income, high-income earners may choose to work less hard. This will reduce the revenue generated by higher taxes. To assess the full social opportunity cost, it is necessary to consider whether top incomes are an accurate measure of the social contribution of high earners or whether part of those incomes is derived at the expense of others, for example, through financial manipulations or overpayment of top executives. If that is the case, then the social loss from reduced work effort will be less than the reduction in income for high-income earners. There is ample evidence that the increased pay of senior executives over recent decades has not produced a commensurate increase in their economic contribution. Similarly, the discussion in chapter 11 suggests that high incomes derived from financial markets do not reflect an economic contribution.

Another opportunity cost is that the higher the tax rates are, the more effort high-income earners, and their lawyers and accountants, may be expected to put into schemes to avoid or reduce tax liabilities. From the viewpoint of someone paying a tax rate of 40 percent, and not concerned with the ethics of tax avoidance, a scheme that turns a dollar of taxable income into 70 tax-free cents is quite worthwhile. The benefit of 70 cents exceeds the opportunity cost of 60 cents of disposable income. So, we can expect higher marginal tax rates to be associated with some increase in the resources devoted to tax avoidance.

On the other side of the transfer, it is often argued that more generous unemployment benefits reduce the opportunity cost of remaining unemployed, namely the income forgone, and therefore make the unemployed less keen to seek work. The evidence on this point is mixed in the US context, but there is probably at least some effect.

Taking all these points into account, the opportunity cost of a $1 billion reduction in the tax paid by top income earners will be a reduction of less than $1 billion in the net benefits that can be paid to the unemployed. For One Lesson economists, that's sufficient to resolve the issue. Cutting taxes on the rich, and impoverishing the poor even further, will generally increase GDP. But GDP is an aggregate, which tells us nothing about the social opportunity costs and benefits of different allocations of rights and obligations.

To assess the desirability of a redistribution of rights, we need to weigh the benefits to the gainers against the opportunity costs to the losers, in this example, the reduction in net income borne by high-income taxpayers.

One part of this assessment is, at least in principle, straightforward. We need to determine the magnitude of the opportunity cost, that is, the reduction in net income for high-income taxpayers that is needed to finance a given increase in net income for welfare recipients.

The other part of the assessment raises trickier issues. Suppose that the opportunity cost of an additional dollar's worth of food for a poor family is a reduction of two dollars in the net income of some well-off taxpayer. Is society better or worse off for the transfer? What if the cost is five dollars or ten dollars? These are value judgments that must be made through political processes and ultimately reflect social judgments. Nevertheless, a proper understanding of opportunity cost is helpful in clarifying the issues.

13.3. Weighing Opportunity Costs and Benefits

Over the past 40 years or so, changes in the regulation of labor and capital markets and in taxation and expenditure policy have greatly enhanced the income and wealth of the best-off members of society (the so-called 1 percent), and have yielded more modest, but still substantial, improvements in the position of those in the top 20 percent of the income distribution (broadly speaking, professionals and business owners and managers).

On the other hand, incomes for the rest of the community have grown more slowly than might have been expected based on the experience of the decades from 1945 to 1975. The substantial technological advances of recent decades have had little impact on the (inflation-adjusted) income of the median US household. For many below the median, incomes have actually fallen as a result of declining real wages and welfare reform.[2]

In the absence of the tax cuts of the 1980s, and the associated cuts in public expenditure and financial and industrial relations policies that benefited business, the incomes of the wealthy would not have increased as much as they have done. Those on median and lower incomes would have done substantially better.[3] But how should we compare those gains and losses?

Economists and philosophers have been looking at this question for a long time and in many different ways. The answers most consistent with opportunity cost reasoning can be derived from the following "thought experiment," developed explicitly by John Harsanyi and John Rawls in the mid-twentieth century, but implicit in the reasoning of earlier writers like Jeremy Bentham, John Stuart Mill, and Friedrich von Wieser.

First, consider yourself in the position of both the high-income beneficiary and the low-income loser from such a change. Next, imagine that you are setting rules for a society, of

---

[2] The term "reform" is commonly used with the sense of "change for the better." However, from a liberal or social democratic perspective, most of the policy changes sold as reform over the past 40 years have been for the worse. At this point, it seems best to use the term neutrally and let readers make their own judgments.

[3] The claim that tax cuts for the rich will ultimately "trickle down" to make everyone better off is discussed at greater length as one of the "zombie ideas" in my book *Zombie Economics*.

which you will be a member, without knowing which of these positions you might be in. One way to think of this is to imagine life as a lottery in which your life chances are determined by the ticket you draw.

Now consider a choice between increasing the income of the better-off and the worse-off person. Presumably, if the dollar increase were the same in both cases, you would prefer to receive it in the case where you are poor rather than in the case where you are rich.

The reasons for this preference are obvious enough. For a very poor person, an additional $100 could mean the difference between eating and not eating. For someone slightly better off, it may mean the difference between paying the rent and being evicted. For a middle-class family, it might allow an unexpected luxury purchase. For someone earning $1 million a year, it would barely be noticed.

Economists typically present this point in terms of the concept of marginal utility, a technical term for the benefits that are gained from additional income or consumption. As argued above, the marginal utility of additional income decreases as income rises. It follows that a policy that increases the income of the rich and decreases that of the poor by an equal amount will reduce the utility of the poor more than it increases the utility of the rich.

Few mainstream economists would reject this analysis outright.[4] However, many prefer to duck the issue, relying on a distinction between "positive" economics, concerned with factual predictions of the outcomes of particular economic policies, and "normative" economics, concerned with "value judgments"

---

[4] The most notable exceptions, somewhat outside the mainstream, are members of the "Austrian School," who have dismissed interpersonal comparisons as "unscientific" and offered a variety of more or less spurious justifications for inequality. As discussed in section 1.5, von Wieser, the originator of the opportunity cost analysis, was an exception to this exception.

like the one discussed above. The debate over the justifiability or otherwise of this distinction has been going on for decades and is unlikely to be resolved any time soon.

More important, constructs derived from economics are often used, implicitly or explicitly, in ways that imply that an additional dollar of income should be regarded as equally valuable, no matter to whom it accrues.

The most important of these constructs is gross domestic product (GDP), the aggregate value of all production in the economy. GDP per person is the ordinary average (or arithmetic mean) income of the community. GDP per person treats additive changes in income equally no matter who receives them. There are many reasons why this is inappropriate, but the failure to take account of the distribution of income is most important.

For anyone who values a more equal society, an increase in the income of a poor person at the opportunity cost of an equal reduction in the income of a better-off person is a change for the better. Yet this redistribution leaves GDP unchanged.

What about the case when the choice is between a given increase for the poor person at the opportunity cost of a larger reduction in the income of the rich person, and therefore a net reduction in GDP. How large must the benefit to the better-off person be before it outweighs the opportunity cost (the forgone opportunity to improve the position of the worse-off person)? This question, raising once again the thought experiment mentioned above, can be answered in many different ways.

One answer, which seems close to the views typically elicited when people are asked questions of this kind, is to treat equal proportional increases in income as being equally desirable. That is, an increase of $1,000 in the income of a person on $10,000 a year (10 percent) is seen as yielding a benefit comparable to that of an increase of $10,000 in the income of a person earning $100,000 a year (also 10 percent). Conversely, if the opportunity cost of the $10,000 benefit to the high-income earner is a loss to the low-income earner of more than $1,000, the cost exceeds the benefit.

The idea that equal proportional increases are equally valuable, and therefore that the geometric mean is a good measure of economic welfare or well-being, is not the only answer to the question posed above. Another, leading to a strong version of egalitarianism, is always to prefer the increase to the worse-off person.[5] In this case, welfare is measured by the minimum income.

There's no way of reaching a final resolution on questions like this. But it's worth observing that a policy aimed at maximizing the geometric mean of income would be substantially more egalitarian than anything that has ever been seen in a market economy.

It's not surprising that political outcomes are less egalitarian than an opportunity cost estimate would suggest. The thought experiment leading to the geometric mean gives everyone equal weight, as in an ideal democracy. In practice, however, the well-off have more weight in democratic systems than do the poor; and the disparity is even greater in undemocratic and partly democratic systems. While there are good arguments for more strongly egalitarian approaches, policies aimed at maximizing geometric mean income will inevitably be found well to the left of center in any feasible political system.

13.4. How Much Should the Top 1 Percent Be Taxed?

Discussions of the opportunity costs associated with choices about income distribution and redistribution have long been hampered by the absence of adequate information, leading to

---

[5] The "difference principle" espoused by philosopher John Rawls is often interpreted to imply this view. However, scholars of Rawls's work disagree on this, and much more.

a situation where much of the debate consists of assertion and counter-assertion. In particular, until recently, hardly anything was known about the income of the very wealthy (those in the top 1 percent, and even the top 0.1 percent) who receive an outsize share of total income and hold an even larger share of total wealth.

Over the past 15 years, this situation has been largely remedied thanks to the work of a group of scholars including Thomas Piketty and Emmanuel Saez (working largely on US and French data) as well as Tony Atkinson and Andrew Leigh (working on UK and Australian data). This work reached the attention of the broader public through Piketty's best-selling book *Capital in the Twenty-First Century*.

On the issue of opportunity cost, one of the most illuminating products of this research program is a paper by Piketty, Saez, and Stefanie Stantcheva, which examines the responses to changes in top marginal tax rates. An increase in top marginal tax rates yields revenue that may be transferred to lower income earners or used to fund public expenditure.

The most obvious opportunity cost is the reduced income of those who pay the extra tax. However, as was argued in section 13.3, in a society with highly unequal incomes, and with moderately egalitarian attitudes, this opportunity cost will be negligibly small; we are trading off increases in luxury expenditures against the capacity to meet basic needs.

As was discussed in section 13.2, there are other opportunity costs that need more attention, most notably "work disincentive" effects and incentives for tax avoidance and evasion. The work of Piketty, Saez, and Stantcheva demonstrates that these opportunity costs are much smaller than has been claimed by advocates of lower and less progressive taxation.

As regards the supposed work incentive, they find no evidence of a correlation between growth in real GDP per capita and the drop in the top marginal tax rate in the period 1960 to the present. Rather, the evidence is consistent with a model whereby gains at the top come at the expense of lower income earners. The lower the tax rate, the stronger the incentive for senior executives and financial firms to change the rules under which corporations operate in order to extract more income for themselves at the expense of everyone else.

The results on tax avoidance are also striking, in terms of economic theory at least. Far from being a response to high tax rates, tax avoidance has increased massively since the 1970s, even as the top rates of income tax declined sharply.

With the release of troves of documents like the Panama Papers, not available at the time the book was written, this conclusion is virtually self-evident. Tax avoidance is driven primarily by the ease with which it can be undertaken in a globalized financial system, and not by the incentive effects of tax rates.

The conclusion of Piketty, Saez, and Stantcheva is that top tax rates of 80 percent or more would provide the best match between social benefits and opportunity costs. Such a rate could apply to the top 1 percent of incomes (those in excess of $360,000 a year) earned mainly by business owners, senior managers, and finance professionals. These rates might seem unthinkable in the light of recent experience. However, as was shown in section 13.1, many low-income earners face effective marginal tax rates as high as this.

Very high top marginal tax rates prevailed during the post–World War II era of widely shared prosperity known as the Great Compression. While these high rates were offset to some extent by generous concessions and loopholes, there is no doubt that the tax system was substantially more progressive then than it is today. Yet economic growth remained strong for decades, and large-scale unemployment was non-existent. There is, therefore, no reason to suppose that an increase in top marginal tax rates would lead to economic stagnation.

13.5. Policies for the Present and the Future

The aim of this book is not to set out a policy program but to show how the Two Lessons of economics may be used to think about policy. Nevertheless, it might be beneficial to summarize the ideas raised in this chapter and suggest some implications for current and future policy.

From the perspective of someone who accepts the general egalitarian position that the benefits of transfers from the rich to the poor are substantially greater than the opportunity costs, a policy program for predistribution and redistribution might be outlined as follows:

- Reverse anti-union policies, increase minimum wage shares, and seek to increase the wage share of national income.
- Limit corporate monopoly power, particularly power based on intellectual property.
- Change corporate bankruptcy laws to make it harder for corporations to avoid their obligations to workers and suppliers.
- (Re)introduce a progressive tax-welfare system in which high-income earners face the highest effective marginal tax rates. This implies increasing top marginal rates of taxation and reducing the severity of "clawbacks" in the welfare system.

These policies would largely involve the reversal of changes made since the 1970s under the influence of One Lesson economics.

As the failures of One Lesson economics have become more evident in recent years, attention has turned to more radical alternatives, notably including the idea of a Universal Basic Income or Guaranteed Minimum Income. These are beyond the scope of this book, but, as I have argued, the concepts of opportunity cost and the effective marginal tax rate are crucial in understanding them.

13.6. Geometric Mean

We've looked above at the idea that a given proportional increase in income is equally desirable, at whatever income level its recipient may be. It's surprisingly easy to turn this way of looking at things into a measure of living standards over time. If we want a measure that treats proportional changes equally, all that is needed is to replace arithmetic mean measures such as income per person with the geometric mean we all learned about in high school (and most of us promptly forgot).

The geometric mean has the property that, if all incomes increase by the same proportion, so does the geometric mean. This indicates that it's a better measure of the growth rate of incomes across the community than the usual arithmetic mean. It can also be justified mathematically, in terms of the theory of expected utility.

The more unequal the income distribution is, the greater the gap between the arithmetic and geometric means. For this reason, the ratio of the arithmetic to the geometric mean is often used as a measure of income inequality.

We can look at the changes in these measures using data from the US Census Office and some simple computations (details available on request). From 1967 to 2013, arithmetic mean income per household (in 2013 dollars) rose from $66,500 to $104,000, an increase of 56 percent. But the geometric mean rose by only 34 percent, from $50,000 to $67,500. The ratio between the two rose from 1.32 to 1.54, indicating a substantial increase in inequality.

Further Reading

The Tax Policy Center (2018) provides useful information on the US tax system. Bakija, Cole, and Heim (2012) show that growth in top incomes has mostly gone to executives, managers, supervisors, and financial professionals. Other references are Western and Rosenfeld (2011); Congressional Budget Office (2012); Piketty and Saez (2003, 2006); Piketty (2014); Piketty, Saez, and Stantcheva (2014); and Stewart (2017).

CHAPTER 14

◾

Policy for Full Employment

The Congress hereby declares that it is the continuing policy and responsibility of the federal government to . . . [foster] conditions under which there will be afforded useful employment for those able, willing, and seeking work, and to promote maximum employment, production, and purchasing power.

—"Declaration of Policy," Employment Act of 1946

The Employment Act of 1946 was the product of the bitter experience of the previous three decades. In the United States, and throughout the developed world, the Great War that ended in 1918 was followed by a lengthy economic slump. The US economy recovered in the "Roaring Twenties" only to fall into an even deeper slump in the Great Depression, which began with the stock market crash of 1929. The orthodox response of "austerity," raising tax rates and cutting public expenditure, only made matters worse. It was not until the introduction of the New Deal by President Franklin D. Roosevelt that the economy recovered, and then only partially.

Yet once demand was stimulated by the outbreak of World War II, unemployment virtually disappeared. The contrast between the Depression and the War made brutally clear the opportunity cost of leaving 15 million workers idle rather than defying the orthodoxy of One Lesson economics.

The global consequences of the Great Depression were even more severe than those in the United States. In Germany, the failure of austerity policies adopted by the conservative Brüning administration led directly to the rise of Hitler. A similar pattern played out in Japan.

After World War II, the victorious allies were determined never to repeat such a disaster. A commitment to full employment, backed up by Keynesian macroeconomic policies, was the product of that determination.[1]

As we saw in chapter 8, recessions and depressions are a crucial example of Lesson Two, where market prices (in this case, wages) do not match opportunity costs. In this chapter we will examine what governments can do to respond to the problem of unemployment.

14.1. What Can Governments Do about Recessions?

If governments are interested in making markets work properly to set prices equal to opportunity costs, in the way Lesson One requires, they should seek to ensure that the economy is as close to full employment as possible.

The crucial point is that, under conditions of high unemployment, the wage received by a newly employed worker is not a measure of the opportunity cost of their labor; the opportunity cost is the time they would otherwise have spent in idleness.

---

[1] The commitment was never complete. The Employment Act was the product of a compromise in which an unconditional commitment to full employment, stated in early drafts, was watered down to an aspirational goal. Nevertheless, the change in attitudes represented by the Act was crucial and helped to sustain near-full employment for decades.

Unfortunately, the key policies required to achieve this goal run counter to intuitions that are derived from our experience in managing household budgets and are reflected in Lesson One. When money is short, the natural response of a household is to "tighten its belt" and forgo unnecessary expenditure, while trying to get as much work as possible to bring in extra income.

This is possible for a household, but it isn't possible for a country as a whole. Since what is produced must be consumed or invested, we can't collectively earn extra income by producing more, while also consuming and investing less.[2]

The opportunity cost of resources, including labor resources, is lower during recessions than under normal conditions, and far lower than under boom conditions. It therefore makes sense for governments to spend money and hire workers during recessions and finance that expenditure by taxes raised during booms.

That in turn entails running deficits during recessions and surpluses during booms in a way that balances out over the course of the economic cycle.[3] It also makes sense to encourage private consumption and investment through temporary tax cuts and lower interest rates.

14.2. Fiscal Policy

The simplest thing governments can do to respond to the existence of unemployed workers and resources is to employ them, by increasing public expenditure. In economic jargon, this is referred

[2] The story is a bit more complicated in an "open economy" where a substantial portion of production is exported and some consumption is derived from imports. But increasing net exports rapidly is quite difficult. This issue is unfortunately beyond the scope of this book.

[3] In a growing economy, the government can run small deficits on average while maintaining a stable ratio of debt to GDP. But "balance over the cycle" is a simpler description that captures the essence of the Keynesian policy prescription.

as countercyclical fiscal policy. "Fiscal policy" is a general term referring to the management of public expenditure and revenue. The term "countercyclical" means that governments "lean against the wind" of the business cycle, by spending more when economic activity is weak. Governments can also encourage private expenditure by offering temporary tax cuts or cash payments.

The case for countercyclical fiscal policy is simple. Since the opportunity cost of productive resources is lower during recessions, governments should seek to increase their use of resources during recessions relative to periods where resources are fully employed, or nearly so.

A countercyclical fiscal policy involves increasing expenditure during recessions, thereby creating budget deficits. During booms, these policies should be reversed, producing surpluses. Over the course of the cycle, these surpluses and balances should balance out in such a way as to maintain a stable ratio of public debt to national income.

The theory of countercyclical fiscal policy was first developed by the great British economist John Maynard Keynes, who published his *General Theory of Employment, Interest and Money* in 1936. Before the development of this theoretical basis, and after the failure of other approaches such as the National Industrial Recovery Act, Franklin D. Roosevelt's New Deal embodied the basic logic of Keynesianism.

The most successful application of countercyclical fiscal policy took place in the immediate aftermath of the Global Financial Crisis. National governments, including that of the Obama administration in the United States, adopted countercyclical fiscal policies, which helped to stop the decline in output and employment, and to stabilize the economy, but at a lower level than before the crisis. However, there was a rapid return to austerity from late 2009 onward. The result was a painfully slow recovery in the United States and renewed recession in many European countries.

14.2.1. Fiscal Policy and the Multiplier

It's difficult to get an intuitive sense about the numbers involved in fiscal policy, but it may be worth a try. The key idea is that of the "multiplier."

As Keynes pointed out, the effects of spending on, say, a public works project did not stop with the project itself. The newly hired workers would spend most of their wages, and this would create additional demand, leading to more hiring, and so on.

Some simple algebra can be used to turn this verbal argument into a number. Suppose that some proportion c of each dollar of initial spending is itself spent on domestically produced goods and services. For illustration, $c = 0.5$, so that half the initial amount is spent again. If the same proportion holds for the second round, then a proportion c^2 of the initial amount will be spent in the third round (in the illustrative example, $c^2 = 0.25$). This is a geometric series and high school algebra shows that the sum eventually approaches $1/(1 - c)$. In the example given here, $1/(1 - 0.5) = 1/0.5 = 2$. This final effect is called the multiplier, or to spell out the initial source, the public expenditure multiplier.

Having worked out the multiplier, it is important to remember the original assumption that all additional production is generated by hiring unemployed workers and resources, rather than by diverting them from the production of other goods and services. That is, there is no opportunity cost, except for the alternative use the workers might have made of their time. Generally speaking, unemployed workers place little if any value on their extra free time (many would be glad to have work for its own sake). This implies that the opportunity cost of the extra resources used is close to zero.

The original analysis of the multiplier was developed in the depths of the Great Depression, when the opportunity cost of putting unemployed workers and resources to work was close to zero. Any addition to demand could be met by hiring the unemployed rather than by diverting workers and resources from other activities.

The situation is very different if the economy is in a position of full employment. In this case, additional production of goods and services is feasible only if resources are drawn away from other productive activities or if workers are induced to work longer hours, giving up leisure time or household work to do so. In this case, the opportunity cost of additional production may be as great or greater than the contribution made by the initial public expenditure. The second-round effects of additional public expenditure and reduced production elsewhere will cancel out, leaving no further multiplier effect.

The relationship between the multiplier and opportunity cost may be expressed in numerical form depending on the range in which the value of the multiplier falls at any given time: greater than 1, between 0 and 1, and 0 or less.

In deep recessions, the multiplier is commonly greater than 1. This means that the opportunity cost of additional spending is negative. Not only does society benefit from the project itself, but the addition to demand generates still more employment and greater benefits. In recessions, public projects can be beneficial even if they would not be undertaken at a time of full employment. Not only are additional workers employed, but their demand for goods and services will stimulate additional production, mostly in the private sector of the economy.

In moderate recessions, the multiplier is likely to be between 0 and 1. Some of the workers and resources employed by public expenditure projects will have been previously unemployed, but some will be diverted from private sector production. This "crowding out" effect forms the basis of standard arguments against Keynesian fiscal policy.

But unless crowding out is complete (the multiplier is zero), the social opportunity cost of public expenditure will be less than the monetary cost of the additional public expenditure. Provided that the social value of the additional expenditure is at least equal to the monetary cost, there will be a net benefit. Even if the social value is less than the monetary cost, it may still exceed the social opportunity cost because some of the resources used were previously unemployed.

In the ideal case of competitive equilibrium, implicit in the parable of the broken window, the multiplier is exactly zero. In competitive equilibrium, an increase in the production of one good can only come at an equal opportunity cost. An increase in public provision of goods and services will crowd out private production and consumption of equal market value.

This means that the social opportunity cost of public expenditure is equal to the monetary cost to the budget. Under these circumstances, the standard rules of benefit-cost analysis apply.

Finally, under boom conditions the multiplier is less than zero. In a boom, typically involving inflation, there is more demand for goods and services of all kinds than the market can supply. So, workers are employed and capital used even when the additional product they generate has less social value than the opportunity cost of workers' time and the depreciation of capital.

Under boom conditions, increased government expenditure will not only divert resources from private sector production but will also increase aggregate demand, which is already excessive.

It was precisely for this reason that Keynes wrote, in 1937, "the boom, not the slump is the time for austerity at the Treasury."

Booms are less common than recessions and are enjoyable while they last. However, the financial bubbles created by booms often burst, leading to recessions that are longer and deeper than usual. Moreover, using monetary policy (higher interest rates) as a response to financial bubbles carries a risk of causing the bust it is aimed at preventing. Because of this, the use of fiscal policy to tamp down excessive booms by reducing excess demand is an important part of macroeconomic stabilization.

14.2.2. Automatic Stabilizers

To some extent, countercyclical fiscal policy happens without the need for a specific policy decision. When the economy slows down, tax revenue declines automatically while some kinds of expenditure, such as unemployment insurance payments, rise.

The decline in tax revenue is most marked for company income tax and for personal income taxes with a progressive tax scale. Company profits generally rise and fall more sharply over the business cycle than does national income as a whole, with the result that company income tax revenue also falls sharply during a recession.

In a progressive income tax system, the average rate of tax paid is lower than the marginal rate, since only part of a tax-payer's income is taxed at the marginal rate associated with their tax bracket while the rest is taxed at lower rates. It follows that when income falls, say by 10 percent, the percentage reduction in tax payments is greater.

For these reasons, when the economy declines, tax revenue declines at a faster rate. In effect, a system in which company income tax and a progressive personal income tax are important revenue sources provides an automatic stabilizer.

Unemployment insurance is another form of automatic stabilizer. Workers who lose their jobs receive payments from the unemployment insurance fund. In the United States, the duration of these payments is normally limited to 26 weeks, which provides a period of automatic stabilization. It is usual in recessions for the US Congress to extend the period of eligibility. In the wake of the Global Financial Crisis, eligibility was extended to

99 weeks, nearly two years. However, the extension was wound back well before the labor market recovered from the crisis.

The existence of automatic stabilizers in the second half of the twentieth century helped to ensure that recessions such as those of the 1970s and 1980s did not turn into depressions.

In the twenty-first century, however, a failure to understand opportunity cost has led to the replacement of automatic stabilizers in fiscal policy with what might be called "automatic destabilizers." The most extreme form of automatic destabilizer is a requirement for government budgets to balance on an annual basis.

More generally, policies of austerity such as those pursued in the European Union have had predictably disastrous results. In Italy, for example, aggregate output in 2018 was barely above the level in the year 2000. Unsurprisingly, the failure of macroeconomic management has opened the way for politicians seeking to blame economic woes on immigrants and to populist advocates of "anti-politics."

14.2.3. Fine Tuning

A problem with countercyclical fiscal policy as a means of stabilizing the economy is that it takes time to plan and implement. Milton Friedman, the most prominent critic of fiscal policy in its heyday, made a major point of the "long and variable lags" involved in the use of fiscal policy.

Friedman's point only applied to "discretionary" fiscal policy, arising from government decisions to increase public spending or to cut taxes in response to evidence of a slowdown in economic activity. It is not applicable to the automatic stabilizers discussed in section 14.2.2.

Friedman's critique of discretionary fiscal policy was particularly sharp when directed at the idea, prevalent in the optimistic decade of the 1960s, that Keynesian fiscal policy could be used to "fine tune" the economy, eliminating even "growth recessions," that is, modest slowdowns in economic growth lasting for six months to a year. It is less relevant in the circumstances prevailing at present in much of the world, where stagnation has gone on for years.

14.3. Monetary Policy

Like fiscal policy, monetary policy is a response to the fact that the opportunity cost of expenditure is lower during recessions than during normal conditions or booms. As we saw in chapter 3, the rate of interest determines the opportunity cost of current consumption in terms of future consumption. The central idea of monetary policy is to reduce interest rates during recessions and increase rates during booms.

A reduction in interest rates makes investments of all kinds, financed by borrowing, more attractive. The opportunity cost of the capital required to make the investment is the principal and interest that must be repaid in the future. The investment is profitable if its returns are greater than this opportunity cost. The lower the interest rate, the lower the opportunity cost.

Central banks like the US Federal Reserve do not set the interest rates levied on households and businesses, at least not directly. Rather, the Fed sets an interest rate at which it is willing to lend to banks (the Federal Funds rate). Changes in this rate are reflected, sometimes wholly and sometimes in part, through the structure of rates charged by banks to borrowers and paid to savers.

The period from the early 1990s to the Global Financial Crisis of 2008 was one of exclusive, and seemingly successful, reliance on monetary policy. Small adjustments in interest rates, usually shifts of 0.25 percentage points, were sufficient to maintain steady rates of growth. The only recession in this period, which took place in 2000, following the bursting of a stock market bubble, was brief and mild by historical standards.

The result was a bubble of complacency centered around the term the "Great Moderation." This bubble burst, along with others, when the Global Financial Crisis brought the economy to the edge of meltdown in 2008. Although total disaster was avoided, expansionary monetary policy proved unable to stimulate a return to normal economic conditions. Even a decade later, the US economy remains well below its previous growth path, and other developed countries are even worse.

14.3.1. The Zero Lower Bound

A critical problem for monetary policy is that bank interest rates can't be reduced below zero, or at least not much below zero. People always have the alternative option of holding money in cash.[4] They may be willing to accept a small negative interest rate in return for the convenience of keeping money in the bank rather than carrying it around or hiding it under the mattress. But if the opportunity cost of putting money in the bank at a negative rate of interest is the zero rate of return on cash, plus the cost of safe storage, people will soon start holding large amounts of cash.

Unfortunately, zero interest rates are most likely to be a problem during deep recessions, precisely the time at which expansionary macroeconomic policy is most needed.

The zero lower bound is one of many reasons why monetary policy is an inadequate tool for macroeconomic management. It

---

[4] There have been numerous proposals to get around this problem by making money depreciate in value over time. Some recent suggestions are from Miles Kimball.

can work well to smooth out relatively minor fluctuations in the economy but fails when it is most needed.

When the use of interest rates as an instrument of monetary policy is constrained by the zero lower bound, as it has been ever since the Global Financial Crisis, the remaining options are limited. The most popular has been "quantitative easing," that is, the large-scale purchase of government bonds or other assets by central banks, using newly created money. This is an important topic, but beyond the scope of this book.

14.4. Labor Market Programs and the Job Guarantee

The central idea of fiscal and monetary policy is to maintain the aggregate demand for goods and services at a level where resources including workers are fully employed, that is, to the point where the opportunity cost of increased economic output would exceed the benefits. At this point, at least in aggregate, the conditions for Lesson One are satisfied.

Another approach to the problem of unemployment created by recessions is to focus directly on putting unemployed workers into jobs created specifically for that purpose. The Works Progress Administration, the New Deal program that employed millions of workers on a wide range of projects, is the classic example.

Job creation programs have a mixed record. Two common characteristics of job creation programs tend to undermine their effectiveness. The first is a punitive approach to the participants, commonly found in "workfare" programs where the payment is designed to replace welfare benefits. In these programs, the main focus is on ensuring that the required hours are worked rather than on generating a socially valuable output or preparing participants for entry into the general labor market.

The other problem arises when the choice of projects is constrained by a concern not to compete with private firms or with the standard activities of governments. The basis for this concern is the possibility of "churning" that arises if the goods and services produced by job creation projects displace existing production and lead to the loss of existing jobs. However, under conditions of deep recessions, such concerns are misplaced. As was discussed in relation to the multiplier, job creation in deep recessions will provide a stimulus to demand and therefore improve the position of existing producers.

The ideal job creation program would be one that created sufficient work such that anyone willing and able to work could do so. This type of goal has been put forward many times, and has recently been popularized under the name Job Guarantee.[5] A central part of the case for such a guarantee is that the pool of workers employed under the guarantee constitutes an "automatic stabilizer" of the kind discussed in section 14.2.

14.4.1. Alternatives to Job Creation

Wage subsidies may also be understood as a response to the gap between wages and social opportunity costs that characterizes a recession. Wage subsidies work best in the early stages of a recovery, when employers are increasing output, but are reluctant to hire new workers until the recovery shows itself to be sustained.

Under normal economic conditions, when employers are hiring in any case, much of the subsidy will be ineffectual, providing a bonus to employers who were going to fill a vacancy anyway. This problem is referred to as (the absence of) "additionality."

---

[5] I advocated a Job Guarantee in my 1994 book, *Work for All* with John Langmore. More recently I've argued for a Job Guarantee as a complement for a Universal Basic Income.

In a deep recession, on the other hand, employers who take advantage of a wage subsidy may lay off existing workers and use the newly hired subsidized workers as substitutes. This problem is referred to as "churning."

Another labor market policy commonly adopted in response to recessions is reliance on training programs. The idea, which makes sense in terms of Lesson One, is that increased skills will raise the productive capacity of workers and therefore the opportunity cost of leaving them unemployed.

In general terms, increased training and education does raise productive capacity and in the long run this is reflected in higher wages. Considered as a response to recessions, however, the advocacy of more training is a misunderstanding. It's true that, under all economic circumstances, better educated workers are more likely to be employed, and less likely to lose jobs when they have them, than less educated workers. But this does not mean that more education and training will reduce unemployment substantially. Average levels of education have risen greatly over the past two centuries, but the rate of unemployment has fluctuated over the business cycle, with no clear trend. Large-scale unemployment does not result from the lack of skills on the part of workers, but from recessions, that is, from failures of the market to match wages with opportunity costs. Lesson Two, not Lesson One, is what matters here.

14.5. One Lesson Economics and Unemployment

Economists like to think of their subject as a science, which, like the natural sciences, advances over time with theoretical improvements. Yet in relation to the mass unemployment associated with the business cycle, One Lesson economics has gone backward over time. This can be seen by comparing Bastiat to

Hazlitt and then to today's leading One Lesson economists, the advocates of "Real Business Cycle theory."

Bastiat was relatively pragmatic on the issue. He qualified his general objection to "job creation" as an objective of public policy, allowing that it might be desirable during depressions:

> As a temporary measure, on any emergency, during a hard winter, this interference [job creation] with the taxpayers may have its use. It acts in the same way as insurance. It adds nothing either to labor or to wages, but it takes labor and wages from ordinary times to give them, at a loss it is true, to times of difficulty.

This isn't quite right. Bastiat does not spell out how it is that the labor and wages added in times of difficulty are offset by a greater loss in ordinary times.

Clearly, Bastiat's intuition is based on Lesson One. He assumes that extra work must always have an opportunity cost and, since there is no such cost in periods of high unemployment (such as a hard winter in which demand for agricultural laborers is low), the cost must arise in normal times. But the opportunity cost of unemployment is the alternative use unemployed workers make of their time, much of which is spent in idleness and depression. Nevertheless, Bastiat is right on the broader point that, like insurance, macroeconomic stabilization reduces the risk faced by workers.

Now let's look at Hazlitt. His *Economics in One Lesson* was published in 1946, just after the end of World War II, and after Keynes's General Theory had begun to influence the US economics profession. In addition, he was writing not long after the Great Depression, by far the deepest in US history. It is natural to ask how this changed his analysis, compared to that offered by Bastiat nearly 100 years previously. The answer, unfortunately, is "hardly at all."

If Hazlitt was aware of this contrast, his book gives no indication of it. In fact, his only explicit allusion to the Great Depression refers to the "depression of 1932," which he mentions in the context of theories blaming unemployment on technology.[6] Hazlitt's discussion of the great macroeconomic problems of unemployment and cyclical booms and busts is both vague and unconvincing. This is Hazlitt's theoretical account of depressions, in its entirety.

> The real causes [of any existing depression] most of the time, are maladjustments within the wage-cost-price structure: maladjustments between wages and prices, between prices of raw materials and prices of finished goods, or between one price and another or one wage and another. At some point these maladjustments have removed the incentive to produce, or have made it actually impossible for production to continue; and through the organic interdependence of our exchange economy, depression spreads. Not until these maladjustments are corrected can full production and employment be resumed.

The inadequacy of such an account of depressions was obvious long before Hazlitt wrote. Even his Austrian School mentors, Hayek and Mises, had a more sophisticated analysis, based on the idea of an over-accumulation of capital investments driven by problems in credit markets.

The maladjustment of relative prices referred to by Hazlitt implies that some prices are higher than the true opportunity

---

[6] Hazlitt mentions this in the context of the short-lived but impressive popularity of the Technocracy movement, which proposed to solve all economic problems by handing them over to engineers. The movement reached its peak of popularity in 1932. However, the Great Depression began with the stock market crash of 1929 and did not properly end until 1939, when preparations for war drove a rapid return to full employment.

cost of the good or service involved, and others are lower. The logic of opportunity costs, discussed above, explains how markets will respond to such a situation.

Where prices exceed opportunity costs, producers will be keen to supply the good or service in question, but they may find no buyers. Conversely, however, there will be unmet demand for those goods and services for which the price is less than the true opportunity cost.

In a recession or depression, however, there are few or no areas of excess demand, contradicting Hazlitt's explanation. Rather than adjusting in relative terms, prices undergo a general decline, referred to as deflation. Moreover, depressions frequently spread from one country to another, which cannot happen if the cause is to be found in market maladjustments triggered by factors operating at the national level, such as unions or minimum-wage laws.

One Lesson macroeconomics was largely discredited by the contrast between the prosperity of the postwar period, in which generally Keynesian policies were pursued, and the misery of the Depression years. However, in the aftermath of the economic crises that began in the late 1960s, One Lesson macroeconomics re-emerged under the name Real Business Cycle (RBC) theory. Despite its impressive theoretical sophistication, RBC theory was even less realistic than the Austrian theories espoused by Hazlitt, and a major step backward from the "insurance" position put forward by Bastiat.[7]

---

[7] Recognized by the award of the 2004 Nobel Memorial Prize to the leading RBC theorists Finn Kydland and Edward Prescott. A few years later, the Prize was awarded to one of their sharpest critics, Paul Krugman. The fact that the Prize can be awarded to people saying exactly opposite things shows that economics is more like literature (no one expects writers to agree among themselves) than like physics (where disagreements are resolved, sooner or later, by evidence, and only discoveries that have been confirmed by the evidence are likely to win the Prize).

The central claim of RBC theory is that there is no divergence between market prices (including wages) and opportunity costs, even in a recession. This means that any attempt by government to reduce unemployment in a recession can only make matters worse.

The simplest version of the theory is that business cycles are caused by technological "shocks" which change the opportunity cost of labor and other resources. Favorable technological shocks arise from new discoveries that generate more opportunities for productive activity. This leads to higher demand for labor and stronger wage growth. The opportunity cost of time spent away from work increases, and employment rises.

Unfavorable shocks arise when technology stagnates and there are fewer new opportunities. In this case, the opportunity cost of time spent away from work falls, and so does employment, at least relative to a long-run trend.

The problem with this idea is that unless technology actually regresses, it can't explain serious recessions in which aggregate production, conventionally measured by GDP, actually falls.

RBC theorists responded by looking at the other side of the relationship between opportunity costs and wages. The idea was that changes in workers' preference for leisure could increase or reduce the opportunity cost of time spent working. That sounds plausible at first blush, but this plausibility collapses once we consider the implications.

At the worst points of the Great Depression, 25 percent of workers were unemployed. Paul Krugman mocked RBC economists for the suggestion that this could be explained by a change in preferences, suggesting they might prefer the name "Great Vacation."

The Global Financial Crisis, which was obviously not caused by technology or a desire for leisure, pushed RBC economists into further contortions. Even though the crisis was obviously generated within the system, RBC advocates suggested that it should be treated as a technological shock, thereby ruling it out as a refutation of their theory.

In the words of the great philosopher of science Imre Lakatos, moves like this, which make a theory impossible to refute, are a sign of a "degenerating research program." Indeed, it's now clear that many of them don't really believe their own theory any more. The years since the crisis have seen an intellectual collapse among One Lesson economists in the United States.

14.6. Summary

In market economics, paid work is a necessity to maintain more than a basic standard of living for most people. Unemployment is therefore one of the most important ways in which markets regularly fail to match prices and opportunity costs.

The experience of the twentieth century shows that, with a combination of political will and sound economic policy, unemployment can be reduced to minimal levels over long periods. The experience of the twenty-first century shows the converse. The failure to understand opportunity cost represented by policies of austerity leads to economic, and ultimately to political, disaster.

Further Reading

Steelman (2013) gives background on the Employment Act of 1946. The disastrous impact of austerity in Germany and Japan is documented by Blyth (2012).

Thanks to Crooked Timber commenter Tim Wilkinson for tracking down the Keynes (1937) quote on austerity.

The idea of the multiplier was first developed by Kahn (1931) and developed further by Keynes (1936). It was popularized by Samuelson's (1948) text, which has appeared in 19 subsequent editions and remains, arguably, the most useful introduction to economics from a Keynesian perspective.

Arguments for an explicit full employment policy are presented by Langmore and Quiggin (1994), Mitchell (1998), and Mosler (1997).

A useful discussion of the failure of One Lesson macroeconomics is Krugman (2009). For the idea of a degenerating research program, see Lakatos (1970). The Technocracy movement is described by Wikipedia: https://en.wikipedia.org/wiki/Technocracy_movement.

CHAPTER 15

∎

Monopoly and the Mixed Economy

> Before the monopoly should be permitted, there must be reason to believe it will do some good—for society, and not just for monopoly holders.
> —Lawrence Lessig, *The Future of Ideas: The Fate of the Commons in a Connected World*

Two hundred years after the birth of Karl Marx, and 50 years after the last upsurge of revolutionary ferment in 1968, terms like "monopoly capitalism" sound quaint and antiquated. In reality, however, the problems of monopoly and associated market failures such as oligopoly and monopsony have never been more significant.

The idea of market failure comes directly from the theory of general equilibrium described in Lesson One. Under the ideal conditions of competitive general equilibrium, market prices for all goods and services would reflect their opportunity cost for society as a whole. But not all markets are competitive. In many sectors of the economy, individual firms have substantial power over the prices they charge and the wages they pay.

One Lesson economists have tried to argue that, in a modern globalized economy, problems of market power are less significant than they once were. In fact, the opposite is the case.

In the twentieth century, the market power of large firms was offset, to a large extent, by the "countervailing power" of trade unions and governments. As unions have declined, and governments have increasingly followed the dictates of financial markets, that countervailing power has dissipated. Meanwhile, as we have seen, the attempt to control monopoly power through antitrust policy has largely been abandoned.

In this chapter, we will consider possible responses to monopoly power, including a revival of antitrust policy and the expansion of public enterprise.

15.1. Monopoly and Monopsony

A crucial requirement of Lesson One is that prices are determined in competitive markets. But free markets are not necessarily competitive. If the technology of production involves economies of scale, as is the case for most kinds of manufacturing and many services, large firms will have lower average costs than small ones.

Over time, therefore, the number of firms will shrink through exits or mergers, until economies of scale are exhausted. In the limiting, but not unrealistic, case of natural monopoly, unrestrained competition will lead to the emergence of a single dominant firm.

Once a firm attains a dominant position, it can hold that position for a long time, even after any initial advantages have disappeared. Suppliers and dealers can be locked into long-term contracts. If these contracts expire at different times, the suppliers and dealers have no "outside option" and therefore little bargaining power.

By cutting prices whenever competition emerges, dominant firms can exclude any entrants lacking the deep pockets to sustain a price war. Where different firms are dominant in different market segments or geographic regions, they may agree (formally if this is legal and informally otherwise) to an "orderly" sharing out of markets and the associated monopoly profits.

If vital parts are produced to a standard design, patents over those parts can be used to exclude competitors. As an example, the AT&T Bell monopoly in the United States required that only phones made by its subsidiary, Western Electric, could be connected to its network. This and other restrictions excluded all competition for decades.

In a natural monopoly industry, production by a single firm is technically efficient. But the price that maximizes profits will be higher than the opportunity cost of production. Some of the potential benefits of technical efficiency will be lost, while the bulk of what remains will go to the monopolist rather than to consumers.[1]

The situation is even worse where monopoly is maintained through costly devices used to exclude competitors. Not only will prices be higher than opportunity costs, but they will also exceed the competitive market price. As free-market economist Gordon Tullock has argued, even the monopolist will dissipate much of its profit in its efforts to exclude competitors.

These problems first emerged on a large scale in the late nineteenth century, as the growth of rail networks made it possible, and profitable, for firms to operate on a national scale. The railways themselves were one of the most important industries in which the benefits of scale economies, along with the appeal of potential monopoly profits, led to a rash of mergers.

---

[1] In a very simple model of monopoly pricing, the monopolist gets half of the potential benefits from the supply of the good, consumers get a quarter, and the remaining quarter is lost because of the divergence between price and opportunity cost.

15.2. Antitrust

The first corporate monopolies of the late nineteenth century were organized using a legal device called a "trust," a predecessor of the "holding company."[2] Along with Standard Oil, discussed in chapter 9, prominent trusts included US Steel, the American Tobacco Company, and the International Mercantile Marine Company.

The trust held shares in a number of corporations and acted to coordinate their activities for mutual benefit. An obvious source of benefits was the exploitation of monopoly or monopsony power to raise prices for consumers while lowering the prices paid to suppliers and the wages paid to workers.

The policy response was a string of "antitrust" laws beginning with the Sherman Act of 1890 and concluding with the Celler-Kefauver Act of 1950. These laws aimed to break up existing trusts and to prevent the emergence of new ones by restricting mergers.

The most radical version of antitrust policy, commonly referred to as "trust-busting," involved breaking up large corporations into separate firms that were expected to compete against one another. The era of trust-busting began with the breakup of Standard Oil and the American Tobacco Company in 1911 and ended with that of AT&T in 1982.

From the 1980s onward, and as a result of the resurgence of One Lesson economics, enthusiasm for trust-busting declined. Critics of trust-busting argued that the AT&T monopoly depended, not on the market power of the company, but on

---

[2] Although trusts as a legal device were rapidly rendered obsolete by the development of more complex corporate structures, the name "antitrust" stuck, and is carried on in the antitrust division of the Justice Department.

state-level regulations of various kinds, and that technological innovation would have undermined the monopoly in the long run anyway. The implication was that if governments simply left markets alone, competition would emerge spontaneously and drive down monopoly profits.

Although the US Department of Justice continued to bring antitrust cases, most were unsuccessful. The biggest was the challenge to the domination of the desktop computer software market by Microsoft. A decade of court action ended with a settlement that did little to constrain Microsoft's market power. Although overshadowed by Apple and Google, both of which also rely heavily on market power for their profitability, Microsoft's continued dominance of the desktop market means that it remains one of the world's most profitable corporations.

The logic of opportunity cost applies to trust-busting, as it does to all kinds of policy. Breaking up monopolies reduces the extent of monopoly power, at the cost of forgoing opportunities for improved scale economies arising from mergers.

There is no simple way of determining the balance of opportunity costs here, other than through the test of experience. As policies have gone back and forth since the mid-nineteenth century, it has become increasingly evident that unrestrained monopoly goes hand in hand with inequality in income, wealth, and political power.

From the passage of the Sherman Act until the 1970s, the loss of scale economies was seen as an acceptable price to pay to keep monopoly in check. Over this period, beginning with the "Gilded Age" of the late nineteenth century and culminating in the "Great Compression" of the mid-twentieth century, inequalities in income declined. By the 1960s, the United States could plausibly be described as a "middle-class society," where the extremes of wealth and poverty were exceptions to a general rule of comfortable prosperity.

The resurgence of One Lesson economics following the economic crises of the mid-1970s reversed the underlying assumptions of antitrust policy. The presumption that monopolies were harmful, with a requirement for evidence to the contrary, was replaced by a "presumption of innocence" with a requirement to prove that intervention to change market outcomes was necessary.

In the decade since the Global Financial Crisis, opinion has begun to shift again. Analysis of the upsurge in inequality since the 1970s has pointed to monopoly and monopsony power as a major factor. To quote Nobel Laureate Joseph Stiglitz:

> As inequality has widened and concerns about it have grown, the competitive school, viewing individual returns in terms of marginal product, has become increasingly unable to explain how the economy works.

The "competitive school" that Stiglitz describes as being "unable to explain how the economy works" is that of One Lesson economics where prices are determined by marginal (opportunity) costs, which in turn reflect the marginal product of capital and labor. The characteristic feature of monopoly is that owners of capital receive a surplus in addition to their marginal contribution to production.

The role of monopoly and oligopoly in generating inequality has also been stressed by bodies such as the Economic Policy Institute and the Open Markets Foundation, as well as by leading economists, including David Autor and Paul Krugman.

So far, however, this change in the views of the economics profession has not been reflected in public policy. Rather, as trust-busting anti-monopoly policies have been abandoned, they have been replaced by largely ineffectual regulation and competition policy.

15.3. Regulation and Its Limits

As trust-busting has declined, attention has turned to various forms of regulation. The core idea of regulation is to fix the prices charged by monopolies at levels that reflect the opportunity cost of resources used in production, but not to allow the extraction of monopoly profits.

The first step is to estimate the value of the capital assets needed to produce the good or service in question, to determine the "regulatory asset base." The monopolist is allowed a rate of return that is supposed to correspond to the opportunity cost of the capital invested in the asset base.

In practice, the rate of return has almost invariably been set too high. The common result has been that regulated monopolies have been highly profitable, while consumers have paid higher prices than necessary.

One illustration of this is the fact that the market value of a regulated monopoly is typically around 40 percent more than the value of its regulatory asset base, as estimated by the regulator. This asset base premium reflects the fact that the regulated price is more than the opportunity cost of the resources used in production.

Regulation constrains the exploitation of monopoly power, but it entails compliance and enforcement costs and may prevent firms and consumers from reaching bargains that are mutually beneficial. Where a natural monopoly business involves large-scale investment, it may prove difficult to set a price that accurately reflects opportunity costs, while providing incentives for efficient investment.

A more fundamental problem of regulation is that of regulatory "capture," where the regulator falls under the sway of the companies it is supposed to regulate and ends up assisting them in maintaining high prices. A classic example is the capture of the Federal Communication Commission by the cable companies it is supposed to regulate. At least when they are being consistent, One Lesson economists recognize the problem of regulatory capture. The problem is that they have no alternative to offer, except that of unregulated monopoly.

The crucial trade-offs in regulation involve the distribution of income and property rights. To encourage appropriate levels of investment, it is desirable to offer high rates of return. However, this implies that monopoly profits will be enhanced at the expense of the community as a whole. One solution, discussed in the next section, is public ownership.

15.4. Public Enterprise

While the United States adopted trust-busting and regulation as solutions to monopoly power, most other developed countries preferred direct public ownership. This was partly due to the greater popularity of socialist ideas and partly to the perceived failure of regulated monopolies to deliver adequate outcomes.

By the middle of the twentieth century, infrastructure services such as railways, telecommunications, water supply, and electricity were provided by public enterprises in most developed countries.[3] These enterprises charged market prices for their services, typically designed to cover the opportunity costs of the resources used in providing the service and a surplus sufficient to cover depreciation and finance new investment. Over time, many of these enterprises were converted to a corporatized

---

[3] There were a variety of exceptions, such as water supply in France and railways in Japan. Conversely, various governments ran businesses more commonly found in the private sector. For example, in Australia, state governments operated in travel agencies for many years. Overall, however, there was remarkable consistency in the structure of the mixed economy.

form and paid dividends, which provided a source of revenue for governments.

Along with redistributive policies of various kinds, the public ownership of monopoly enterprises contributed to the historically unprecedented reduction in inequality that took place in the decades after 1945, sometimes referred to as the "Great Compression."

Moreover, the period of public ownership was one of substantial expansion of infrastructure networks. Electricity supply, which had previously been patchy and often confined to urban areas, became almost universal. Highway systems expanded greatly, with the US Interstate System the most prominent example. Telephone systems grew from local services to national and international networks, with steadily declining costs.

However, public enterprises were subject to two significant criticisms. First, they were viewed as overstaffed and inefficient. Second, although they generated sufficient revenue to cover the opportunity costs of production in aggregate, the prices charged for particular services did not necessarily reflect the opportunity cost of providing those services. There were extensive cross-subsidies between rural and urban users and between households and businesses.[4]

These criticisms emerged gradually over the postwar decades. However, as long as Keynesian macroeconomic policies delivered full employment and continued economic growth, faith in the ability of governments to manage the economy extended to a judgment that the benefits of public enterprise outweighed the costs. Although there were shifts back and forth, with enterprises being nationalized for various reasons,

---

[4] Some of these were justified because of the desire to provide universal service, but others were simply the result of political pork-barreling.

and others privatized, the general trend was toward greater public ownership.[5]

The economic crises of the 1970s, and the failure of Keynesian policies to control them, put an end to this. From the 1980s onward, the trend toward greater public ownership was reversed. Beginning with the Thatcher government in the United Kingdom, public enterprises of all kinds were privatized.

Much of the political appeal of privatization arose from the appearance of a "free lunch" for governments selling assets. The proceeds of the asset sales could be used to finance current government expenditure, or new investments in desirable infrastructure, without the need to raise taxes or issue debt.

As is usually the case, the appearance of a free lunch was illusory. The opportunity cost of privatizing a public asset is the loss of the income flowing to the government from ownership of the asset (dividends or earnings retained and reinvested).

In most of the privatizations undertaken after 1980, assets were underpriced, so that the value realized in the sale was less than the opportunity cost associated with lower future income. Once the sale proceeds were spent, governments were permanently poorer because of the loss of earnings flowing from the now-private enterprises.

One Lesson economists who advocated privatization were mostly happy to let governments chase the free lunch of revenue from asset sales. However, their real hope was that, with government enterprises out of the way, competitive markets would emerge, and that Lesson One would once again be relevant.

One Lesson advocates of privatization produced a range of studies suggesting that the problems of natural monopoly had

---

[5] This term was not much used; the prevailing term "denationalized" reflected the fact that such movements were counter to the general trend.

been overstated and were easily soluble.[6] As a result, they largely ignored the earlier failures of regulation, assuming that regulation would be needed only for a transitional period, until a fully competitive market emerged.

As usual, One Lesson economists disregarded concerns about the distribution of income and wealth. When forced to respond to such concerns, they argued that the efficiency benefits associated with privatization would be sufficient to provide lower prices for consumers, higher returns for investors, and even some kind of compensation for displaced workers.

Initial evaluations of privatization were highly positive. The World Bank, in particular, was an influential booster, and continues to promote the idea, though with an increasingly defensive tone.

Over time, however, problems became more evident. The cost savings from firing large numbers of technical workers were partially or completely offset by the expansion of marketing and finance divisions, and by an explosion in the salaries and bonuses paid to a growing number of senior managers, who also required support staff.

Moreover, the promised benefits to consumers often did not occur. Sometimes prices rose instead of falling. In other cases, lower prices were accompanied by reduced quality of services. Other costs have been slower to become apparent. A UN report in 2014 noted that privatization of education had harmed educational opportunities for women and girls.

On the other hand, privatization has proved a highly reliable method of enriching those who have managed to secure control

---

[6] One popular idea, important in the case for airline deregulation, was that monopolies did not pose a problem if they were "contestable." Experience after deregulation showed, however, that fares were substantially higher on routes served by only one or two airlines.

of the process. Many of the great fortunes that symbolize the rise of the global "1 percent," notably including those of Russian oligarchs, have been derived from privatization.

These failures have led to a slowing down in the push to privatization, and even to some reversals. Examples include the renationalization of the British railway track system and of the entire New Zealand rail network, and Australia's creation of a publicly owned National Broadband Network following the failure of its privatized telecom company to create such a network.

In the end, the choice between public ownership and regulated private monopoly involves the need to strike a balance between different opportunity costs. That balance has shifted over time, partly in response to technological changes and partly as a result of ideological shifts in thinking. Since the 1970s, excessive faith in Lesson One has led to a sharp movement away from public ownership, without any clear attempt to assess the balance of costs and benefits. Such a reassessment is long overdue.

15.5. The Mixed Economy

In any modern society, goods and services are provided in many different ways.[7] Some are sold in markets where competing firms choose what to supply, and how much to charge, with little in the way of oversight or regulation. Others are supplied under conditions of more or less stringent regulation, with prices determined through rule-setting processes. Still others

---

[7] Even in Communist states, private farms and quasi-legal private services played an essential role. More generally, the failure of the Communist attempt to bring all economic activity under public ownership is an "exception that proves the rule" for many of the points made here.

are supplied by governments, or government-funded organizations, often without any explicit price.

The result is what has been called a "mixed economy." In terms of ownership, the mixed economy sits between the extremes of a centrally planned command economy and the idealized laissez-faire economy found in One Lesson tracts.

The pattern of activity in mixed economics differs from place to place and from time to time. For example, water for household use is mostly supplied by private companies in France but by publicly owned utilities in much of the United States.

Despite these variations, there is a surprising degree of consistency regarding the kinds of services that are likely to be provided by private markets, by governments, and by combinations of the two. For example, consumer goods such as household appliances and grocery items have almost invariably been supplied by private firms, and attempts to regulate their prices have usually been unsuccessful.

By contrast, health and education services have mostly been provided or funded by governments. The involvement of for-profit firms in these areas of activity has been limited and often highly problematic.

The typical structure of the mixed economy can be explained in terms of the Two Lessons. In some sectors of the economy, such as the provision of many kinds of consumer goods and services, most of the conditions for competitive equilibrium, discussed in section 2.4, are met, at least approximately. All consumers face the same prices and are aware of the prices that they face. Since consumers are familiar with goods and services that they consume regularly, they can be assumed to make choices that reflect their own needs and preferences. Because there are large numbers of buyers and sellers, no one can influence prices significantly. Externalities in production can be managed through environmental policies (see chapter 16) without the need for public ownership. In these cases, Lesson One is broadly correct.

At the other extreme are services such as health and education. In these cases, if prices are charged, they rarely bear any close relationship to the opportunity cost of the services in question. "Consumers" (patients and students) rely on the expertise and professionalism of "producers" (health professionals and educators) rather than on their own knowledge of the services in question. Moreover, in the case of health, many of the largest costs arise in emergency situations, where patients often have no say in their treatment, let alone the option of "shopping around" for the best price and quality.

Another area where public provision has played a substantial role is that of infrastructure and public utilities, especially those characterized by natural monopoly. In this case, the main failures of Lesson One arise from monopoly power and externalities.

Finally, the legal, judicial, and enforcement systems underlying the structure of property rights within which economic activity takes place relies, inevitably, on state power. Some parts of these systems may be contracted out to the private sector; examples include private prisons and systems of private arbitration. Leaving aside the unsatisfactory performance of many experiments of this kind, the fact that some functions are performed by private entities does not change the direct dependence of the system on state power. The same is true, even more directly, of national defense.

Setting the boundaries of the public and private sectors in a mixed economy is a trade-off which may be explained in terms of opportunity cost. Public provision of a good or service involves forgoing the benefits of market prices in providing information about opportunity costs and incentives to align production and consumption with those opportunity costs. On the other hand, public ownership provides a variety of options for dealing with the various forms of market failure that we have discussed, thereby taking the full range of opportunity cost into account.

The trade-off between these two forms of opportunity cost will be determined by the relative importance of Lesson One and Lesson Two in any given context. That is why any serious approach to economic policy requires an understanding of both lessons.

15.6. *I, Pencil*

The things that markets can achieve seem miraculous. The thousands of steps required to produce this book and put it in your hands (or on your computer/phone/tablet) are taken with little central direction or coordination. Trees planted decades ago are harvested and turned into paper, to be printed perhaps in a different continent, with text produced by a complex computer system controlled by skilled typesetters.

Even the production of such a mundane object as a pencil draws on the labor of millions of different workers, the capital of many different investors, and the resources of many countries. This observation is the basis of a well-known pro-market tract "*I, Pencil*," written by Leonard Read.

Read's essay is a description of the incredibly complex "family tree" of a simple pencil, making the point that the production of a pencil draws on the work of millions of people, not one of whom could actually make a pencil from scratch, and most of whom don't know or care that their work contributes to the production of pencils.[8] So far, so good. Read goes on to say that

---

[8] In fact, given the raw materials, the process of pencil-making per se is simple enough for a single person to understand and undertake unaided. Henry David

There is a fact still more astounding: the absence of a master mind, of anyone dictating or forcibly directing these countless actions which bring me into being. No trace of such a person can be found. Instead, we find the Invisible Hand at work.

Hold on a moment! A closer look suggests that large parts of the process of making a pencil are in fact centrally directed.

Read's first-person pencil starts the story like this:

My family tree begins with what in fact is a tree, a cedar of straight grain that grows in Northern California and Oregon.

That would probably have been in a forest managed by the US Forest Service or the Bureau of Land Management, or maybe a similar state agency. And why is this? Starting in the late nineteenth century, the US government (most notably under Theodore Roosevelt) judged that the nation's forests were not likely to be adequately managed to ensure a supply of timber for, among other things, the production of pencils for future generations if they relied on existing private property rights and the workings of the invisible hand. Similar judgments have been made in Australia and many other countries. The fact that pencils were still being made in the 1950s depended, to a substantial extent, on conscious planning undertaken 50 years earlier.

Read's pencil goes on to mention "all the persons and the numberless skills" that are involved in forestry and in the

---

Thoreau and his family made pencils by hand and dominated the US market for some time. Thoreau invented improvements to the process, which has changed only marginally since then, except that the processes are now undertaken by machines. Thoreau wrote his classic, *Walden*, with one of his family's pencils, a notable example of what economists call "vertical integration."

various subsequent stages of production. Most of those people would have acquired their basic skills in public schools, and learned more in colleges, trade schools, and so on, mostly public or publicly funded.

Education is a prime example of a service that (except in marginal cases, or for very specific vocational skills) has almost nowhere been successfully provided on a market-driven for-profit basis. Successful "private" schools are almost invariably nonprofit, and commonly benefit from direct or indirect public funding. The near-total failure of for-profit school companies like EdisonLearning, and the reliance of the for-profit higher education sector on fraudulent exploitation of federal grants, are cases in point. In Sweden, long the poster child for for-profit schooling, similar problems are now emerging. As with forests, the availability of skilled and educated workers to produce Read's pencil depends on planning decisions made years or decades previously.

Next up is the rail trip to San Leandro, California. Read's pencil doesn't mention the line, but the train was most likely to have started on the Northwest Pacific railroad, then connected to the Southern Pacific, successor to the Central Pacific. The Central Pacific, along with the Union Pacific, was one of two railroads created by an Act of Congress under Abraham Lincoln, with the plan of building a railway line across the continent, famously meeting at the Golden Spike at Promontory Summit, Utah. Reliance on the invisible hand to produce coherent railway networks was a failure wherever it was tried. The same is proving true today wherever governments seek to turn the road network over to private toll road operators. In complex transport networks, central planning is essential.

And, while we learn how the pencil is produced by sandwiching a graphite tube between two wooden slates, the pencil forgets to mention its invention and patenting by Nicolas Conte in the late eighteenth century. As we have discussed previously, the patent system is a temporary government-created monopoly, and a classic example of the mixed economy.

Finally, let's look at Eberhard Faber, the company that made the pencil. It's now a subsidiary of Newell Rubbermaid, a multi-national consumer goods conglomerate with more than 20,000 employees and dozens of different brands. Obviously, someone sees a fair bit of benefit in "dictating and forcibly directing" the work of these thousands of employees, rather than relying exclusively on transactions in the marketplace. And the shareholders prefer to organize all this activity under the state-created protection of the limited liability corporation, rather than acting as independent entrepreneurs.

A corporate firm, or even an unincorporated business firm, is a complex social construction, embodying both cooperation —to make and sell the firm's products, and conflict—between workers and owners over wages and conditions, between shareholders and managers over corporate control, and between long-term and short-term stakeholders over strategic directions. Out of this mix of cooperation and conflict, the firm produces a distribution of the income it generates: always unequal, but more equal at some times and places than others.

What can we learn from all this? As Read argues, following Adam Smith, markets can indeed organize very complex production processes, to an extent that might well seem miraculous to anyone who tried to reason about it in the abstract. But that doesn't mean that markets are the only, or invariably the best, way to organize production.

The question of why production is so commonly organized within firms, rather than in markets, was first addressed in a classic 1937 article by Ronald Coase. Coase's ideas were developed in large literature centered around the idea of the firm as a nexus of contracts.

The majority of economic activity takes place without any direct connection to markets. This includes activity undertaken in the household or government sector, or within large corporations that trade in the market sector but use central planning to organize their own activities. The boundaries are constantly shifting as some activities shift between household, government, and market sectors, and as households, governments, and firms outsource some activities and integrate others.

The fact that a particular form of organization exists and functions does not prove that it is optimal. It is certainly possible to imagine forms of modern society in which markets and private property play no role, or forms in which there are "markets in everything." And, within the broad class of mixed economies, there's a wide range of possibilities—most goods and services have somewhere and sometime been provided by governments, and somewhere and sometime by private markets.

Nevertheless, the broad outlines of the mixed economy have remained stable since the 1940s. It survived the challenge from comprehensive central planning in the Soviet Union. More recently, the mixed economy has outlasted the push for privatization that began in the 1980s and ended (as a program with a credible theoretical foundation, if not as an ideological agenda) in the Global Financial Crisis. Any serious policy program has to take account of this fact.

Further Reading

The quote at the beginning of the chapter is from Lessig (2001). The term "countervailing power" was coined by Galbraith (1969).

The relationship between monopoly/monopsony and inequality has become a hot topic recently. Useful sources include Autor et al. (2017); Bivens, Mishel, and Schmidt (2018);

Christophers (2016); Lynn (2011); Khan and Vaheesan (2017); Krugman (2016); Naidu, Posner, and Weyl (2018); and Stiglitz (2016).

Koloko (1970, 1977) discusses regulatory capture. Esguerra (2008) and Walker (2008), writing from very different perspectives, examine the capture of the Federal Communications Commission. Thompson, MacDonald, and Mouliakis (2016) provide evidence on the excess returns to regulated monopolies in Australia.

I've written extensively on public ownership and the mixed economy, including in my previous book, *Zombie Economics*. The term "mixed economy" was popularized by Shonfield (1965, 1984).

I, Pencil was originally published as Read (1958) and is available on the Internet. My response was published on the Crooked Timber blog in 2011. See also Rodrik (2011). The ideas of Coase (1937) were developed by Williamson (1986).

Other references include CEDAW (2014) and Tullock (1967). The discussion of Standard Oil and the history of antitrust draws on Wikipedia.

CHAPTER 16

■

Environmental Policy

People "over-produce" pollution because they are not paying
for the costs of dealing with it.
    —Ha-Joon Chang, *23 Things They Don't
Tell You about Capitalism*

As we saw in chapter 10, pollution externalities represent one
of the most pervasive and intractable market failures in a market economy. Almost every kind of economic activity produces
harmful by-products, which are costly to dispose of safely. The
cheapest thing to do is to dump the wastes on land, in waterways, or into the atmosphere.

Under the market conditions that prevailed until relatively
recently, that's precisely what happened. This is a classic case of
Lesson Two. Polluters paid nothing for dumping waste while
society bore the cost.

Economists have long had a solution to this problem, or
rather, several variants of the same solution. As far back as the
1920s, A. C. Pigou had argued that the divergence between private and social opportunity costs could be removed if taxes were
imposed on firms generating negative externalities. This would
make the (tax-inclusive) prices paid by those firms reflect social
cost. The level of pollution would depend on the value to firms
of the processes that generate it.

An alternative approach developed from the work of Ronald Coase, whose classic article in 1960 stressed the role of property rights.[1] In the Coasian approach, rather than setting a price for pollution, society (through courts or governments) decides how much pollution can be tolerated and creates property rights reflecting that decision. Companies that want to dispose of waste must pay for the rights to do so. Whereas the Pigovian approach determines a price and lets markets determine the volume of polluting activity, the Coasian approach sets the volume and lets the market determine the price.

The ideas of Pigou and Coase provide a theoretically neat answer to the market failure problem, which is an important part of Lesson Two. Unfortunately, they run into the more fundamental problem of income distribution and property rights.

Whether property rights are created explicitly, as in the Coasian approach, or implicitly, through Pigovian taxes, there are losers as well as gainers from the resulting change in the distribution of property rights and, therefore, market income. In many cases, those potential losers have provided effective resistance to market-based policies to control pollution.

The strongest resistance arises when businesses that have previously dumped their waste into airways and waterways free of charge are forced to bear the opportunity costs of their actions, by paying taxes or purchasing emissions rights. Such businesses can call on an array of lobbyists, think tanks, and friendly politicians to defend their interests.

Sometimes the result has been to prevent any action. In other cases, pollution has actually increased in anticipation of changes in property rights structures. Faced with these

[1] Coase later won the Nobel Memorial Prize in Economics, primarily for this work.

difficulties, governments have often fallen back on the less cost-effective but simpler option of regulation.

In this chapter, we'll look at regulation as well as market-based responses and consider whether the two can be made to work together.

16.1. Regulation

The simplest and most direct response to pollution is to ban it by prohibiting the discharge of waste. Alternatively, polluters may be required to adopt specific technologies which either reduce pollution at the source or disperse it farther away. Such a policy is described, often pejoratively, as "command and control" or, more neutrally, as "regulation."

Although there had been some environmental laws even in the nineteenth century, the first systematic attempts to regulate pollution were the Clean Air Act in Britain (1956) and the United States (1970).[2] These Acts relied on direct controls, such as a requirement for the use of smokeless fuels in urban areas, to achieve their goals. The US Clean Water Act followed in 1972, along with similar legislation in Britain and Europe.[3]

Since little attention had been paid to the problem of pollution, such requirements often achieved significant reductions in pollution at relatively low cost. The famous "pea-souper" smogs of London are now a distant memory. Pollution control policies

---

[2] The 1970 Clean Air Act established the command-and-control approach to federal environmental legislation. It replaced a series of more limited pieces of federal legislation going back to the Air Pollution Control Act (1955), along with a variety of partial measures at the state and local levels.

[3] As with the Clean Air Act, the Clean Water Act replaced earlier, less systematic legislation dating back to the 1899 Rivers and Harbors Act.

have solved many of the most acute problems of air and water pollution. The Thames, once so toxic that entering it was likely to be fatal, is now home once again to fish, seals, and dolphins, and even, I have read, a visiting whale. Los Angeles, likewise, has blue rather than brown skies once again.[4] These achievements show that there is no necessary conflict between a (mixed) market economy and preservation of the environment.

Conversely, central planning does not necessarily solve environmental problems. Soviet planners saw pollution and environmental degradation as part of the price of progress and largely ignored it, producing a string of environmental disasters, notably including the Chernobyl meltdown and the near-destruction of Lake Baikal in Siberia. In some post-Communist countries like Poland, which have persisted with largely unregulated coal mining and coal-fired power, the air remains hazardous to breathe.

Despite the successes of regulation, the problem of air pollution has not been solved. In many cases, regulation served to shift pollution rather than to reduce it.

For example, the 1956 UK Clean Air Act sought to solve pollution problems by requiring taller chimneys. The result was that pollutants, rather than creating smog in British cities, were blown out to sea by the prevailing westerly winds. Unfortunately, the smoke did not stop there. Instead it blew all the way to Scandinavia, where the sulfur dioxide combined with rainwater to produce a dilute form of sulfuric acid, the infamous acid rain. This was one of the first instances of the problem of "transborder pollution."

In other cases, sources of pollution, such as the manufacturing industry, have shifted to newly industrializing countries,

[4] Recent reports suggest smog may be making a comeback, partly as a result of climate change.

notably including China. In Beijing, pollution is so bad that serious consideration has been given to the creation of "biodomes" in which the wealthy could breathe filtered air. The situation is just as bad in India. Even so, regulation remains the first and simplest response to uncontrolled pollution. A recent example is that of the Chinese government, which has announced a ban on coal-fired power stations in the vicinity of Beijing and other heavily polluted cities.

Regulations work well when there are only a few sources of pollution and only limited ways to fix it. Such cases are often referred to as "point-source pollution." In this case, the polluter can simply be required to adopt the necessary measures to control pollution. As a trivial example, truckers carrying items such as coal may be required to cover their loads.

Another case well suited for regulation is when a technology is so polluting that it must be banned altogether. The case of chlorofluorocarbons (CFCs), discussed in chapter 10, provides an example.

More difficult problems arise in cases where many different activities contribute to pollution and where it is not feasible simply to prohibit such activities.

16.2. Environmental Taxes

By the end of the 1970s, problems with regulatory approaches were becoming evident. Further reductions in pollution, while still clearly necessary, could only be achieved at substantial cost if policy continued to rely on direct regulation.

The Two Lessons explain why. In the end, firms will always try to respond to the price signals they face. If the opportunity cost of pollution is not reflected in the prices they face, firms will seek to work around regulations in order to minimize their costs of production.

Moreover, there were several different technological approaches to reducing emissions, and it was far from clear which would be the most effective. Plants could change their fuel mix, or their boilers, or install equipment on their output stacks to capture and neutralize emissions. Setting a price on emissions encourages firms to adopt the most cost-effective way of reducing them.

In Europe, environmental taxes based on the Pigovian principle have been adopted widely. The Paris-based Organization for Economic Cooperation and Development has been a strong advocate for such taxes, arguing that they provide "incentives for further efficiency gains, green investment and innovation and shifts in consumption patterns."

In the United States, by contrast, political institutions and attitudes are more favorable to regulation than to taxes. The closest approximation to Pigovian taxes is container deposit legislation modeled on the Oregon Bottle Bill and currently in force in ten states. The idea is to include a refundable deposit as part of the price of bottles and other containers. The deposit is refunded when the item is returned for recycling and is forfeited if the item is not returned.

Container deposits are, in effect, a tax on discarding containers and also a subsidy for collecting and returning them.[5]

Pigou's reasoning has also been used as an argument for higher rates of taxation on goods that are considered to be generating negative externalities, including cigarettes and alcohol. In the first two cases, the negative externalities include both direct effects on others from consumption (second-hand smoke and alcohol-fueled bad behavior and drunk driving) and the costs imposed on the public health system by smokers and drinkers.

---

[5] The Academy Award–nominated documentary *Redemption* looks at the life of "canners" who collect containers and redeem the deposits for a living.

16.3. Tradeable Emissions Permits

The benefit of reducing pollution is the same, no matter who does it, while the opportunity costs differ from firm to firm. So, there are potential gains from exchange.

The first policy to capture these gains arose in response to the problem of "acid rain" and came into prominence in Europe and North America in the 1980s. Acid rain comes about mainly because of sulfur dioxide in the atmosphere, arising from the burning of high-sulfur coal, mainly in power stations. Sulfur dioxide combines with water vapor in the atmosphere to form dilute sulfuric acid. Falling as rain, it kills trees and changes the acid-alkaline balance of lakes, causing potentially severe ecological damage.

Unlike the pollution problems that had been addressed in the 1950s and 1960s, such as urban smog and the dumping of waste in rivers, the problem of acid rain was not local in its nature. The source of sulfur dioxide might be hundreds of miles from the point at which it fell to Earth as acid rain.

To resolve the problem of acid rain, it was necessary to reduce the amount of sulfur dioxide emitted by power plants. The traditional way of doing this, which had proved successful in dealing with problems such as urban smog, would be to impose rules specifying requirements for pollution control equipment, or prohibiting the use of high-sulfur coal.

In the case of acid rain, however, it appeared certain that this would be very costly, perhaps prohibitively so. It is very difficult to retrofit pollution control equipment to old plants. On the other hand, applying the rules only to new plants and "grandfathering" old ones would delay a solution to the problem, creating what is probably an unacceptable delay.

An alternative policy response was to create a system of emissions permits, allowing the holder to generate a given quantity of emissions. In effect, these permits were newly created property rights. At the same time, the previously existing general right to emit was withdrawn from anyone who did not hold a permit.

The crucial innovation in the system is that permits are tradeable. A firm that holds permits equal to its current emissions can choose to reduce emissions through the installation of pollution control equipment and then sell the surplus permits to another firm that lacks them. The opportunity cost of selling the permit, for the first firm, is the cost of reducing its emissions. Conversely, for the second firm, the opportunity cost of emissions is the price paid for the permit.

If the permit price is equal to the social opportunity cost of pollution, then the conditions of Lesson One are restored.

In practice, it's very difficult to determine the social opportunity cost of pollution. An emissions trading scheme works by setting a cap on total emissions, lower than the level prevailing in the absence of controls. In most cases, the allowable quantity of emissions declines over time. This can be managed by making permits time-limited. As old permits expire, they are replaced by a smaller quantity of new ones.

The other aspect of Lesson Two relates to income distribution. In the original version of the emissions trading scheme, most permits were allocated, free of charge, to existing polluters. In effect, these firms had their right to pollute somewhat reduced, while potential entrants had no rights.

A more satisfactory approach, which does not reward past pollution, is to auction permits. The auction proceeds may either be allocated to specific purposes such as offsetting environmental damage or added to general government revenue.

16.4. Global Pollution Problems

Policies to reduce air and water pollution have been remarkably successful at the local and national levels, at least in developed countries. Rapidly developing countries like China and India have, until recently, tolerated high levels of pollution as the price of economic growth. However, increasing evidence and public awareness of the health damage and other effects have prompted change. For example, China has closed down coal-fired power stations near major cities like Beijing and is now attempting to replace coal used for home heating with cleaner natural gas.

At the same time as progress is made at the local and national levels, global pollution problems have come to constitute a graver threat than ever to the whole of humanity. Two of the most notable have been the potential destruction of the ozone layer and human-induced climate change.

The threat to the ozone layer arose from a novel class of chemicals called chlorofluorocarbons (CFCs). Under normal conditions, these chemicals are almost completely inert, a fact that made them ideal for use as refrigerants and propellants for spray cans. That same inertness allowed CFCs to drift into the upper atmosphere, where they reacted with ozone, the form of oxygen that absorbs ultraviolet light.

Only prompt action in the 1980s and 1990s, a response to inspired, and lucky, scientific research, prevented the destruction of the ozone layer that protects us from deadly ultraviolet radiation from the Sun. The Montreal Protocol was an international agreement to phase out CFCs.

16.5. Climate Change

The global threat of CFCs was a dress rehearsal for a much bigger problem. During the 1980s and 1990s, it became increasingly evident that emissions of greenhouse gases, most importantly carbon dioxide, were changing the global climate, leading to an increase in average temperatures, changes in rainfall patterns, and an increase in the frequency of extreme climate events. The resulting increase in global temperatures threatens the future of everyone on the planet.

Since the great majority of energy in modern societies is produced by the burning of carbon-based fuels, solving this problem will require changes in a vast range of economic activities. If these changes are to be achieved without reducing standards of living or obstructing the efforts of less developed countries to lift themselves out of poverty, it is important to find a path to emissions reductions that minimizes opportunity costs.

16.5.1. Carbon Budgets

But how should we think about the opportunity cost of carbon dioxide emissions? We could look at the costs imposed on the world's population as a whole from climate change and measure how this changes with additional emissions. But this is an almost impossibly difficult task. The only thing we know for certain about the costs of climate change is how much we don't know. We can be reasonably sure that, if global temperatures keep on increasing, the costs will be substantial, but the possibilities range from manageable damage to total catastrophe. There is no easy way to put probabilities on these outcomes.

A better way to think about the problem is in terms of carbon budgets. We have a reasonably good idea of how much more carbon dioxide (and other greenhouse gases) the world as a whole can afford to emit while keeping the probability of dangerous climate change (more than about 2 degrees Celsius) reasonably low. A typical estimate is 2,900 billion tons compared to 2,000 billion tons already emitted since the Industrial Revolution, most of it in the past 30 years.

Within any given carbon budget, an additional ton of CO_2 emitted from one source requires a reduction of one ton somewhere else. So, it is the cost of this offsetting reduction that determines the opportunity cost of the additional emission.

As the Two Lessons show, opportunity costs are closely related to prices. A price for CO_2 emissions high enough to keep total emissions within the carbon budget would ensure that the opportunity cost of increasing emissions would be equal to the price.

Prices can tell us about the relative costs of different kinds of emissions. But such prices do not arise spontaneously from existing markets, since the costs of carbon dioxide emissions are borne by everyone on the planet, not just those directly or indirectly responsible for them.

A price on carbon dioxide emissions, or any kind of pollution, will arise only from policy actions that create markets in one form or another. Such market-based instruments sometimes compete with, and sometimes complement, regulatory policies.

16.5.2. Emissions Permits vs. Taxes

The biggest unresolved question is whether to implement carbon taxes, tradeable emissions permits, or some hybrid of the two. Both have been implemented successfully, both ensure the existence of a price for CO_2 emissions, and both can be set up to distribute the costs of emissions in a lot of different ways.[6]

Permits have a number of advantages.

First, while the natural starting point for both systems is one in which the government collects the entire implied value of emissions, either as tax revenue or as the proceeds from

---

[6] The provincial government in British Columbia implemented a carbon tax in 2008. The European Union has operated an emissions trading scheme since 2005. Despite initial problems arising from excessive allocations of permits, the scheme is working successfully to reduce emissions. At the time of writing, a national scheme in China is in its early stages of operation.

auctioning permits, the emissions trading system allows for (but doesn't require) free allocation of some permits. Particularly in transitional stages when not all sources are covered, this can be used to offset unanticipated distributional consequences of the scheme, and thereby increase its political feasibility.

Second, since we are uncertain about the elasticity of demand for emissions, we are faced with a choice between allowing this uncertainty to be reflected in uncertainty about reaching the targeted level of reductions in emissions, uncertainty about the price, or some combination of the two. Given the risk that we will fail altogether if individual countries fall short of their targets, some uncertainty about the price appears preferable.

Third, and most important, the ideal outcome is an international agreement to reduce emissions in the most cost-effective way possible. The obvious way to do this is through the creation of international markets for emissions permits. By contrast, in a world of sharply varying exchange rates, it would be very difficult to set up a coordinated global system of carbon taxes.

16.5.3. One Lesson Economics and Climate Change

The question of how to respond to externalities such as pollution has long been a difficult one for the advocates of One Lesson economics.

Henry Hazlitt, in a 1984 interview with the propertarian magazine *Reason*, admitted as much, noting that one of the issues "that I find very tough is the question of pollution. A lot of these issues I haven't written about at all."

Surprisingly, back in the nineteenth century Bastiat did write about pollution. Decades before Arrhenius described the greenhouse effect, Bastiat gave us an eerily prescient preview of the climate change debate and the One Lesson response to it.

Suppose that a professor of chemistry were to say: "The world is threatened by a great catastrophe; God has not taken proper precautions. I have analyzed the air that comes from human lungs, and I have come to the conclusion that it is not fit to breathe; so that, by calculating the volume of the atmosphere, I can predict the day when it will be entirely polluted, and when mankind will die of consumption, unless it adopts an artificial mode of respiration of my invention."

Another professor steps forward and says: "No, mankind will not perish thus. It is true that the air that has already served to sustain animal life is vitiated for that purpose; but it is fit for plant life, and what plants exhale is favorable to human respiration. An incomplete study has induced some to think that God made a mistake; a more exact inquiry shows a harmonious design in His handiwork. Men can continue to breathe as Nature willed it."

What should we say if the first professor overwhelmed the second with abuse, saying: "You are a chemist with a cold, hard, dried-up heart; you preach the horrible doctrine of laissez faire; you do not love mankind, since you demonstrate the uselessness of my respiratory apparatus."

This is the sum and substance of our quarrel with the socialists. Both they and we desire harmony. They seek it in the innumerable schemes that they want the law to impose on men; we find it in the nature of men and things.

Although Bastiat's first professor (a chemist, like Arrhenius) is set up as a straw man, he correctly identifies the problem gases that give rise to climate change. Humans exhale both carbon dioxide and methane, but livestock emit far more methane and the burning of fossil fuels produces far more carbon dioxide.

Moreover, although these gases are poisonous in high concentrations, the real problem is the greenhouse effect, which means that a mere doubling of the pre-industrial concentration is potentially disastrous.

Even more striking is Bastiat's anticipation of the response of his protagonist, the second professor (of theology, it would appear), who assures us that everything will be alright. He doesn't show an error in the chemist's calculation, but simply assures us that Divine Providence, standing in for the free market, will solve the problem in some unspecified fashion. A hundred and fifty years later, this is, for all practical purposes, the response of those who describe themselves as "climate skeptics." This group, dominating the US Republican Party and conservative parties in other English-speaking countries, overlaps very closely with the group of supporters of One Lesson economics.

The debate over climate change illustrates the (literally) poisonous effects of rigid adherence to One Lesson economics. Cost-effective solutions to the problem of reducing CO_2 emissions must include market-based policy instruments, including taxes and new forms of property rights. But for One Lesson ideologues, taxes are an anathema, and the fact that property rights are created by governments is a shameful secret.

16.6. Summary

The environment is, by definition, all around us. We depend on it in every economic activity, and everything we do affects our environment. Only if the structure of rights and obligations, and the prices facing producers and consumers, reflects the environmental impacts of human activity can a market economy work to yield socially and environmentally sustainable outcomes. Two Lesson economics gives us the tools we need.

Further Reading

The classic work of Pigou (1920) and Coase (1960) has already been cited. The Environmental Protection Agency (2018a, 2018b) provides a history of the Clean Air Act and an overview of clean air markets.

Worland (2016) reports on the return of smog in Los Angeles and the link to climate change. Wikipedia provides information on the history of container deposit legislation: https://en.wikipedia.org/wiki/Container_deposit_legislation_in_the_United_States.

Environmental taxes are discussed by Castiglione et al. (2016); Ekins (1999); OECD (2018); and Suter and Felix (2001). The disastrous effects of pollution in Poland are described by Kozlowska (2017).

The discovery of the greenhouse effect by Eunice Foote is described by Darby (2016). The passage from Bastiat is taken from an essay, *Justice and Fraternity*, reproduced and translated as Bastiat (1995).

CONCLUSION

For every complex problem there is an answer that is clear, simple, and wrong.
> —Attributed to H. L. Mencken[1]

It is difficult to get a man to understand something, when his salary depends on his not understanding it.
> —Upton Sinclair, in *I, Candidate for Governor: And How I Got Licked*

Two lessons are harder than one. The appeal of One Lesson economics may be explained in part by the human desire for simple and plausible solutions to complex problems. The appeal of such simple solutions is enhanced, in many respects, when they appear to provide a deeper insight than that possessed by the uninitiated. Many students of economics are so struck by the power of the price mechanism, illustrated in Lesson One, that they never go any further. When they encounter problems such as externalities, unemployment, and the distribution of property rights, they wave them away with superficially plausible but ultimately untenable talking points.

Equally human, though less defensible, is the tendency to ignore facts that threaten your income and social position. For those who benefit from the unfettered growth of industrial production, pollution and climate change externalities represent, in

---

[1] As is often the case, this is an improvement on the original statement by Mencken: "Explanations exist; they have existed for all time; there is always a well-known solution to every human problem—neat, plausible, and wrong." From "The Divine Afflatus" in *New York Evening Mail* (November 16, 1917).

the words of Al Gore, an inconvenient truth. Similarly, defenders of a market economy, like Hazlitt, don't want to admit that mass unemployment is a possibility, unless it can be attributed to the bad actions of governments and unions. Most obviously, those who benefit from the existing structure of property rights never want to admit that these rights were created, and are maintained, by the actions of governments.

The dogmatic certitudes of One Lesson economics will always have plenty of appeal, especially to those who stand to benefit from its prescriptions. But faced with problems like unemployment, growing inequality, and climate change, One Lesson economics has nothing useful to say. To understand how markets work, we must also understand how they can fail, and what can be done about it. In this book, I have tried to show how Economics in Two Lessons can provide the understanding we need.

BIBLIOGRAPHY

Akerlof, George, and Shiller, Robert. 2015. *Phishing for Phools: The Economics of Manipulation and Deception*. Princeton, NJ: Princeton University Press.

Ariely, Daniel. 2016. "Mental Depletion Complicates Financial Decisions for the Poor." AZquotes, citing interview with Kristen Doerer, www.pbs.org. January 19, https://www.azquotes.com/quotes/topics /opportunity-cost.html.

Arneil, Barbara. 1996. *John Locke and America: The Defence of English Colonialism*. Oxford: Clarendon Press.

Arrow, Kenneth, and Debreu, Gerard. 1954. "Existence of an Equilibrium for a Competitive Economy." *Econometrica* 22(3): 265–90.

Atkinson, Anthony B. 2018. *Inequality: What Can Be Done*. Cambridge, MA: Harvard University Press.

Autor, David et al. 2017. "Concentrating on the Fall of the Labor Share." *American Economic Review: Papers & Proceedings* 107(5): 180–85.

Azar, Jose, Marinescu, Ioana, and Steinbaum, Marshall. 2017. Labor Market Concentration. Working paper. https://ssrn.com/abstract =3088767.

Bacon, Robert, Ley, Eduardo, and Kojima, Masami. 2010. Subsidies in the Energy Sector: An Overview. World Bank Group Energy Sector Strategy, http://siteresources.worldbank.org/EXTESC/Resources /Subsidy_background_paper.pdf.

Baker, Dean, Jayadev, Arjun, and Stiglitz, Joseph. 2017. Innovation, Intellectual Property, and Development: A Better Set of Approaches for the 21st Century. Access IBA, http://ip-unit.org/wp-content /uploads/2017/07/IP-for-21st-Century-EN.pdf.

Bakija, Jon, Cole, Adam, and Heim, Bradley. 2012. Jobs and Income Growth of Top Earners and the Causes of Changing Income

Inequality: Evidence from US Tax Return Data, http://piketty.pse
.ens.fr/files/Bakijaetal2010.pdf.

Bank for International Settlements (BIS). 2016. Triennial Central
Bank Survey of Foreign Exchange and OTC Derivatives Markets in
2016, https://www.bis.org/publ/rpfx16.htm.

Barkai, Simcha. 2016. Declining Labor and Capital Shares. Working
paper. https://research.chicagobooth.edu/~/media/5872fbeb10424
5909b8f0ae8a84486c9.pdf.

Barro, Robert. 2001. Why the War Against Terror Will Boost the
Economy. *Business Week*, November 5. https://www.bloomberg.com
/news/articles/2001-11-04/why-the-war-against-terror-will-boost
-the-economy.

Bastiat, Frédéric. 1995. "Justice and Fraternity." In *Selected Essays
on Political Economy*, edited by Seymour Cain, trans. George B.
de Huszar. Irvington-on-Hudson, NY: Foundation for Economic
Education, http://bastiat.org/en/justice_fraternity.html.

Bastiat, Frédéric. 2012a. *Essays on Political Economy*. Amazon Digital
Services. https://www.econlib.org/library/Bastiat/basEss.html

Bastiat, Frédéric. 2012b. *"The Law," "the State," and Other Political Writings, 1843–1850 (the Collected Works of Frédéric Bastiat)*.
Auburn, AL: Ludwig von Mises Institute.

Bastiat, M. Frédéric. 2013. *That Which Is Seen and That Which Is
Not Seen: The Unintended Consequences of Government Spending*.
Auburn, AL: Ludwig von Mises Institute.

Bator, Francis. 1958. "The Anatomy of Market Failure." *Quarterly
Journal of Economics* 72(3): 351–79.

Baumol, William. 1977. "On the Proper Cost Tests for Natural
Monopoly in a Multi-Product Industry." *American Economic Review*
67(5): 809–22.

Bebchuk, L. A., and Fried, J. 2004. *Pay Without Performance: The
Unfulfilled Promise of Executive Compensation*. Cambridge, MA:
Harvard University Press.

Becker, Gary S., and Murphy, Kevin M. 1993. "A Simple Theory of
Advertising as a Good or Bad." *Quarterly Journal of Economics*
108(4): 941–64.

Beckett, Andy. 2003. Ready, Ken? *The Guardian*, February 10, https://www.theguardian.com/politics/2003/feb/10/london.congestioncharging.

Bernanke, Ben S. 2004. *Essays on the Great Depression*. Princeton, NJ: Princeton University Press.

Biasi, Barbara, and Moser, Petra. 2018. Effects of Copyrights on Science—Evidence from the US Book Republication Program. National Bureau of Economic Research, https://www.gwern.net/docs/economics/2018-biasi.pdf.

Bilotkach, Volodymyr. 2017. *The Economics of Airlines*. Newcastle, UK: Agenda Publishing.

Bivens, Josh, Mishel, Lawrence, and Schmitt, John. 2018. It's Not Just Monopoly and Monopsony: How Market Power Has Affected American Wages. Economic Policy Institute, https://www.epi.org/publication/its-not-just-monopoly-and-monopsony-how-market-power-has-affected-american-wages/.

Blanchard, Olivier, and Summers, Lawrence. 2017. Rethinking Stabilization Policy. Back to the Future. "Rethinking macro policy" conference at the Peterson Institute for International Economics, October.

Blaug, M. 2007. "The Fundamental Theorems of Modern Welfare Economics, Historically Contemplated." *History of Political Economy* 39(2): 185–207.

Blyth, Mark. 2012. *Austerity: The History of a Dangerous Idea*. Oxford: Oxford University Press.

Brand, Stewart. 1987. *The Media Lab: Inventing the Future at MIT*. New York: Viking Penguin.

Brotman, Stuart. 2017. Revisiting the Broadcast Public Interest Standard in Communications Law and Regulation. Brookings Institution, https://www.brookings.edu/research/revisiting-the-broadcast-public-interest-standard-in-communications-law-and-regulation/.

Bureau of Labor Statistics. 2018a. American Time Use Survey: Average Hours Per Day Spent in Selected Activities by Sex and Day. https://www.bls.gov/charts/american-time-use/activity-by-sex.htm.

Bureau of Labor Statistics. 2018b. Job Openings and Labor Turnover Survey. https://www.bls.gov/jlt/.

Burnham, James. 1941. *The Managerial Revolution: What Is Happening in the World*. New York: John Day.

Byrne, Rhonda. 2006. *The Secret*. New York: Atria Books.

Card, D., and Krueger, A. B. 1994. "Minimum Wages and Employment: A Case Study of the Fast-Food Industry in New Jersey and Pennsylvania." *American Economic Review* 84(4): 772–93.

Card, D., and Krueger, A. B. 1995a. *Myth and Measurement: The New Economics of the Minimum Wage*. Princeton, NJ: Princeton University Press.

Card, D., and Krueger, A. B. 1995b. "Time-Series Minimum-Wage Studies: A Meta-Analysis." *American Economic Review* 85(2): 238–43.

Casciani, Dominic. 2014. Did Removing Lead from Petrol Spark a Decline in Crime? BBC News, https://www.bbc.com/news/magazine-27067615.

Castiglione, Concetta, Infante, Davide, and Smirnova, Janna. 2016. Environmental Taxation and Its Determinants in Europe. Is There Any Relationship with Rule of Law, ICT and Imports? Working Paper.

CEDAW. 2014. Privatization and Its Impact on the Right to Education of Women and Girls. United Nations Committee on the Elimination of Discrimination against Women.

Chambers, Robert G., and Quiggin, John. 2000. *Uncertainty, Production, Choice and Agency: The State-Contingent Approach*. Cambridge, UK: Cambridge University Press.

Chandler, Alfred. 1990. *Scale and Scope: The Dynamics of Industrial Capitalism*. Cambridge, MA: Harvard University Press/Belknap.

Christophers, Brett. 2016. *The Great Leveler: Capitalism and Competition in the Court of Law*. Cambridge, MA: Harvard University Press.

Ciriacy-Wantrup, Siegfried, and Bishop, Richard. 1975. "'Common Property' as a Concept in Natural Resource Policy." *Natural Resources Journal* 15(4): 713–27.

Coase, Ronald. 1937. "The Nature of the Firm." *Economica* 4: 368–405.

Coase, Ronald. 1960. "The Problem of Social Cost." *Journal of Law and Economics* 3(1): 1–44.

Coase, Ronald H. 1964. "Discussion." *American Economic Review* 54(3): 192–97.

Cohan, Steven, and Hark, Ina Rae. 1997. *The Road Movie Book*. New York: Routledge.

College Board. 2016. *Trends in College Pricing*. New York: College Board.

Commonwealth of Australia. 1945. *Full Employment in Australia*. Canberra: Commonwealth Government Printer.

Congressional Budget Office. 2012. Effective Marginal Tax Rates for Low- and Moderate-Income Workers. https://www.cbo.gov /publication/43709.

Cornes, Richard, and Sandler, Todd. 1996. *The Theory of Externalities, Public Goods, and Club Goods*. Cambridge, UK: Cambridge University Press.

Council of Economic Advisers. 2016. "Benefits of Competition and Indicators of Market Power." In *Economic Report of the President*, chap. 5. Washington, DC: Council of Economic Advisers.

Cowen, Tyler. 2014. The Lack of Major Wars May Be Hurting Economic Growth. *New York Times*, June 13, https://www.nytimes .com/2014/06/14/upshot/the-lack-of-major-wars-may-be-hurting -economic-growth.html.

Coyle, Diane. 2015. *GDP: A Brief but Affectionate History*. Princeton, NJ: Princeton University Press.

Crain, Caleb. 2007. There She Blew. *New Yorker*, http://www.new yorker.com/magazine/2007/07/23/there-she-blew.

Crawford, Neta. 2016. US Budgetary Costs of Wars Through 2016: $4.79 Trillion and Counting. Watson Institute, Boston University. http://watson.brown.edu/costsofwar/figures/2016/us-budgetary -costs-wars-through-2016-479-trillion-and-counting.

Crouch, David. 2015. Pitfalls of Rent Restraints: Why Stockholm's Model Has Failed Many. *The Guardian*, August 15, https://www .theguardian.com/world/2015/aug/19/why-stockholm-housing -rules-rent-control-flat.

Dahlman, Carl. 1980. *The Open Field System and Beyond*. Cambridge, UK: Cambridge University Press.

Darby, Megan. 2016. "Meet the Woman Who First Identified the Greenhouse Effect." *Climate Home News*, http://www.climate changenews.com/2016/09/02/the-woman-who-identified-the -greenhouse-effect-years-before-tyndall/.

Dasgupta, Partha. 1982. *The Control of Resources*. Oxford: Basil Blackwell.

Davala, Sarath, Jhabvala, Renana, Mehta, Soumya K., and Standing, Guy. 2015. *Basic Income: A Transformative Policy for India*. London: Bloomsbury Paperbacks.

De Loecker, Jan, and Eeckhout, Jan. 2017. The Rise of Market Power and the Macroeconomic Implications. National Bureau of Economic Research, http://www.janeeckhout.com/wp-content/uploads /RMP-pres.pdf.

Debreu, Gerard. 1959. *Theory of Value*. New York: Wiley.

Defoe, Daniel. 2003. *Robinson Crusoe*. Harmondsworth: Penguin Classics.

del Granado, Francisco J. A., Coady, David, and Gillingham, Robert. 2012. "The Unequal Benefits of Fuel Subsidies: A Review of Evidence for Developing Countries." *World Development* 40(11).

Demsetz, Harold. 1969. "Information and Efficiency: Another Viewpoint." *Journal of Law and Economics* 12(1): 1–22.

Diamond, Jared. 1987. "The Worst Mistake in the History of the Human Race." *Discover*, May, http://discovermagazine.com/1987 /may/02-the-worst-mistake-in-the-history-of-the-human-race/.

Diamond, Patrick, and Chwalisz, Claudia. 2015. *The Predistribution Agenda: Tackling Inequality and Supporting Sustainable Growth*. London: I.B. Tauris.

Diamond, Peter A., and Mirrlees, James A. 1971a. "Optimal Taxation and Public Production I: Production Efficiency." *American Economic Review* 61(1): 8–27.

Diamond, Peter A., and Mirrlees, James A. 1971b. "Optimal Taxation and Public Production II: Tax Rules." *American Economic Review* 61(3): 261–78.

Dolin, Eric Jay. 2008. *Leviathan: The History of Whaling in America.* New York: W. W. Norton.

Easterley, William. 2006. Why Doesn't Aid Work? *Cato Unbound*, April 2, https://www.cato-unbound.org/2006/04/02/william -easterly/why-doesnt-aid-work.

Easterley, William. 2017. This Common Argument for U.S. Foreign Aid Is Actually Quite Xenophobic. *Washington Post*, March 31, https://www.washingtonpost.com/news/global-opinions/wp/2017 /03/31/this-common-argument-for-u-s-foreign-aid-is-actually-quite -xenophobic/?utm_term=.5a971fa9e106.

Eggertsson, Gauti B., Robbins, Jacon, and Wold, Ella. 2018. Kaldor and Piketty's Facts: The Rise of Monopoly Power in the United States. NBER Working Paper 24287.

Eisenhower, Dwight. 1953. "The Chance for Peace." Address to the American Society of Newspaper Editors, http://www.edchange.org /multicultural/speeches/ike_chance_for_peace.html.

Eisenhower, Dwight. 1961. "Farewell Address." http://www.american rhetoric.com/speeches/dwightdeisenhowerfarewell.html.

Ekins, Paul. 1999. "European Environmental Taxes and Charges: Recent Experience, Issues and Trends." *Ecological Economics* 31(1): 39–62.

Environmental Protection Agency. 2018a. Clean Air Act Require- ments and History. https://www.epa.gov/clean-air-act-overview /clean-air-act-requirements-and-history.

Environmental Protection Agency. 2018b. Clean Air Markets. https:// www.epa.gov/airmarkets.

Esguerra, Richard. 2008. The FCC and Regulatory Capture. *Electronic Frontier Foundation*, https://www.eff.org/deeplinks/2008/08/fcc -and-regulatory-capture.

Fama, Eugene. 1970. "Efficient Capital Markets: A Review of Theory and Empirical Work." *Journal of Finance* 25(2): 383–417.

Farrant, Andrew, McPhail, Edward, and Berger, Sebastian. 2012. "Pre- venting the 'Abuses' of Democracy: Hayek, the 'Military Usurper' and Transitional Dictatorship in Chile." *American Journal of Eco- nomics and Sociology* 71(3): 513–38.

Farrell, Henry, and Quiggin, John. 2011. "How to Save the Euro—and the EU: Reading Keynes in Brussels." *Foreign Affairs* 90(3): 96–103.

Farrell, Henry, and Quiggin, John. 2017. "Consensus, Dissensus, and Economic Ideas: The Rise and Decline of Keynesianism during the Economic Crisis." *International Studies Quarterly* 61(2): 269–83.

Federal Reserve Bank of St. Louis. 2017. Federal Reserve Economic Database (FRED): Interest Rates. https://fred.stlouisfed.org /categories/22.

Fein, Ellen, and Schneider, Sherrie. 1996. *The Rules: Time-Tested Secrets for Capturing the Heart of Mr. Right*. New York: Grand Central Publishing.

Feldstein, Martin. 2009. Economic Conditions and U.S. National Security in the 1930s and Today. NBER Working Paper 15290.

Ferraro, Paul J., and Taylor, Laura O. 2005. "Do Economists Recognize an Opportunity Cost When They See One? A Dismal Performance from the Dismal Science." *B.E. Journal of Economic Analysis & Policy* 4(1): 1–14.

Fine, Ben. 2016. *Microeconomics: A Critical Companion*. London: Pluto Press.

Fine, Ben, and Dimakou, Ourania. 2016. *Macroeconomics: A Critical Companion (IIPPE)*. London: Pluto Press.

Fontevecchia, Agustino. 2012. Despite $50b in Damages, Hurricane Sandy Will Be Good for the Economy, Goldman Says. *Forbes*, November 6, https://www.forbes.com/sites/afontevecchia/2012/11/06 /despite-50b-in-damages-hurricane-sandy-will-be-good-for-the -economy-goldman-says/#d06c17d6ad71.

Fox, Justin. 2009. *The Myth of the Rational Market: A History of Risk, Reward, and Delusion on Wall Street*. New York: HarperBusiness.

Franklin, Benjamin. 1748. From His Advice to a Young Tradesman from an Old One. http://founders.archives.gov/documents /Franklin/01-03-02-0130.

Freeman, Richard. 2007. Do Workers Still Want Unions? More Than Ever. Economic Policy Institute Briefing Paper 182, http://www .gpn.org/bp182.html.

Friedman, M. 1975. *There's No Such Thing as a Free Lunch*. Chicago: Open Court Publishing.

Friedman, Milton, and Boorstin, Daniel. 1951. "How to Plan and Pay for the Safe and Adequate Highways We Need." In *Roads in a Market Economy*, edited by Roth, Gabriel J., 223–45. Avebury: Ashgate.

Frost, Robert. 1921. *Mountain Interval*. New York: Henry Holt.

Fry, Cristy. 2017. Spring Herring Season Kicks Off. *Homer News*, March 29, http://homernews.com/seawatch/2017-03-30/spring -herring-season-kicks.

Fukuyama, Francis. 1992. *The End of History and the Last Man*. New York: Free Press.

Furman Center for Real Estate and Urban Policy. 2012. Rent Stabilization in New York City. http://furmancenter.org/research /publication/rent-stabilization-in-new-york-city.

Galbraith, John Kenneth. 1958. *The Affluent Society*. New York: Houghton Mifflin.

Galbraith, John Kenneth. 1969. *The New Industrial State*. Harmondsworth: Penguin.

Galbraith, J. K. 1971. *Economics, Peace and Laughter*. New York: Houghton Mifflin.

Gigerenzer, Gerd, Hertwig, Ralph, and Pachur, Thorsten. 2015. *Heuristics: The Foundations of Adaptive Behavior*. Oxford: Oxford University Press.

Gigerenzer, Gerd, and Selten, Reinhard. 2002. *Bounded Rationality: The Adaptive Toolbox*. Cambridge, MA: MIT Press.

Gigerenzer, Gerd, Todd, Peter M., and ABC Research Group. 2000. *Simple Heuristics That Make Us Smart*. Oxford: Oxford University Press.

Gold, Bela. 1981. "Changing Perspectives on Size, Scale, and Returns: An Interpretive Survey." *Journal of Economic Literature* 19(1): 5–33.

Goldstein, Jacob. 2013. Is It Nuts to Give to the Poor Without Strings Attached? *New York Times*, August 13, http://www.nytimes.com /2013/08/18/magazine/is-it-nuts-to-give-to-the-poor-without -strings-attached.html?_r=0.

Gordon, H. S. 1954. "The Economic Theory of a Common Property Resource: The Fishery." *Journal of Political Economy* 62(1): 124–47.

Graaff, J. de V. 1968. *Theoretical Welfare Economics*. Cambridge, UK: Cambridge University Press.

Graeber, David. 2011. *Debt: The First 5,000 Years*. Brooklyn, NY: Melville House.

Grant, Simon, and Quiggin, John. 2005. "What Does the Equity Premium Mean?" *Economists' Voice* 2(4): Article 2.

Greenwood, Robin, and Scharfstein, David. 2013. "The Growth of Finance." *Journal of Economic Perspectives* 27(2): 3–28.

Hacker, Jacob. 2011. The Institutional Foundations of Middle-Class Democracy. *Policy Network*, May 6.

Hacker, Jacob S., and Pierson, Paul. 2017. *American Amnesia: How the War on Government Led Us to Forget What Made America Prosper*. New York: Simon & Schuster.

Hardin, Garrett. 1968. "The Tragedy of the Commons." *Science* 162(3859): 1243–48.

Harrison, Todd. 2013. Chaos and Uncertainty: The FY 14 Defense Budget and Beyond. Center for Strategic and Budgetary Assessments (CSBA), http://csbaonline.org/research/publications/chaos-and-uncertainty-the-fy-14-defense-budget-and-beyond.

Harvard University. 2016. Cost of Attendance. https://college.harvard.edu/financial-aid/how-aid-works/cost-attendance.

Hattam, Victoria C. 1993. *Labor Visions and State Power: The Origins of Business Unionism in the United States (Princeton Legacy Library)*. Princeton, NJ: Princeton University Press.

Haushofer, J., and Shapiro, J. 2013. Household Response to Income Changes: Evidence from an Unconditional Cash Transfer Program in Kenya. Massachusetts Institute of Technology. http://jeremyp shapiro.com/papers/Household%20Response%20to%20Income%20Changes-%20Evidence%20from%20an%20Unconditional%20Cash%20Transfer%20Program%20in%20Kenya%20November%202013.pdf.

Hayek, Friedrich. 1937. "Economics and Knowledge." *Economica* 4(1): 33–54.

Hayek, Friedrich. 1944. *The Road to Serfdom*. Chicago: University of Chicago Press.

Hayek, Friedrich. 1945. "The Use of Knowledge in Society." *American Economic Review* 35(3): 519–30.

Hayek, Friedrich. 1966. *Monetary Theory and the Trade Cycle*. New York: Augustus M. Kelley.

Hazlitt, Henry. 1946. *Economics in One Lesson*. New York: Harper & Brothers.

Hazlitt, Henry. 1959. *The Failure of the "New Economics."* New York: Van Nostrand.

Hazlitt, Henry. 1967. How Should Prices Be Determined? https://fee .org/articles/how-should-prices-be-determined/.

Hazlitt, Henry. 1993. *The Wisdom of Henry Hazlitt*. Auburn, AL: Ludwig von Mises Institute.

Heinlein, Robert A. 1966. *The Moon Is a Harsh Mistress*. New York: Berkley.

Homer, Sidney, and Sylla, Richard. 2005. *A History of Interest Rates, Fourth Edition (Wiley Finance)*. New York: Wiley.

Howard, Peter, and Sylvan, Derek. 2015. Expert Consensus on the Economics of Climate Change. Institute for Policy Integrity, New York University School of Law, New York, http://policyintegrity .org/files/publications/ExpertConsensusReport.pdf.

Howe, Walt. 2016. A Brief History of the Internet, http://www .walthowe.com/navnet/history.html.

Ingraham, Christopher. 2017. Massive New Data Set Suggests Economic Inequality Is About to Get Even Worse. *Washington Post*, January 4, https://www.washingtonpost.com/news/wonk/wp/2018 /01/04/massive-new-data-set-suggests-inequality-is-about-to-get -even-worse/?utm_term=.b6c6fad16126.

Jaumotte, Florence, and Buitron, Carolina. 2015a. Inequality and Labor Market Institutions. International Monetary Fund Staff Discussion Note 15/14, https://www.imf.org/~/media/Websites/IMF /imported-full-text-pdf/external/pubs/ft/sdn/2015/_sdn1514.ashx.

Jaumotte, Florence, and Buitron, Carolina. 2015b. "Power from the People." *Finance & Development* 52(1): 29–31.

JC. 2005. Comment. http://marginalrevolution.com/marginal revolution/2005/09/opportunity_cos.html.

Johnson, Ted. 2017. "Stations Set to Reap $10 Billion as FCC Closes Auction of Broadcast Airwaves." *Variety*, http://variety.com/2017/biz/news/fcc-incentive-auction-10-billion-1202030079/.

Jones, Ernest. 1867. "Democracy Vindicated." *Elliot*, http://www.gerald-massey.org.uk/jones/b_jones_democracy.htm.

Jorda, Oscar, Knoll, Katharina, Kuvshinov, Dmitry, Schularick, Moritz, and Taylor, Alan M. 2017. The Rate of Return on Everything, 1870–2015. National Bureau of Economic Research Working Paper No. 24112, http://www.nber.org/papers/w24112.

Kahn, Richard F. 1931. "The Relation of Home Investment to Unemployment." *Economic Journal* 41(162): 173–98.

Kahneman, Daniel. 2013. *Thinking, Fast and Slow*. New York: Farrar, Straus and Giroux.

Kay, John. 2004. *The Truth About Markets: Why Some Nations Are Rich but Most Remain Poor*. New York: Penguin.

Kenny, C. 2015. Give Poor People Cash. *The Atlantic*, September 25, https://www.theatlantic.com/international/archive/2015/09/welfare-reform-direct-cash-poor/407236/.

Kerouac, Jack. 1957. *On the Road*. New York: New American Library.

Keynes, John Maynard. 1923. *A Tract on Monetary Reform*. London: Macmillan.

Keynes, John Maynard. 1936. *The General Theory of Employment, Interest and Money*. London: Macmillan.

Keynes, John Maynard. 1937. How to Avoid a Slump. *The Times*.

Khan, Lina, and Vaheesan, Sandeep. 2017. "Market Power and Inequality: The Antitrust Counterrevolution and Its Discontents." *Harvard Law and Policy Review* 11: 235–94.

Kitroeff, Natalie. 2015. Law School Applications Set to Hit 15-Year Low. *Bloomberg News*, https://www.bloomberg.com/news/articles/2015-03-19/law-school-applications-will-hit-their-lowest-point-in-15-years.

Klekociuk, Andrew, and Krummel, Paul. 2017. After 30 Years of the Montreal Protocol, the Ozone Layer Is Gradually Healing. https://theconversation.com/after-30-years-of-the-montreal-protocol-the-ozone-layer-is-gradually-healing-84051.

Kondratieff, Nikolai D. 2014. *The Long Waves in Economic Life*. East-ford, CT: Martino Fine Books.

Kozlowska, Hanna. 2017. "When It Comes to Air Pollution, Poland Is the China of Europe." *Quartz*, https://qz.com/882158/with-air-pollution-skyrocketing-warsaw-is-severely-hit-by-polands-smog-problem/.

Kruger, Justin, and Dunning, David. 1999. "Unskilled and Unaware of It: How Difficulties in Recognizing One's Own Incompetence Lead to Inflated Self-Assessments." *Journal of Personality and Social Psychology* 77(6): 1121–34.

Krugman, Paul. 2009. How Did Economists Get It So Wrong? *New York Times*, September 2, http://www.nytimes.com/2009/09/06/magazine/06Economic-t.html.

Krugman, Paul. 2016. Robber Baron Recessions. *New York Times*, April 18, https://www.nytimes.com/2016/04/18/opinion/robber-baron-recessions.html.

Lakatos, Imre. 1970. "Falsification and the Methodology of Scientific Research Programmes." In *Criticism and the Growth of Knowledge*, edited by Lakatos, I., and Musgrave, A. Cambridge, UK: Cambridge University Press.

Lancaster, Kelvin, and Lipsey, Richard. 1956. "The General Theory of Second Best." *Review of Economic Studies* 24(1): 11–32.

Lange, Oskar. 1936. "On the Economic Theory of Socialism: Part One." *Review of Economic Studies* 4(1): 53–71.

Lange, Oskar. 1937. "On the Economic Theory of Socialism: Part Two." *Review of Economic Studies* 4(2): 123.

Langmore, John, and Quiggin, John. 1994. *Work for All: Full Employment in the Nineties*. Carlton, Victoria: Melbourne University Press.

Latson, Jennifer. 2013. The Burning River That Sparked a Revolution. *Time*, June 22.

Leonard, Thomas C. 2000. "The Very Idea of Applying Economics: The Modern Minimum-Wage Controversy and Its Antecedents." *History of Political Economy* 32(Suppl. 1): 117–44.

Lessig, Lawrence. 2001. *The Future of Ideas: The Fate of the Commons in a Connected World*. New York: Random House.

Leswing, Kif. 2016. The 4 Most Valuable Public Companies Are All Tech Companies. *Business Insider*, https://www.businessinsider .com.au/4-most-valuable-public-companies-all-tech-companies -2016-8?r=US&IR=T.

Lev-Ram, Michal. 2008. The Box Office Indicator: When Times Get Tough, Consumers Beeline to the Movies. *Fortune*, August 22, http://archive.fortune.com/2008/08/21/news/companies/Movies .fortune/index.htm?postversion=2008082215.

Lindbeck, Assar. 1972. *Political Economy of the New Left: An Outsider's View*. New York: Joanna Cotler Books.

Little, Ian. 1950. *A Critique of Welfare Economics*. Oxford: Clarendon Press.

Lynn, Barry C. 2011. *Cornered: The New Monopoly Capitalism and the Economics of Destruction*. New York: Wiley.

Mackay, Charles. 1841. *Extraordinary Popular Delusions and the Madness of Crowds*. Litrix Reading Room.

Madia, Matthew. 2008. Life's Value Shrinks at EPA. Center for Effective Government.

Malkiel, Burton G. 2007. *A Random Walk Down Wall Street: The Time-Tested Strategy for Successful Investing (Revised and Updated)*. New York: W.W. Norton.

Manne, Henry. 1965. "Mergers and the Market for Corporate Control." *Journal of Political Economy* 73(1): 110–20.

Manning, Alan. 2003. "The Real Thin Theory: Monopsony in Modern Labour Markets." *Labour Economics* 10(2): 105–31.

Marshall, Alfred. 1920. *Principles of Economics* (8th ed.). London: Macmillan.

Martin, Felix. 2015. *Money: The Unauthorized Biography—from Coinage to Cryptocurrencies*. New York: Vintage.

Marx, Karl, and Engels, Friedrich. 1848. "The Communist Manifesto." *Penguin*, https://www.marxists.org/archive/marx/works/1848 /communist-manifesto/ch01.htm.

McCloskey, Deirdre N. 1982. *The Applied Theory of Price*. New York: Collier Macmillan.

McKean, Roland. 1965. "The Unseen Hand in Government." *American Economic Review* 55(3): 496–506.

McNeil, Leila. 2016. This Lady Scientist Defined the Greenhouse Effect But Didn't Get the Credit, Because Sexism. http://www.smithsonianmag.com/science-nature/lady-scientist-helped-revolutionize-climate-science-didnt-get-credit-180961291/.

Medema, Steven G. 2004. Mill, Sidgwick, and the Evolution of the Theory of Market Failure. CAE Working Papers 03, Aix-Marseille Université, CERGAM, https://ideas.repec.org/p/cgm/wpaper/03.html.

Mill, John Stuart. 2007. *On Liberty*. London: Penguin Classics.

Mirowski, Philip. 2011. Why Is There a Nobel Memorial Prize in Economics? (Video). https://www.youtube.com/watch?v=dLtEo8lplwg.

Mises, Ludwig von. 1920. *Economic Calculation in the Socialist Commonwealth*. Auburn, AL: Ludwig von Mises Institute.

Mises, Ludwig von, Rothbard, Murray N., Haberler, Gottfried, and Hayek, Friedrich A. 1996. *The Austrian Theory of the Trade Cycle and Other Essays*. Auburn, AL: Ludwig von Mises Institute.

Mishel, Lawrence. 2012a. Entry-Level Workers' Wages Fell in Lost Decade. Economic Policy Institute, Issue Brief 327, http://www.epi.org/files/2012/ib327.pdf.

Mishel, Lawrence. 2012b. Unions, Inequality, and Faltering Middle-Class Wages. Economic Policy Institute Briefing Paper 342, http://www.epi.org/publication/ib342-unions-inequality-faltering-middle-class/.

Mishel, Lawrence. 2013. Declining Value of the Federal Minimum Wage Is a Major Factor Driving Inequality. *Economic Policy Institute*, https://www.epi.org/publication/declining-federal-minimum-wage-inequality/.

Mitchell, W. 1998. "The Buffer Stock Employment Model—Full Employment Without a Nairu." *Journal of Economic Issues* 32(2): 547–55.

Morris, Ian. 2014. *War! What Is It Good For?: Conflict and the Progress of Civilization from Primates to Robots*. New York: Farrar, Straus and Giroux.

Morrison, Catherine J., and Schwartz, Amy Ellen. 1994. "Distinguishing External from Internal Scale Effects: The Case of Public Infrastructure." *Journal of Productivity Analysis* 5(3): 249–70.

Moshakis, Alex. 2018. Fresh Air for Sale. *The Guardian*, January 21, https://www.theguardian.com/global/2018/jan/21/fresh-air-for-sale.

Mosler, W. 1997. "Full Employment and Price Stability." *Journal of Post Keynesian Economics* 20(2): 167–82.

Musgrave, Richard A., and Musgrave, Peggy. 1973. *Public Finance in Theory and Practice*. New York: McGraw Hill.

Naidu, Suresh, Posner, Eric, and Weyl, Glen. 2018. More and More Companies Have Monopoly Power Over Workers' Wages. That's Killing the Economy. https://www.vox.com/the-big-idea/2018/4/6/17204808/wages-employers-workers-monopsony-growth-stagnation-inequality.

Nash, John. 1950. "The Bargaining Problem." *Econometrica* 18(2): 155–62.

Nash, John. 1953. "Two-Person Cooperative Games." *Econometrica* 21(1): 128–40.

Neumark, D., and Wascher, W. 1995. "Minimum Wage Effects on Employment and School Enrollment." *Journal of Business and Economic Statistics* 13(2): 199–206.

Nuccitelli, Dana. 2016. 95% Consensus of Expert Economists: Cut Carbon Pollution. *The Guardian*, January 4, https://www.theguardian.com/environment/climate-consensus-97-per-cent/2016/jan/04/consensus-of-economists-cut-carbon-pollution.

Nunn, Ryan. 2018. How Occupational Licensing Matters for Wages and Careers. Brookings Institution: Hamilton Project, https://www.brookings.edu/research/how-occupational-licensing-matters-for-wages-and-careers/.

Nye, Robert A. 1977. *Anti-Democratic Sources of Elite Theory: Pareto, Mosca, Michels*. New York: Sage.

Offer, Avner, and Söderberg, Gabriel. 2016. *The Nobel Factor: The Prize in Economics, Social Democracy, and the Market Turn*. Princeton, NJ: Princeton University Press.

Olson, Elizabeth. 2014. Law School Is Buyers' Market, with Top Students in Demand. *New York Times*, December 1, https://dealbook.nytimes.com/2014/12/01/law-school-becomes-buyers-market-as-competition-for-best-students-increases/.

Olson, Elizabeth. 2017. Whittier Law School Says It Will Shut Down. *New York Times*, April 19, https://www.nytimes.com/2017/04/19 /business/dealbook/whittier-law-school-to-close.html?_r=0.

Oreskes, N. 2004. "Beyond the Ivory Tower: The Scientific Consensus on Climate Change." *Science* 306(5702): 1686.

Oreskes, Naomi, and Conway, Erik M. 2011. *Merchants of Doubt*. New York: Bloomsbury Press.

Organization for Economic Co-operation and Development (OECD). 2017. OECD Employment Outlook 2017. https://read.oecd-ilibrary .org/employment/oecd-employment-outlook-2017_empl_outlook -2017-en#page5.

Organization for Economic Co-operation and Development (OECD). 2018. Environmental Taxation. https://www.oecd.org/env/tools -evaluation/environmentaltaxation.htm.

Ortmann, Andreas, and Spiliopoulos, Leonidas. 2017. "The Beauty of Simplicity? (simple) Heuristics and the Opportunities Yet to Be Realized." In *Handbook of Behavioural Economics and Smart Decision-Making: Rational Decision-Making within the Bounds of Reason*, edited by Altman, Morris, 119. Cheltenham, UK: Edward Elgar.

Orwell, George. 1968. "James Burnham and the Managerial Revolution." In *The Collected Essays, Journalism and Letters of George Orwell*. 4 Volumes, 160–80. London: Martin Secker & Warburg Ltd.

Ostrom, Elinor. 1990. *Governing the Commons: The Evolution of Institutions for Collective Action*. Cambridge, UK: Cambridge University Press.

Packard, Vance. 1957. *The Hidden Persuaders*. New York: Random House.

Passell, Peter. 1995. Economic Scene; in the Cloud of a Natural Disaster, Some See a Silver Lining. *New York Times*, January 26, http:// www.nytimes.com/1995/01/26/business/economic-scene-in-the -cloud-of-a-natural-disaster-some-see-a-silver-lining.html.

Paul, L. A. 2015. *Transformative Experience*. Oxford: Oxford University Press.

Pigou, Arthur. 1920. *The Economics of Welfare*. London: Macmillan.

Piketty, Thomas. 2014. *Capital in the Twenty-First Century*. Cambridge, MA: Harvard University Press.

Piketty, Thomas, and Saez, Emmanuel. 2003. "Income Inequality in the United States, 1913–1998." *Quarterly Journal of Economics* 118(1): 1–39.

Piketty, Thomas, and Saez, Emmanuel. 2006. "The Evolution of Top Incomes: A Historical and International Perspective." *American Economic Review* 96(2): 200–205.

Piketty, Thomas, Saez, Emmanuel, and Stantcheva, Stefanie. 2014. "Optimal Taxation of Top Labor Incomes: A Tale of Three Elasticities." *American Economic Journal: Economic Policy* 6(1): 230–71.

Pingali, Prabhu, and Feder, Gershon. 2017. *Agriculture and Rural Development in a Globalizing World: Challenges and Opportunities (Earthscan Food and Agriculture).* New York: Routledge.

Pinstrup-Andersen, Per (ed.). 1988. *Food Subsidies in Developing Countries: Costs, Benefits, and Policy Options.* Baltimore, MD: Published for the International Food Policy Research Institute (IFPRI) by Johns Hopkins University Press.

Poole, Heather. 2015. How Much Do Flight Attendants Really Make? *Mashable*, http://mashable.com/2015/02/24/how-much-do-flight-attendants-make/#yaeXAhiDuOqo.

Potter, Joel, and Sanders, Shane. 2012. "Do Economists Recognize an Opportunity Cost When They See One? A Dismal Performance or an Arbitrary Concept." *Southern Economic Journal* 79(2): 248–56.

Poynder, John. 1841. *Literary Extracts from English and Other Works; Collected During Half a Century: Together with Some Original Matter Volume 1—2015 Edition.* Arkose Press.

Prochasson, Christophe. 2010. "Intellectuals and Writers." In *A Companion to World War I*, edited by Horne, J., 323–37. New York: Wiley-Blackwell.

Quiggin, A. Hingston. 1949. *A Survey of Primitive Money: The Beginning of Currency.* London: Methuen.

Quiggin, John. 1988. "Private and Common Property Rights in the Economics of the Environment." *Journal of Economic Issues* 22(4): 1071–87.

Quiggin, John. 1994. "The White Paper and After: Policies for Full Employment." *Just Policy* 1(1): 27–38.

Quiggin, John. 1996. *Great Expectations: Microeconomic Reform and Australia.* St. Leonards, NSW: Allen & Unwin.

Quiggin, John. 2006. Becker and Murphy on Advertising. http:// johnquiggin.com/2006/05/11/becker-and-murphy-on-advertising/.

Quiggin, John. 2008. "Stern and His Critics on Discounting and Climate Change." *Climatic Change* 89(3–4): 195–205.

Quiggin, John. 2010. Hayek's Zombie Idea. *Crooked Timber,* http:// crookedtimber.org/2010/10/01/hayeks-zombie-idea/.

Quiggin, John. 2011a. Accounting for Natural Disasters. Paper presented at Western Economic Association International Conference, Brisbane.

Quiggin, John. 2011b. *Zombie Economics: How Dead Ideas Still Walk Among Us* (Paperback Edition). Princeton, NJ: Princeton University Press.

Quiggin, John. 2014. Discussion of How the Private Sector Can Improve Public Transportation Infrastructure. *RBA Annual Conference Volume, 2014.*

Quiggin, John. 2015a. John Locke Against Freedom. *Jacobin,* June 28, https://www.jacobinmag.com/2015/06/locke-treatise-slavery -private-property/.

Quiggin, John. 2015b. John Locke's Road to Serfdom. *Jacobin,* October 18, https://www.jacobinmag.com/2015/10/locke-classical -liberalism-treatise-nozick-constitution/.

Quiggin, John. 2016. Locke's Folly. *Jacobin,* August 14, https://www .jacobinmag.com/2016/08/locke-property-manifest-destiny -jefferson-slavery-indigenous/.

Quiggin, John. 2018. "The Importance of 'Extremely Unlikely' Events: Tail Risk and the Costs of Climate Change." *Australian Journal of Agricultural and Resource Economics* 62(1): 4–20.

Rae, Ian. 2012. "Saving the Ozone Layer: Why the Montreal Protocol Worked." *The Conversation,* https://theconversation.com/saving -the-ozone-layer-why-the-montreal-protocol-worked-9249.

Read, Leonard. 1958. I, Pencil: My Family Tree as Told to Leonard E. Read. *The Freeman,* December, http://www.econlib.org/library /Essays/rdPncl1.html.

REALS. 2015. A Seedbank Which Survives: Pavlovsk Experimental Station. http://realsproject.org/a-seedbank-which-survives-pavlovsk -experimental-station/.

Reardon, Marguerite. 2015. "FCC Rakes in $45 Billion from Wireless Spectrum Auction." *CNET News*, https://www.cnet.com/news /fcc-rakes-in-45-billion-from-wireless-spectrum-auction/.

Rensin, Emmett, and Shor, David. 2014. Blaming Parents, and Other Neoliberal Pastimes. *The Baffler*, December 29, https://thebaffler .com/latest/blaming-parents.

Reyes, Jessica Wolpaw. 2007. "Environmental Policy as Social Policy? The Impact of Childhood Lead Exposure on Crime." *BE Journal of Economic Analysis & Policy* 7(1): 1796.

Ricardo, David. 1817. *On the Principles of Political Economy and Taxation. In the Works and Correspondence of David Ricardo*, Volume 1. Edited by Piero Sraffa, with the Collaboration of Maurice Dobb. Cambridge, UK: Cambridge University Press.

Richards, David. 2007. "Did Passenger Fare Savings Occur After Airline Deregulation?" *Journal of the Transportation Research Forum* 46(1): 73–93.

Riggenbach, Jeff. 2010. Was Robert A. Heinlein a Libertarian? *Mises Daily*, https://mises.org/library/was-robert-heinlein-libertarian.

Robbins, Lionel. 1932. *An Essay on the Nature and Significance of Economic Science*. London: Macmillan.

Robin, Corey. 2013a. *The Reactionary Mind: Conservatism from Edmund Burke to Sarah Palin*. Oxford: Oxford University Press.

Robin, Corey. 2013b. If You're Getting Lessons in Democracy from Margaret Thatcher, You're Doing It Wrong. http://coreyrobin.com /2013/07/16/if-youre-getting-lessons-in-democracy-from-margaret -thatcher-youre-doing-it-wrong/.

Rodrik, Dani. 2011. Milton Friedman's Magical Thinking. *Project Syndicate*, https://www.project-syndicate.org/commentary/milton -friedman-s-magical-thinking.

Romer, Paul M. 1994. "The Origins of Endogenous Growth." *Journal of Economic Perspectives* 8(1): 3–22.

Rosen, Jay. 2010. The View from Nowhere: Questions and Answers. http://pressthink.org/2010/11/the-view-from-nowhere-questions -and-answers/.

Rosenberg, Jeremy. 2012. How Los Angeles Began to Put Its Smoggy Days Behind. https://www.kcet.org/history-society/how-los-angeles -began-to-put-its-smoggy-days-behind.

Rosenfeld, Jake, Denice, Patrick, and Laird, Jennifer. 2016. Union Decline Lowers Wages of Nonunion Workers. Economic Policy Institute, https://www.epi.org/publication/union-decline-lowers -wages-of-nonunion-workers-the-overlooked-reason-why-wages-are -stuck-and-inequality-is-growing/.

Roth, Gabriel. 1998. *Roads in a Market Economy.* Avebury: Ashgate.

Ruane, Kathleen. 2011. Fairness Doctrine: History and Constitutional Issues. Congressional Research Service, https://digital.library.unt .edu/ark:/67531/metadc822082/.

Saez, Emmanuel. 2016. U.S. Top One Percent of Income Earners Hit New High in 2015 Amid Strong Economic Growth, http://equitable growth.org/research-analysis/u-s-top-one-percent-of-income-earners -hit-new-high-in-2015-amid-strong-economic-growth/.

Saint-Paul, Gilles. 2004. "Are Intellectual Property Rights Unfair." *Labour Economics Labour Market Consequences of New Information Technologies* 11(1): 129–44.

Samuelson, Paul. 1948. *Economics.* New York: McGraw-Hill.

Samuelson, Paul. 2009. "An Enjoyable Life Puzzling Over Modern Finance Theory." *Annual Review of Financial Economics* 1(1): 19–35.

Samuelson, Paul A. 1954. "The Pure Theory of Public Expenditure." *Review of Economics and Statistics* 36(4): 387–89.

Schwartz, Barry. 2005. *The Paradox of Choice.* New York: Harper Perennial.

Sears, Louis, and Coady, David. 2015. Evidence for Developing Countries. International Monetary Fund 15250, https://www.imf.org /external/pubs/ft/wp/2015/wp15250.pdf.

Sharkey, William W. 1982. *The Theory of Natural Monopoly.* Cambridge, UK: Cambridge University Press.

Shonfield, Andrew. 1965. *Modern Capitalism: The Changing Balance of Public and Private Power*. Oxford: Oxford University Press.

Shonfield, Andrew. 1984. *In Defence of the Mixed Economy*. Oxford: Oxford University Press.

Simon, Herbert Alexander. 1957. *Models of Man: Social and Rational Mathematical Essays on Rational Human Behavior in a Social Setting*. New York: Wiley.

Sinclair, Upton. 1906. *The Jungle*. New York: Doubleday.

Skorup, Jarrett. 2011. Natural Disasters Are Good? *Mackinac Center*, https://www.mackinac.org/14753.

Smith, Adam. 1776. *Wealth of Nations* (1976 edition). Raleigh, NC: Hayes Barton Press.

Smith, Adam (George Goodman). 1968. *The Money Game By 'Adam Smith.'* New York: Random House.

Staunton, C., and Collins, M. 2013. Evaluating the Effectiveness of Cash Transfers Versus Food Aid: A Case Study in Rural Zimbabwe. Concern Worldwide, http://www.tcd.ie/Economics/assets/pdf/TCD_Econ_Seminar_Cash_and_Food_Aid_April_2011.pdf.

Steelman, Aaron. 2013. Employment Act of 1946. *Federal Reserve History*, https://www.federalreservehistory.org/essays/employment_act_of_1946.

Stern, Nicholas. 2007. *The Economics of Climate Change—the Stern Review*. Cambridge, UK: Cambridge University Press.

Stewart, James. 2017. A Tax Loophole for the Rich That Just Won't Die. *New York Times*, November 9, https://www.nytimes.com/2017/11/09/business/carried-interest-tax-loophole.html.

Stigler, George J. 1961. "The Economics of Information." *Journal of Political Economy* 69(3): 213–25.

Stiglitz, Joseph E. 1996. *Whither Socialism? (Wicksell Lectures)*. Cambridge, MA: MIT Press.

Stiglitz, Joseph E. 2016. *The Great Divide: Unequal Societies and What We Can Do About Them*. New York: W. W. Norton.

Streissler, E. W. 1990. "Menger, Böhm-Bawerk, and Wieser: The Origins of the Austrian School." In *Neoclassical Economic Theory, 1870 to 1930*, edited by Hennings, K., 151–80. New York: Springer.

Suter, Stefan, and Walter, Felix. 2001. "Environmental Pricing: Theory and Practice: The Swiss Policy of Heavy Vehicle Taxation." *Journal of Transport Economics and Policy* 35(3): 381–97.

Swartz, Omar. 2004. "Defending Labor in *Commonwealth v. Pullis*: Contemporary Implications for Rethinking Community." *Murdoch University Electronic Journal of Law* 11(1).

Taleb, Nassim. 2007. *The Black Swan: The Impact of the Highly Improbable*. New York: Random House.

Taleb, Nassim Nicholas. 2010. *The Bed of Procrustes*. New York: Random House.

Tax Policy Center. 2018. Briefing Book. *Urban Institute and Brookings Institution*, https://www.taxpolicycenter.org/briefing-book/what-are-sources-revenue-federal-government.

Taylor, S. 2016. Rising Monopoly Power May Partly Explain US Inequality and Productivity Slowdown, https://www.simontaylorsblog.com/2016/05/16/rising-monopoly-power-may-partly-explain-us-inequality-and-productivity-slowdown/.

Thaler, R. 1990. "Anomalies: Saving, Fungibility, and Mental Accounts." *Journal of Economic Perspectives* 4(1): 193–205.

Thompson, Derek. 2013. "How Airline Ticket Prices Fell 50% in 30 Years (and Why Nobody Noticed)." *Atlantic Magazine*, https://www.theatlantic.com/business/archive/2013/02/how-airline-ticket-prices-fell-50-in-30-years-and-why-nobody-noticed/273506/.

Thompson, Sarah, Macdonald, Anthony, and Mouliakis, Joyce. 2016. Ausgrid Price Explained; 1.41-Times Rab. *Australian Financial Review*, October 20.

Tietenberg, Thomas H., and Lewis, Lynne. 2013. *Environmental Economics and Policy*. New York: Pearson.

Timms, Claire. 2013. Has London's Congestion Charge Worked? http://www.bbc.com/news/uk-england-london-21451245.

Tribe, M. A., and Alpine, R.L.W. 1986. "Scale Economies and the '0.6 Rule'." *Engineering Costs and Production Economics* 10(1): 271–78.

Tullock, G. 1967. "The Welfare Costs of Tariffs, Monopolies, and Theft." *Economic Inquiry* 5(3): 224–32.

Tversky, Amos, and Kahneman, Daniel. 1974. "Judgment Under Uncertainty: Heuristics and Biases." *Science* 185: 1124–31.

United Nations Conference on Trade and Development (UNCTAD). 2017. Global Foreign Direct Investment Slipped in 2017.

US Agency for International Development (USAID). 2017. Afghanistan. https://www.usaid.gov/afghanistan/education.

US Department of Agriculture. 2017. Food Security Status of U.S. Households in 2016. https://www.ers.usda.gov/topics/food-nutrition -assistance/food-security-in-the-us/key-statistics-graphics.aspx.

US History. 2018. Unemployment Statistics During the Great Depression. http://www.u-s-history.com/pages/h1528.html.

US News and World Report. 2015. Top 100—Lowest Acceptance Rates. https://www.usnews.com/best-colleges/rankings/lowest -acceptance-rate.

Van Duijn, J. J. 2006. *The Long Wave in Economic Life*. Abingdon: Routledge.

Vidal, John. 2010. Pavlovsk Seed Bank Faces Destruction. *The Guardian*, August 9, https://www.theguardian.com/environment/2010 /aug/08/pavlovsk-seed-bank-russia.

Von Wieser, Friedrich. Trans. Ford Hinrichs, with a preface by Wesley Clair Mitchell. 1927. *Social Economics*. London: George Allen & Unwin.

Von Wieser, Friedrich Freiherr. 1893. *Natural Value*. London; New York: Macmillan.

Wadwah, Tina. 2016. America's Biggest Banks Are Closing Hundreds of Branches. *Business Insider*, October 23, http://www.business insider.com/bank-branches-around-the-world-are-shrinking-in -favor-of-digital-models-2016-10.

Walker, Jesse. 2008. The Central Committee Is in Session: The Trouble with the Federal Communications Commission. *Reason*, June 12, http://reason.com/archives/2008/06/12/the-central-committee-is-in-se.

Waring, Marilyn. 1988. *Counting for Nothing: What Men Value and What Women Are Worth*. Toronto: University of Toronto Press.

Weinhold, Diana, and Nair-Reichert, Usha. 2009. "Innovation, Inequality and Intellectual Property Rights." *World Development* 37(5): 889–901.

Weissman, Jordan. 2013. "How Wall Street Devoured Corporate America." *Atlantic Magazine*, https://www.theatlantic.com /business/archive/2013/03/how-wall-street-devoured-corporate -america/273732/.

Wells, Herbert George. 1921. *The Outline of History: Being a Plain History of Life and Mankind*. London: Cassell.

Western, B., and Rosenfeld, J. 2011. "Unions, Norms, and the Rise in U.S. Wage Inequality." *American Sociological Review* 76(4): 513–37.

White, Lawrence J. 2006. "The Fishery as a Watery Commons: Lessons from the Experiences of Other Public Policy Areas for U.S. Fisheries Policy." *SSRN Electronic Journal*, http://www.ssrn.com /abstract=945390.

Widerquist, Karl. 2005. "A Retrospective on the Negative Income Tax Experiments: Looking Back at the Most Innovative Field Studies in Social Policy." In *The Ethics and Economics of the Basic Income Guarantee*, edited by Widerquist, Karl, Lewis, Michael Anthony, and Pressman, Steven. Abingdon: Routledge.

Wikipedia. 2016. *Commonwealth v. Pullis*. https://en.wikipedia.org /wiki/Commonwealth_v._Pullis.

Wikipedia. 2017. There Ain't No Such Thing as a Free Lunch. https:// en.wikipedia.org/wiki/There_ain%27t_no_such_thing_as_a_free _lunch.

Wilder, Thornton. 1931. *The Happy Journey to Camden and Trenton: Play in One Act*. New York: Samuel French.

Williamson, Oliver E. 1986. *Economic Organization: Firms, Markets and Policy Control*. London: Wheatsheaf.

Worland, Justin. 2016. Worst Smog in Years Hits Southern California. *Time*, August 11, time.com/4448813/worst-smog-in-years-southern -california/.

World Inequality Database. 2018. http://wid.world/country/usa/.

World Trade Organization. 2017. World Trade Statistical Review 2017. https://www.wto.org/english/res_e/statis_e/wts2017_e/wts17 _toc_e.htm.

Yellen, Janet L. 1984. "Efficiency Wage Models of Unemployment." *American Economic Review* 74(2): 200–205.

Zelveh, Jubin 2009. Military Spending as Fiscal Stimulus? *New Republic*, September 1, https://newrepublic.com/article/68876/military -spending-fiscal-stimulus.

Zucman, G. 2018. Towards Real Taxation of the Digital Giants. *International Politics and Society*, August 4, https://www.ips-journal.eu /topics/european-union/article/show/towards-real-taxation-of-the -digital-giants-2835/.

Zupan, M. 1984. Interview with Henry Hazlitt. *Reason*, December 1, http://reason.com/archives/1984/12/01/interview-with-henry -hazlitt/print.

INDEX

1/N rule, 231
1 percent, 282–84, 319

acid rain, 196, 203–4, 207, 331, 334
additionality, and wage subsidies,
    300
adverse selection, 227n, 228
advertising: on "free" media, 80–83,
    180; as good or bad, 80–83
Affordable Care Act, 260
Afghan War, 122–24, 206n10
agriculture: discovery of, 52–53; prop-
    erty rights based on, 142–44
airfares, 71–75
airlines: deregulation of, 71–75, 318n;
    economies of scope in, 174–75;
    overbooking by, 73, 73n
air travel security, 123
Akerlof, George, 231, 258
Amazon, 179, 183
American Tobacco Company, 311
annual percentage rate (APR), 51
antitrust policy, 309, 311–13; Chicago
    critique of, 181, 184
Apple, 182–83, 256, 258, 312
Ariely, Dan, 69
arithmetic mean, 281, 286
Arrhenius, Svante, 205, 339–40
Arrow, Kenneth, 31n3, 43n

The Art of the Deal (Trump), 35
asymmetric information, 227–28
Atkinson, Tony, 283
AT&T monopoly, 310, 311–12
austerity: disastrous European results
    of, 164n6, 291, 296; after Global
    Financial Crisis of 2008, 157, 158,
    291; during Great Depression, 157,
    288; Keynes on response to boom
    and, 294; as mistaken response to
    depression, 156; political conse-
    quences of, 296, 306
*Austerity: The History of a Dangerous
    Idea* (Blyth), 157
Australia: airline deregulation in,
    83; gains from trade with US,
    38–40; minimum wage in, 252–53;
    National Broadband Network, 319;
    negotiating with pharmaceutical
    companies, 261; *White Paper on
    Full Employment*, 121–22
Austrian School of economics: depres-
    sions and, 303; inequality and, 280;
    market fundamentalism of, 27;
    opportunity cost and, 27; theory of
    the business cycle in, 163n
automatic stabilizers of economy,
    295–96; Job Guarantee providing,
    300
Autor, David, 313

balanced government budget, destabilizing, 296

bankruptcy: corporate, 241, 264, 265, 285; nonexistent until mid-nineteenth century, 263, 264

Bankruptcy Reform Act of 1978, 265

bargaining between employers and workers, 187, 188–91, 242, 243, 248–49; with full employment, 189, 244; imbalance in favor of employers, 250, 251–52

bargaining situations, 187–88

barter, 15–16, 187

Base Erosion and Profit Shifting, 267

Bastiat, Frédéric: climate change and, 238n, 339–41; Hazlitt's reworking of, 2; natural distribution of property rights and, 138–39; parable of broken window, 114, 115, 167, 168; on "that which is not seen," 2, 26, 99, 124, 139; unemployment and, 301–2, 304; using idea of opportunity cost, 26

Bator, Francis, 172n1

Becker, Gary, 181n

benefit-cost analysis, 220, 294

Bentham, Jeremy, 279

Bitcoin, 232–34, 257n

black market, 88

Black Swans, 230

Blair, Tony, 246

Blanchard, Olivier, 156n

blockchain, 257n

Blyth, Mark, 157

Bohr, Niels, 127n

bonds: corporate investment-grade, 58; junk bonds, 58, 265; of US government, 58, 64, 222, 299

booms: as feature of capitalism, 154; fiscal policy in response to, 291, 294–95; raising taxes during, 290

bounded rationality, 228–32

Brand, Stewart, 214, 218

Bretton Woods system, 160

broken window. See glazier's fallacy

bubbles. See dot-com boom of 1990s; financial bubbles and busts

Build Own Operate Transfer (BOOT), 97

Burnham, James, 146n

Burrow, Sharan, 150

Bush (George W.) administration, and Medicare Part D, 260

business cycle, 153–55; Austrian School's theory of, 163n; automatic stabilizers and, 295–96, 300; countercyclical fiscal policy and, 291, 295, 296–97; defined, 150; monetary and fiscal policy to smooth out, 151; RBC theory and, 304–6, 304n; running deficits or surpluses during, 290, 290n, 291. See also booms; recessions; unemployment

cap-and-trade. See tradeable emissions permits

capital, underemployed in recessions, 163

capital gains: as share of market income, 242; wealth made possible by, 264

capital incomes, share of market income going to, 242, 242n, 247

Capital in the Twenty-First Century (Piketty), 191, 283

capitalism: Keynes's macroeconomic theory and, 153; property rights and, 143–44; recession as feature of, 154

carbon budgets, 337–38

carbon dioxide emissions, 196, 197, 204–7, 208, 336–39, 341. *See also* tradeable emissions permits

carbon taxes, 338–39, 338n

Card, David, 186, 251–52

carried interest, 274n

Cato Institute, 108, 108n, 208n

Cavailles, Jean, 127

Celler-Kefauver act of 1950, 311

central planning: for complex transport networks, 324; corporations organized by, 326; criticized by One Lesson economists, 230n; environmental problems and, 331; in Soviet Union, 326, 331

Chain, Ernst, 126

Chang, Ha-Joon, 328

Chapter 11 bankruptcy, 265

Chicago School, 2n, 14, 181n; critique of antitrust policy, 181, 184. *See also* Friedman, Milton

China, pollution in, 332, 336

chlorofluorocarbons (CFCs), 204, 205–6, 332, 336

choice: anxiety about too much of, 231; opportunity cost and, 15, 25–26

Christophers, Brett, 192

Church of Scientology, 258

churning: job creation programs and, 300; wage subsidies and, 301

clawbacks, 272–73, 275, 285

Clean Air Acts, 330, 330n2, 331

Clean Water Act, 330, 330n3

climate change, 203–8, 336–41; beneficiaries of unfettered industry and, 343–44; cost of dealing with, 206–7, 206n; as market failure, 5, 206; scientists' estimates of, 206, 206n

climate science denial, 208, 208n, 238, 238n

climate skeptics, 341

Clinton, Bill, 246

close corporation, 266

Coase, Ronald, 31n2, 199–200, 207, 325, 329

cognitive modules, 228, 229

college education, 75–77

"commercial-in-confidence" intellectual property, 258

commodity futures markets, 224

common knowledge of rationality, 230

common property rights, 103–5, 106–7, 108

Commonwealth v. Pullis, 243

communications technology. *See* information technology; telecommunications networks

comparative advantage, 38–40

competitive equilibrium: compared to competitive oligopoly, 185; in consumer sector, 320–21; crowding out and, 294; economic rent and, 44; free lunch and, 31–32, 35, 40–44; glazier's fallacy and, 117; market failure and, 171–73, 308; market prices in, 31–32; Pareto optimality and, 136–37; perfect, 35, 43–44, 136–37, 173, 185; property rights and, 131, 136–38, 172

competitive markets: cost of production in, 18; for labor, 21

computers: delays in development of, 126–28; dramatic increase in capacity of, 55n; market for, 182–83

condominiums, 104

congestion externalities, 198

consumers: firms exploiting bounded rationality of, 231; interest rates and, 56–57; in mixed economy, 320–21; opportunity costs and, 22–23

container deposits, 333
Conte, Nicolas, 324–25
conventional wisdom, 112
copyrights, 181–82, 192, 240, 254–59, 261–62. *See also* intellectual property
Copyright Term Extension Act of 1998, 256, 258
corporate bankruptcy, 241, 264, 265, 285
corporate bonds, 58, 265
corporations: bargaining power with workers and, 248–49; central planning used by, 326; hierarchical decision-making in, 30–31; intellectual property and, 258–59, 285; limited liability of, 139, 264–65, 325; policy decisions favoring, 248; policy to limit monopoly power of, 285; property rights and, 240–41, 263; as social constructions, 248, 325; taxation of, 266–67, 271 (*see also* tax avoidance)
cost of production, 17–19; fixed, 18–19, 174–75; marginal, 19, 313; negative externalities and, 198–99; sunk, 20; variable, 18–19
countercyclical fiscal policy: automatic stabilizers and, 295; fine tuning by, 296–97; Keynes on, 291, 294; overview of, 291
countercyclical stocks, 64, 64n
Cowen, Tyler, 125
Creative Commons, 262
crowding out, 293–94
Crusoe, Robinson, 15–16, 61–62, 187–88

Dasgupta, Partha, 105
Debreu, Gerard, 31n3, 43n

debt: default risk and, 58–59; origin of, 54–55
debt crises, following Financial Crisis of 2008, 157
debtors' prison, 263, 264
decisions under uncertainty, 230–31
default risk, 58–59
deficits, during recessions, 290, 290n3, 291
deflation, 304
degenerating research program, 306
democracy: hostility of Pareto, Hayek, and Mises toward, 147; Mill's support for, 146
depressions: chronic in much of developed world, 5; Hazlitt on, 303; macroeconomic analysis and, 132, 151; opportunity cost and, 132; typical features of, 156. *See also* Great Depression; Lesser Depression; recessions
deregulation of airlines, 71–72, 74–75, 318n
derivative markets, 232, 233
destruction: as economically beneficial, 114–15, 121, 122; Hazlitt on, 114–18. *See also* natural disasters; war
development aid. *See* foreign aid
Diamond, Peter, 27
disagreement point, 188, 190
disasters. *See* insurance markets; natural disasters
Disney Corporation, intellectual property of, 256
division of labor, 45–48
Doblin, Wolfgang, 127
Domesday Book, 139
dot-com boom of 1990s: bursting of bubble, 161, 298; efficient markets hypothesis and, 232; expansion of

patent rights during, 257; failed
   startups of, 180, 232

Earned Income Tax Credit, 272
Easterley, William, 94, 94n, 95
economic cycle. *See* business cycle
economic rent, 44–45
Economics in One Lesson (Hazlitt),
   1–4, 5–6, 131, 183, 302
economies of co-location, 176–77, 211
economies of scale, 174, 175; external,
   176, 196, 198, 211; insurance markets and, 227; internal, 176, 211;
   monopoly and, 178–79, 197, 309,
   310, 312; technological progress
   and, 47
economies of scope, 174–75
economies of size, 173–74, 177; to
   achieve natural monopoly, 179
education: cost of college, 75–77;
   failure of for-profit model, 324; as
   kind of predistribution, 241; legal,
   77–79; privatization of, 318; public
   provision of, 321, 324; redistribution involving, 241–42; tax
   revenues used for, 271
effective marginal tax rates, 272–75,
   285
efficient markets hypothesis (EMH),
   218–21; Bitcoin bubble and, 232,
   234; decisions under uncertainty
   and, 230; information and,
   218–20, 223
egalitarianism, 145, 282, 283, 285
80–20 distribution, 146
Einstein, Albert, 126
Eisenhower, Dwight, 114, 124–25
elasticity of demand for labor, 250,
   251
Emanuel, Rahm, 246–47

emissions permits, tradeable, 108,
   329, 334–35, 338–39, 338n
employment. *See* bargaining between
   employers and workers; full
   employment; labor markets;
   unemployment
Employment Act of 1946, 288, 289n
employment at will, 140, 250
employment-population ratio, 158,
   159–60, 161
endogenous growth, 211
Engels, Friedrich, 25
environmental taxes, 328, 329,
   332–33, 338–39, 341
equilibrium. *See* competitive equilibrium; general equilibrium model
equity premium puzzle, 58, 65,
   222–23
exchange. *See* gains from trade
excludable goods, 217–18, 254. *See
   also* non-excludability
executive compensation, 277, 284
expected utility: geometric mean and,
   286; maximization of, 230
externalities, 196–200; classification
   of, 198; defined, 4, 196; of infrastructure and public utilities, 321;
   origins of the concept, 4, 196,
   210–11; positive, 196, 198, 199, 211;
   property rights and, 199–200; public goods and, 197, 210, 210n; social
   opportunity costs and, 4–5. *See also*
   market failure; pollution
Exxon, 183

Facebook: intellectual property rights
   and, 258; market power of, 183;
   positive network externalities in,
   198; startup strategy of, 179–80
Fairness Doctrine, 109–10

Farrell, Henry, 164n6

fast food industry, minimum wages in, 186, 251

Federal Communications Commission (FCC), 109, 110; regulatory capture of, 315

Federal Reserve, 297

Federal Reserve Economic Database (FRED), 65, 170

financial bubbles and busts, 220, 226, 294–95. *See also* dot-com boom of 1990s

financial crisis of 2008. *See* Global Financial Crisis of 2008

financial executives, tax rate for, 274n, 284

financial markets: Bitcoin and, 232–34; bounded rationality in, 230–31; complex tax-avoiding corporations and, 265–66; dramatic growth of, 220–21, 225–26, 246; efficient markets hypothesis and, 218–20; extreme volatility of, 222; failures of, 221–22; governments following dictates of, 171, 309; high incomes derived from, 277, 284; speculation and, 223–26; uncertainty in, 63–64

firms, production organized within, 325–26

First Fundamental Theorem of Welfare Economics, 137, 148

fiscal policy, 290–97; countercyclical, 291, 295, 296–97; defined, 291; fine tuning by, 296–97; multiplier and, 292–95; to tamp down excessive booms, 295

fisheries, 100–108; opportunity cost and, 101; overfishing in, 100–102; property rights and, 103–8

fixed costs, 18–19; economies of scope and, 174–75

Fleming, Alexander, 126

Florey, Howard, 126

food aid, international, 90

food stamps: compared to giving money, 90–93; effective marginal tax rate and, 273; opportunity cost of increase in, 275–76; tax revenues used for, 271

food subsidies, 85–86

Foote, Eunice, 205

foreign aid: arguments that it is a failure, 93–96; compared to war expenditure, 122, 123–24; effective type of assistance, 90, 96

foreign exchange markets, 225

fossil fuels, 197, 205, 206, 341

Franklin, Benjamin, 13, 14–15, 26

free lunch: economic rent and, 44–45; "free" radio, TV, and Internet services, 79–82; ideal competitive equilibrium and, 31–32, 35, 40–44; Pareto-optimality and, 148; two kinds of, 33–34. *See also* TANSTAAFL; TISATAAFL

free market: bankruptcy and limited liability laws and, 264; existing property rights and, 1n; Hazlitt's defense of, 1–2

"free" TV, radio, and Internet content, 79–82

Friday. *See* Crusoe, Robinson

Friedman, Milton: copyright term extension and, 258; critique of discretionary fiscal policy, 296–97; on road pricing, 99; TANSTAAFL and, 32. *See also* Chicago School

Frisch, Ragnar, 152n

Frost, Robert, 11, 15

full employment: assumed in One Lesson economics, 23, 151, 153, 164, 166, 289; bargaining power of workers and, 189, 244; Hazlitt's

assumption of, 6, 117–18; illusion that normal state is, 159, 161–62; resources required for Vietnam War and, 120; World War II and, 121–22, 160, 244
fundamental theorems of welfare economics, 137, 148
futures markets, 224

gains from trade, 34, 35–37; comparative advantage and, 38–40; division of labor and, 45, 48; effective marginal tax rate and, 274–75; of emissions permits, 334–35
Galbraith, John Kenneth, 67
game theory: Nash's work in, 188; predatory pricing and, 181
gaze heuristic, 229, 229n
GDP. *See* gross domestic product
general equilibrium model: assuming full employment, 166; market failure and, 171–72, 308. *See also* competitive equilibrium
General Theory of Employment, Interest and Money (Keynes), 5, 36n, 164, 291
geometric mean of income, 282, 286
Gigerenzer, Gerd, 229, 231
glazier's fallacy, 115–18, 151, 167–69
global economy: market power in, 308–9. *See also* financial markets
Global Financial Crisis of 2008: countercyclical fiscal policy following, 291; derivative markets and, 232, 233; efficient markets hypothesis and, 220, 232; employment-population ratio and, 159–60; failed austerity policies following, 157, 158; financial sector profits and, 221; immediate aftermath of, 162; Keynesian stimulus as immediate response

to, 157; Lesser Depression beginning with, 156, 157–58; monetary policy and, 297–98, 299; privatization trend discredited after, 326; RBC theory and, 305–6; social and political consequences of, 157, 158–59; stagnation following, 161, 297, 298; state of recession since, 162; unemployed persons per job opening and, 189–90; unemployment insurance extension during, 295–96
global warming, 205, 206n9, 207, 336–37. *See also* climate change
gold standard: failure of, 164n6; Keynes's critique of, 193
Google: intellectual property rights and, 258; market power of, 182–83, 182n, 312; startup strategy of, 179–80
Google tax, 267
Gordon, H. Scott, 103n
Gore, Al, 344
government action: to allocate and enforce property rights, 7, 107–8, 110, 139–40, 200, 344; efficient markets hypothesis and, 220; Hazlitt's case against, 3–4, 44, 131; opposed by One Lesson economists, 140, 184, 184n; to smooth out the business cycle, 151. *See also* public policy
government bonds, US, 58, 64, 222, 299
government failure, theory of, 184n
government sector, economic activity in, 326. *See also* public ownership
government services, opportunity cost of, 32–33
Great Compression: income inequalities declining in, 312, 316; progressive taxation in, 284; public ownership of monopoly enterprises and, 316

Great Depression, 155–57; alleviated by war economy, 121–22, 162, 288; austerity as initial response to, 157, 288; caused by financial market failure, 221–22; employment-population ratio and, 159–60; failure of gold standard in, 164n6; global consequences of, 289; Hazlitt's lack of attention to, 302–3; Keynesian model as response to, 2; Lesser Depression worse than, 156n; RBC theory and, 305; revenue from movies during, 64n. *See also* New Deal

The Great Leveler (Christophers), 192

Great Moderation, 160–61, 233, 298

Great Society, 120

Great Vacation, 305

greenhouse effect, 204–6, 341

greenhouse gas emissions, 206n9, 336–39, 341. *See also* carbon dioxide emissions; tradeable emissions permits

gross domestic product (GDP): defined, 24; misused as measure of well-being, 24; redistribution and, 281; top marginal tax rate and, 283–84

growth recessions, 297

Guaranteed Minimum Income, 285

Hacker, Jacob, 239

Hardin, Garret, 103n, 104–5, 104n

Harsanyi, John, 279

Hayek, F. A.: depressions and, 303; opportunity cost and, 27; politics of, 137n, 147, 147n; rejecting Keynes's *General Theory*, 36n; theory of the business cycle, 163n; on use of knowledge in society, 59–61

Hazlitt, Henry: as advocate of free market, 1–2; case against government action, 3–4, 44, 131, 140; critique of Keynes, 2, 5, 53n; defenses of monopoly, 183–84; distribution of income and, 44; distribution of property rights assumed by, 25, 138–39; *Economics in One Lesson*, 1–4, 5–6, 131, 183, 302; full employment assumed by, 6, 117–18; glazier's fallacy and, 114–18, 167–69; labor market and, 191; limited liability or personal bankruptcy and, 264; on minimum wages, 89n; pollution not discussed by, 207, 339; unemployment and, 5–6, 302–3

health care: high costs in US, 260–61, 260n; public provision of, 321; tax revenues used for, 271

health insurance, subsidized by US government, 260

Heinlein, Robert, 32

heuristics, 229, 231

Hitchhiker's Guide to the Galaxy, 165n

Hitler, Adolf, 256n, 289

holding company, 311

Homo economicus, 229

households: hours spent on activities in, 24n; opportunity costs and, 22–24; women's work in, 24, 47n

"hub and spoke" networks, 72, 175

human capital, 47

Hume, David, 134

I, Pencil (Read), 322–25

IBM, 182

immigrants, blamed for effects of bad policy, 296

incentive effects of tax increase, 276–77, 283–84

income distribution: arithmetic vs. geometric mean and, 281–82, 286; changed by limited liability and bankruptcy, 264; generated by a firm, 325; gross domestic product and, 281; Hazlitt's argument against government intervention and, 44; minimum wages and, 249; opportunity cost and, 240–42; Pareto's 80–20 distribution, 146; pollution control strategies and, 329; privatization and, 318; system of property rights and, 6, 25; between wages and capital incomes, 242, 242n. *See also* inequality of income and wealth; predistribution; redistribution

income taxes, types of, 271

individual transferable quotas (ITQs), 103, 105, 106, 108

inequality of income and wealth: Austrian School and, 280; corporate bankruptcy and limited liability and, 265, 267; decline in unionization and, 247, 248; declining value of minimum wage and, 253; economic rent and, 45; GDP misused as measure of well-being and, 24; between highly educated and manual workers, 247; intellectual property rights for corporations and, 258; middle-class prosperity after World War II and, 244, 316; monopoly power and, 191–93, 312, 313; Pareto's argument for, 146; policies favoring corporations and, 248; rapidly growing, 5; ratio of arithmetic to geometric mean and, 286; system of property rights and, 6; von Wieser on, 26–27. *See also* income distribution

inflation: global upsurge of 1960s, 245–46; high in 1970s, 160; in wartime, 120

information: asymmetric, 227–28; efficient markets hypothesis and, 218–20, 223; importance to Robinson Crusoe, 61–62; insurance markets and, 63, 227–28; limited capacity to reason about, 232; price system and, 59–61, 214, 215–18; technological innovation and, 34; uncertainty and, 214–15

information technology: growth in productivity of, 55, 55n; intellectual property rights and, 144, 257; reduced cost of financial transactions and, 225. *See also* computers

infrastructure services: dependence of business on, 145; under public ownership, 315–17, 321

insurance markets, 63, 226–28

intellectual property (IP), 254–62; alternatives to, 259–62; corporations and, 258–59, 285; costs vs. benefits of, 255; damage caused by enforcement of, 257–59; historical expansion of rights to, 255–57, 258; inequality and, 258; monopoly rights associated with, 181–82, 192, 285; natural rights theory of property and, 144; One Lesson economists' disagreements about, 140; pharmaceutical profits and, 258, 260–61; as public good, 254–55; tax avoidance and, 258–59. *See also* copyrights; patents

interest rates: basic concept of, 51, 54; consumer side and, 56–57; differences in, 57–59; expressed as APR, 51; monetary policy and, 294–95, 297–99; as opportunity cost of not waiting, 51, 54; own-rate of

interest rates (*continued*)
 interest, 54–55, 55n; production
 side and, 52–56; reduced during
 recessions, 290; risk-free value of, 51,
 56, 57; wheat rate of interest, 53, 54
International Mercantile Marine
 Company, 311
International Monetary Fund: decline
 of unionization and, 247; full
 employment after World War II
 and, 160
international trade, 37–40
Internet: confusing options in type
 of service, 231; "free" content on,
 79–82, 180; Google's dominance
 on, 182–83; possible expansion of
 public domain on, 261–62. *See also*
 dot-com boom of 1990s
Investor–State Dispute Settlement
 (ISDS) provisions, 240–41
invisible hand, 323, 324
IP. *See* intellectual property
Iraq War, 122, 206n10
Ireland, as corporate tax haven, 259,
 266
ITQs (individual transferable quotas),
 103, 105, 106, 108

Jefferson, Thomas, 143
job creation programs, 299–301, 302
Job Guarantee, 300, 300n
job training: in Australia, 253; not effective response to recessions, 301
Juglar, Clement, 154–55
junk bonds, 58, 265

Kahneman, Daniel, 229
Keynes, John Maynard: on the long
 run, 164, 164n7, 182, 193; on
 wheat rate of interest, 53

Keynesian economics: alleged need
 for microfoundations, 165–66;
 *General Theory of Employment,
 Interest and Money*, 5, 36n, 164,
 291; Hayek's ideas and, 36, 36n;
 Hazlitt's critique of, 2, 5, 53n; macroeconomics and, 5, 152, 152n, 165;
 unemployment and, 5–6, 152
Keynesian policies: countercyclical
 fiscal policy, 291, 294; crowding
 out and, 293–94; failure to control
 crises of 1970s, 317; fine tuning of
 economy and, 297; after World War
 II, 160, 162, 289, 291, 304
Keynesian stimulus: after Global
 Financial Crisis of 2008, 157, 291;
 of New Deal, 157, 291
Kimball, Miles, 298
knowledge, Hayek on, 59–61, 216. *See
 also* information
Kondratiev, Nikolai, 154–55
Krueger, Alan, 186, 251–52
Krugman, Paul, 14, 304n, 305, 313
Kydland, Finn, 304n

labor markets: competitive, 21, 186;
 performing better in Australia than
 US, 252–53; in recession or depression, 6. *See also* monopsony; wages
labor share of national income, 242,
 242n, 247, 258
labor unions. *See* unions
Laffer curve, 276
laissez-faire, 2
Lakatos, Imre, 306
land, creation of property rights in,
 139–40, 142–44
"The Law" (Bastiat), 2
law schools, 77–79
lead pollution in atmosphere, and
 crime, 202

Leigh, Andrew, 283
Lesser Depression, 157–59; caused by financial market failure, 221–22; different from typical recession, 156; employment-population ratio and, 158, 160; worse than Great Depression in some ways, 156n
Lessig, Lawrence, 308
Lesson One. *See* One Lesson economics
Lesson Two. *See* Two Lesson economics
libertarians, 32n, 108n, 147n. *See also* propertarians
licensed occupations, 248
limited liability of corporations, 139, 264–65, 325
Lincoln, Abraham, 324
Lindbeck, Assar, 85
Livingstone, Ken, 98–99
Locke, John: "natural rights" in property and, 132–33, 142–43
London, congestion charge of, 98–99
long waves, 154–55
lump-sum taxation, 137–38

macroeconomics: alleged need for microfoundations, 165–66; defined, 5; distinguished from microeconomics, 132, 151–52; Keynes and, 5, 152, 152n, 165; market failure and, 151
marginal cost of production: defined, 19; monopoly and, 313
marginal tax rate: effective, 272–75, 285; top level of, 240, 283–84
marginal utility, 26, 27, 280
market concentration, 191–93
market failure, 171–73; broad categories of, 8–9, 173; climate change as, 5, 206; growing importance of, 171; Lesson One and, 171–72,

308–9; Lesson Two and, 131–32, 197; opportunity costs and, 5, 132, 172–73, 197; opposition to government intervention for, 184n; public ownership and, 322; typologies of, 172. *See also* externalities; monopoly; pollution; unemployment
market fundamentalism, 27
market imperfections, 173, 197
market liberalism, 2n, 256
market power, 308–9
market price. *See* prices
markets: economic activity mostly outside of, 173, 325–26; property rights as framework for, 7
Marshall, Alfred, 4, 211
Marx, Karl, 25, 154, 154n, 171, 237, 308
mass unemployment: Hazlitt's denial about, 344; illustrating Two Lesson economics, 151, 152, 163; invalidating One Lesson economics, 133, 166; as regular occurrence, 164; seen as rare exception, 159
means testing, 272, 274
Medicaid, 260
Medicare, 260
Mencken, H. L., 343, 343n
mergers, 309, 310, 311, 312
microeconomics: assuming full employment, 166; defined, 3, 132; distinguished from macroeconomics, 132, 151–52; of Lesson One, 166
Microsoft: antitrust case against, 312; intellectual property rights and, 258; market power of, 182, 183
military-industrial complex, 124–25
Mill, John Stuart, 145, 146, 279
minimum wages, 249–54; in Australia compared to US, 252–54; claimed to reduce employment, 186; current US level of, 252; in fast food

minimum wages (*continued*)
industry, 186, 251; as kind of price control, 89n; Lesson One analysis of, 249–50, 251; policy program including increase in, 285

Mirrlees, James, 27

Mises, Ludwig von, 27, 147, 303

Mishel, Lawrence, 253

mixed economy, 319–22; national variations in, 315n; opportunity costs and, 321–22; patent system as example of, 325; wide range of possibilities for, 326

monetary policy, 155, 294–95, 297–99

money: giving to the poor, 89–96; opportunity cost and, 16; origin of, 54–55

monopoly, 173, 177–84; defenses of, 183–84; defined, 177; inequality and, 191–93, 312, 313; natural, 178–80, 309–10, 314, 317–18, 321; regulation of, 314–15, 318, 319; unnatural, 180–83. *See also* antitrust policy; intellectual property

monopsony, 185–87; bargaining power and, 252; continuing problems of, 308; corporate monopolies and, 311; inequality and, 191, 192, 313

The Moon is a Harsh Mistress (Heinlein), 32

moral hazard, 227n

Moseley, Henry, 127, 127n

Moss, David, 264

multiplier, 167n, 292–95

Mussolini, Benito: Pareto's support for, 137n, 145, 147

Nash, John, 188

National Bureau of Economic Research (NBER), 153–54, 155, 161–62, 189

natural disasters, 115, 118–19, 226–27

natural distribution of property rights: assumed by Hazlitt, 25, 138–39; flaws in arguments for, 141, 142–45; Locke on, 132–33, 142–43

natural law, 142

natural monopoly, 178–80, 309–10; advocates of privatization and, 317–18; of infrastructure and public utilities, 321; regulation of, 314

natural resources, wealth derived from, 144

neoliberalism, 2n

network externalities, 198

New Deal: Keynesian orientation of, 157, 291; labor movement and, 243–44, 248; partial recovery associated with, 288; unemployment remaining in spite of, 159; Works Progress Administration in, 299

Nixon wage-price freezes, 246

noncompete agreements, 190

non-excludability, 209, 210; of market information, 216. *See also* excludable goods

non-rivalry, 209, 210; of ideas, 255; of market information, 216. *See also* rival goods

normative economics, 280–81

Obama, Barack: business's dependence on infrastructure and, 145; Global Financial Crisis and, 291; Rahm Emanuel in administration of, 246

Obamacare, 260

occupational licensing, 248

oil resources, wealth derived from, 144

oligopoly, 184–85, 308, 313

One Lesson economics: beneficiaries of, 344; climate change and, 207–8, 339–41, 344; continuing relevance of, 50; full employment assumed in, 23, 151, 153, 164, 166, 289; Great Depression produced by, 122; intellectual collapse of, 306; labor market and, 191; leaving markets alone, 2, 3; microeconomics and, 151; monopoly and, 183–84; policy program to reverse the influence of, 285; pollution and, 207, 339; prices in competitive equilibrium and, 31–32, 40–44; privatization and, 317–19; property rights and, 140–41; rational agents and, 229–30; recessions and, 150; statement of, 7–8, 31–32; terms used to describe, 1n; unchanged since Hazlitt wrote, 2; unemployment and, 301–6, 344; welfare economics and, 148. See also *Economics in One Lesson*; Hazlitt, Henry

1/N rule, 231

the 1 percent: enriched by privatization, 319; taxation of, 282–84

open source software, 262

opportunity cost: Bastiat's use of concept, 26; of carbon dioxide emissions, 338; cost of production and, 17–19; of creation of property rights, 139–40, 200; defined, 3, 15; free lunch and, 33, 34, 44; income distribution and, 240–42; individual vs. social, 4–5; intellectual history of, 25–27; interest and, 51, 54; market failure and, 5, 132, 172–73, 197; market prices and, 7–8, 31–32, 61, 132, 164, 173; mixed economy and, 321–22; of policies affecting taxation and public expenditures, 271; in recession, 6, 132, 290, 291;

of redistribution, 275–78; as "that which is not seen," 99, 128; tricky question about, 69–71; uncertainty and, 62–63; unemployment and, 162–64, 289; of war, 119–25. *See also* social opportunity costs

optimal tax, 27

Organization for Economic Co-operation and Development, 333

Orwell, George, 146n

Ostrom, Elinor, 105

overheads, 18n

own-rate of interest, 54–55, 55n

ozone layer, 204, 206, 207, 336

Panama Papers, 266n, 284

parable of the broken window. *See* glazier's fallacy

Pareto, Vilfredo: political and economic ideas of, 145–47

Pareto-efficient allocations, 148

Pareto optimality, 133, 137, 145, 147–48

Pareto's Law, 146

patents, 181, 192, 254–62, 310; for pencil, 324–25; of pharmaceutical corporations, 258, 260–61. *See also* intellectual property

patent trolls, 257, 259–60

Pavlovsk Experimental Station, 127

payday lenders, 58

payroll taxes, 271

pencil, 322–25

perfect competitive equilibrium, 35, 43–44, 136–37, 173, 185. *See also* competitive equilibrium

pharmaceutical corporations: government support of, 260–61; patents of, 258, 260–61

Phishing for Phools (Akerlof and Shiller), 231

Pigou, A. C.: Coase's challenge to ideas of, 199, 200; concept of externalities and, 4, 198, 211; taxation of negative externalities and, 328, 329, 333

Piketty, Thomas, 191, 283, 284

pin factory, 45–47, 173–74

Pinochet, Augusto: Hayek's support for, 137n

point six power rule, 174

point-source pollution, 332

policy. *See* public policy

policy program, for predistribution and redistribution, 285

political power, of corporations and the wealthy, 241

pollution, 200–203; beneficiaries of unfettered industry and, 343–44; as externality, 4, 196; global problems of, 335–36; market-based approaches to, 328–30, 338, 341 (*see also* environmental taxes; tradeable emissions permits); not discussed by Hazlitt, 207, 339; regulation of, 330–32. *See also* externalities

populism, 296

positive economics, 280

positive externalities, 196, 198, 199, 211

poverty: giving money to the poor and, 89–96. *See also* food stamps; welfare benefits

poverty traps, 275

predatory lending practices, 58–59

predatory pricing, 181

predistribution: defined, 237, 239; to help the poor, 93; policy changes for, 240–42, 285. *See also* corporate bankruptcy; intellectual property; limited liability of corporations; minimum wages; unions

Prescott, Edward, 304n

price controls, 85–89, 111, 120, 246

prices: in ideal competitive equilibrium, 31–32; in industry with dominant firm, 310, 310n; information coordinated by, 59–61, 214, 215–18; marginal cost of production and, 19, 313; opportunity costs and, 7–8, 31–32, 61, 132, 164, 172–73

price wars, 180, 185, 309

private goods, defined, 254

private property, vs. private goods, 254

privatization: benefiting the rich and powerful, 107; efficient markets hypothesis and, 220; at end of Soviet communism, 141; of fisheries, 103, 106; Hardin's case for, 104; in legal and enforcement systems of state, 321; mixed economy surviving push for, 326; as trend beginning in 1980s, 317–19, 326

"The Problem of Social Cost" (Coase), 199–200

productivity, rate of growth in, 55–56

progressive income tax, 27, 285, 295

propertarians: distribution of property rights and, 239; government services and, 32–33; libertarians and, 32n, 108n, 147n; limited liability or personal bankruptcy and, 264; transferable quotas and, 108

property: defined, 138–39; private, vs. private goods, 254

property rights: assumption of natural distribution of, 25, 132–33, 138–39, 141, 142–45; common, 103–5, 106–7, 108; constantly changing, 131, 134–35; creation of, 107–8, 110, 139–40, 142–44, 200, 344; of employers, 250; end of communism in Russia and,

141; externalities and, 199–200; as framework of market economy, 6–7; "free market" concept and, 1n; gains from exchange and, 37; income distribution and, 6, 25; market equilibrium and, 136–38, 172; monopolies changing distribution of, 193; pollution control by means of, 329, 341; as social constructions, 132–33, 239, 262–63; social opportunity costs and, 172; starting point for, 138–42; telecommunications spectrum and, 110–11; tradeable emissions permits and, 108, 329, 334–35, 338–39, 338n; unlimited number of possible allocations of, 131, 136, 137, 147–48. *See also* intellectual property; predistribution; privatization

public bads, 197n

public domain, desirability of expansion of, 261–62

public expenditure multiplier, 292–95

public expenditures, and opportunity costs, 271

public goods: common meaning of, 208; economists' concept of, 208–10; externalities and, 197, 210, 210n; market information as, 216–18; private property rights and, 254–55

public health measures, 210

public ownership, 315–19; market failure and, 322

public policy: benefiting high-income earners, 240–41, 278–79; changes to promote predistribution and redistribution, 240–42, 285; favoring monopoly over competition, 192; Hazlitt's assumptions about, 44; improved allocation of resources and, 34; mass unemployment and,

133; opportunity cost and, 271; to remedy market failures, 5. *See also* government action

public–private partnership, 97

public services: changes in property rights and, 141–42; redistribution and, 270; tax revenues used for, 271

public utilities, 321

pure public good, 209; market information as, 216–18. *See also* public goods

quantitative easing, 299

racism: Trump's supporters and, 159; union movement and, 244–45

radio: "free" content on, 79–82; regulation of, 108–11

railway networks: failure of private ownership of, 324; public ownership of, 315; renationalization of, 319; scale economies of, 310

rational agents, 229–30

rationing, 88–89

Rawls, John, 279, 282n

Read, Leonard, 322–25

Reagan, Ronald, 246

Real Business Cycle (RBC) theory, 304–6, 304n

recessions: automatic stabilizers and, 296; bursting of bubble in 2000 and, 298; chronic in much of developed world, 5; countercyclical stocks in, 64, 64n; critical feature of, 151; effective government response to, 290; equity premium and, 222–23; fiscal policy in, 290–97; frequently chronic, 5; general features of, 150; growth recessions, 297; informal definition

recessions (*continued*)
of, 159; macroeconomic analysis
and, 151; monetary policy in, 298;
multiplier in, 293–94; National
Bureau of Economic Research
and, 153–54; NBER definition of,
154, 155; opportunity cost and,
6, 132, 290, 291; as ordinary part
of market economy, 150; running
deficits during, 290, 290n3, 291;
typical pattern of, 155; unemployment insurance during, 295–96;
wage subsidies in, 300–301. *See also*
depressions; unemployment
recycling of containers, 333
redistribution: defined, 239, 270;
egalitarian doctrine and, 145–46;
example of opportunity cost for,
275–78; gains and losses of last
40 years and, 278–82; by giving
money to the poor, 93; Pareto's
argument against, 146; policy
changes for promotion of, 240–42,
285; privatization leading to, 107.
See also income distribution
regulation: to allocate scarce goods
and services, 111; of monopolies,
314–15, 318, 319; of pollution,
330–32; price control as, 85–89;
speculators exploiting inconsistencies in, 225; of telecommunications
spectrum, 108–11. *See also* deregulation of airlines
regulatory asset base, 314
regulatory capture, 314–15
renationalization, 319
rent control, 68, 85; in New York
City, 86–87, 87n
rents: created by property rights, 140.
See also economic rent
rent-seeking, 45

resource allocation, improvements
in, 34
Ricardo, David, 38
right-wing extremism, and failures of
capitalism, 158–59
risk-free interest rate, 51, 56, 57
rival goods, 254. *See also* non-rivalry
roads: failure of private management,
324; pricing of, 96–100, 203n
The Road to Serfdom (Hayek), 36, 36n
Robbins, Lionel, 27
Rockefeller, John D., 180
Rogers, Will, 270
Roosevelt, Franklin D., 126, 156–57,
288, 291
Roosevelt, Theodore, 323
Rosenfeld, Jake, 247
rule of 70, 51, 57
Russian communism, privatizations at
end of, 141
Russian oligarchs, 141, 319

Saez, Emmanuel, 283, 284
Samuelson, Paul, 1, 149
Schwartz, Barry, 231
Schwarzschild, Karl, 127
Second Fundamental Theorem of
Welfare Economics, 137, 148
Sen, Amartya, 14
sexism, and union movement,
244–45
Shaw, George Bernard, 14
Sherman Antitrust Act, 180–81, 311,
312
Shiller, Robert, 231
Silk Road, 233
Simon, Herbert, 229
Sinclair, Upton, 343
slavery: Locke's wealth and, 142,
142n; master-servant relationship

and, 243; US Constitution and, 262n

Smith, Adam: on collusion of firms, 171, 177; critical of corporations, 263–64; division of labor and, 45–47, 173–74; free lunches and, 33; production organized by markets and, 325; *Wealth of Nations*, 33, 45, 173

smoking, health dangers of, 208, 208n

socialism: Bastiat on, 340; Mises and Hayek on, 65–66. *See also* central planning

socialist calculation debate, 65–66

social opportunity costs: allocation of property rights and, 172; climate change and, 207; defined, 4–5; market failure and, 5, 172, 199; natural monopoly and, 180; of pollution, 201, 328, 335; of public expenditure, 294; of traffic congestion, 202–3. *See also* opportunity cost

Social Security: as choice involving property rights, 239; opposed by One Lesson economists, 141; taxes for funding of, 271

Sonny Bono Copyright Term Extension Act, 256, 258

South Sea Bubble, 222, 263

Soviet Union: central planning in, 326, 331; end of communism in, 141; investment in economic growth, 95–96

speculation, and financial markets, 223–26

speculative stocks, 63–64

Standard Oil Trust, 180–81, 311

Stantcheva, Stefanie, 283, 284

Stern, Nicholas, 5, 206

Stigler, George, 181n

Stiglitz, Joseph, 14, 313

stock market investment: counter-cyclical stocks in, 64, 64n; equity premium puzzle, 58, 65, 222–23

subsidies of vital goods, 85–86

subsidized housing, 91

Summers, Lawrence, 156n

sunk costs: of law degree, 78; of production, 20; tricky question about, 71

Supplemental Nutrition Assistance Program (SNAP). *See* food stamps

supply and demand, 13–14

Taft-Hartley Act of 1947, 245, 248

TANSTAAFL, 32–35, 79. *See also* free lunch

taxation: automatic stabilizer associated with, 295; of corporations, 266–67, 271; environmental, 328, 329, 332–33, 338–39, 341; federal types of, 271; financial engineering to minimize, 225; of firms generating negative externalities, 328; lump-sum taxes, 137–38; opportunity costs and, 271; property rights created by, 136; redistribution through, 93, 270; sources of, 271; state and local, 271; of top 1 percent, 282–84

tax avoidance: by corporations of vast complexity, 266–67; driven by ease of accomplishing, 284; effective marginal tax rate and, 275; incentive effects of tax rates and, 277, 283, 284; intellectual property and, 258–59; massively increased since 1970s, 284

tax credits, 272

tax cuts: of 1980s, benefiting the wealthy, 279; temporary, during

tax cuts (*continued*)
recessions, 290, 291; at the top, costing lower income earners, 283–84; "trickle down" claim about, 279n3

tax havens, 266

Tea Party, 157

Technocracy movement, 303n

technological progress: as free lunch, 33–34, 41; growth in productivity and, 55–56, 55n; monopoly profits and, 312; Smith on, 45, 47; telecommunications spectrum and, 110

technological shocks, 305, 306

technology: economies of scale in, 174, 197; war and, 125–28

telecommunications networks, public ownership of, 315, 316, 319

telecommunications spectrum, 108–11

television: "free" content on, 79–82; as public good, 197, 209; regulation of, 109–11, 315

Temporary Assistance to Needy Families, 271

terrorist attacks, cost of protection from, 123

Thatcher, Margaret: anti-union position of, 246

Thatcher government, privatization under, 317

Thatcherism, 2n

"that which is not seen": Bastiat on, 2, 26, 99, 124, 139; opportunity cost as, 99, 128

thick markets, 217, 224

thin markets, 217

Thoreau, Henry David, 322n

time as money, 13, 14–15

TISATAAFL, 33–34. *See also* free lunch

tobacco industry, 208, 208n

top marginal tax rates: benefits of increase in, 284, 285; experience of postwar prosperity and, 284; reduced from 70 percent to 39.6 percent, 240; responses to changes in, 283–84

trade: international, 37–40; lowering opportunity costs, 34; seen as zero-sum game, 34, 35–36. *See also* gains from trade

tradeable emissions permits, 108, 329, 334–35, 338–39, 338n

traffic congestion charge, 99

"The Tragedy of the Commons" (Hardin), 103n, 104–5

transaction costs, 199–200

transfer payments: changes in property rights and, 141–42; redistribution and, 270, 272

Treasury bonds, 58

triangular trade, 40n

true value, 35

Trump, Donald: employment at will and, 250; right-wing extremism and, 159; zero-sum thinking of, 35

Trump administration, and existing property rights, 32n

trust-busting, 311–12

trusts, 311, 311n

Tullock, Gordon, 310

Turing, Alan, 126

Tversky, Amos, 229

Twitter, startup strategy of, 179–80

Two Lesson economics: financial markets and, 64; macroeconomics and, 151–52; market failure and, 131–32, 197; mass unemployment and, 151, 152, 163; recession conditions and, 164; statement of, 8, 132; welfare economics and, 148–49.

See also market failure; recessions; unemployment

Tyndall, John, 205

uncertainty, 62–64; decision-making under, 230–31; as inescapable problem, 16; information and, 214–15

unemployed persons per job opening, 189–90

unemployment: business cycle and, 132; in chaotic 1970s, 160; difficulty of changing jobs and, 21; fiscal policy to address, 290–94; glazier's fallacy and, 118, 151; Hazlitt's treatment of, 5–6, 302–3; of high school graduates, 76; job creation programs and, 299–301, 302; Keynes on, 5–6, 152; in Lesser Depression, 156n, 157–58, 160; One Lesson economics and, 301–6, 344; opportunity cost and, 162–64, 289; of people giving up looking for work, 158, 161, 162, 190; in recessions, 151. *See also* employment-population ratio; Great Depression; mass unemployment

unemployment insurance: as automatic stabilizer, 295–96; not provided by the market, 227; opportunity cost of unemployment and, 277; public programs of, 228; tax revenues used for, 271

unions, 242–49; airline deregulation and, 75; bargaining by, 187, 190–91; decline of, 171, 186, 245–48, 309; economic rent and, 45; historical development of, 242–47; public sector, 244, 246–47; reversing policies against, 247–49, 285; twentieth-century power of, 171, 308–9

Universal Basic Income, 285

unnatural monopoly, 180–83

"The Use of Knowledge in Society" (Hayek), 59–61, 216

US Steel, 311

utility: expected, 230, 286; marginal, 26, 27, 280; Pareto's attack on Mill and, 146

value: theory of, 27; true value, 35

Value of Statistical Life, 123

variable costs, 18–19

Vietnam War, 120

vocational training, 254

volatility of market prices, 217

von Wieser, Friedrich, 26–27, 279, 280n

Voyer, René de, 2

wages: lower in monopoly situations, 192; occupational licensing and, 248; opportunity costs and, 6, 21, 152–53; share of market income going to, 242, 242n, 247, 285. *See also* bargaining between employers and workers; minimum wages; unions

wage subsidies, 300–301

Wagner Act, 243–44, 248

war: cost of US interventions, 122–24; as economic stimulus, 114–15; failure of US interventions, 122, 122n; opportunity cost of, 119–25; technology and, 125–28

Washington Consensus, 2n

The Wealth of Nations (Smith), 33, 45, 173

welfare benefits: opposed by One Lesson economists, 141; redistribution through, 93; tax revenues used for, 271; workfare programs in place of, 299

Welfare Economics: First Fundamental Theorem of, 137, 148; Second Fundamental Theorem of, 137, 148

welfare reform, 279, 279n2

welfare systems: clawbacks in, 272–73, 275, 285; property rights created by, 136

Western, Bruce, 247

Western Electric, 310

"What Is Seen and What Is Unseen" (Bastiat), 2

wheat rate of interest, 53, 54

When All Else Fails (Moss), 264

White, Laurence, 102

Whitehouse, Sheldon, 196

Whittle, Frank, 126

Wilde, Oscar, 30

William the Conqueror, 139

women, household work done by, 24, 47n

work disincentive effects, 276–77, 283–84

workfare programs, 299

work for hire, copyright of, 256

Works Progress Administration, 299

World Bank: postwar Keynesian policies and, 160; promoting privatization, 318

World War II: Great Depression ended by, 121–22, 162; success of Keynesian economics following, 160, 162; technological advances and, 125–28

zero lower bound, 298–99

zero-sum game, trade viewed as, 34, 35–36

Zucman, Gabriel, 266

Zuse, Konrad, 127–28